THE IDEA OF COMMUNISM VOLUME 2

THE IDEA OF COMMUNISM
VOLUME 2

EDITED BY SLAVOJ ŽIŽEK

V

VERSO

London • New York

First published by Verso 2013
© the collection Verso 2013
© individual contributions the contributors 2013

1 3 5 7 9 10 8 6 4 2

Verso
UK: 6 Meard Street, London W1F 0EG
US: 20 Jay Street, Suite 1010, Brooklyn, NY 11201

www.versobooks.com

Verso is the imprint of New Left Books

ISBN-13: 978-1-84467-980-5 (PBK)
ISBN-13: 978-1-84467-981-2 (HBK)

British Library Cataloguing in Publication Data
A catalogue record for this book is available from the British Library

Library of Congress Cataloging-in-Publication Data
A catalog record for this book is available from the Library of Congress

Typeset in Cochin by Hewer Text UK Ltd, Edinburgh
Printed in the US by Maple Vail

Contents

Introduction

In 2011 we witnessed (and participated in) a series of emancipatory events which surprised everyone, including their actors: from the Arab Spring to the Occupy Wall Street movement, from the Greek revolt to the UK riots. Now, a year later, every day brings new evidence of how fragile and inconsistent this awakening was, its many facets displaying the same signs of exhaustion: the enthusiasm of the Arab Spring is mired in compromises and religious fundamentalism; OWS has lost momentum to such an extent that, in a nice case of the 'cunning of reason', the police clean-up of Zuccotti Park and other sites of the Occupy protests cannot but appear as a blessing in disguise, covering up the immanent loss of momentum. And the same story continues around the world: the Maoists in Nepal seem to be outmanoeuvred by the reactionary forces; Venezuela's 'Bolivarian' experiment appears to be regressing into a caudillo-run populism, and so on.

What are we to do in such times? The first thing to demonstrate is that the subterranean work of dissatisfaction is continuing: rage is accumulating and a new wave of revolts will follow. So it is important to set the record straight, to locate these events in the totality of global capitalism, which means showing how they relate to its central antagonism. The present book endeavours to contribute to such a 'cognitive mapping' (Fredric Jameson) of our constellation. It brings together the interventions of 'Communism: A New Beginning', a conference – third in the series, after London in 2009 and Berlin in 2010 – dedicated to the idea of communism and held at the Cooper Union in New York on 14–16 October 2011.

Slavoj Žižek

1 The Communist Idea and the Question of Terror

Alain Badiou

In the nineteenth century, the communist Idea was linked to violence in four different ways.

First of all, it went hand in hand with the fundamental issue of revolution. Revolution was conceived of – since the French Revolution, at least – as the violent act whereby one social group, one class, overthrows the domination of another group or class. All revolutionary imagery was, and to a great extent still is, focused on the legitimate violence by means of which the people in arms seize the seats of power. The word 'communism' thus implied the word 'revolution' in the sense of an ideological and political legitimation of insurrection or people's war, and therefore of collective violence directed at the exploiters and their police and military apparatuses.

Second, the communist Idea also went hand in hand with the repression deployed by the new popular power against the attempts at counter-revolution led by the former ruling classes. These attempts were based on what remained of the old state apparatus. Marx himself thus considered that a transitional period was necessary during which the new popular, working-class power would really destroy everything that remained of the apparatuses that constituted the state of the oppressors. He called this period the 'dictatorship of the proletariat'. He conceived of it as a short period, of course, but an indubitably violent one, as indicated by the word 'dictatorship'. Thus, the word 'communism' also implied the legitimation of destructive violence perpetrated by the new power.

Third, the communist Idea went hand in hand, in this case over a long period of time, with different types of violence linked to the radical transformation not of the state now, but of society as a whole. The collectivization of land in the domain of agriculture; centralized industrial development; the formation of a new military apparatus; the struggle against religious obscurantism; and the creation of new cultural and artistic forms – in short, the whole transition to a collective 'new world' created powerful conflicts at every level. A great deal of violence – in the form of constraints exerted on a mass scale, often resembling real civil wars, particularly in the countryside – had to be accepted. 'Communism' was often the name of something for the construction of which this violence was unavoidable.

Fourth, and last of all, all the conflicts and uncertainties about the birth of an entirely new society without precedent in history were formalized as the 'struggle between two ways of life' – the way of life of the proletariat and the way of life of the bourgeoisie, or the communist way of life and the capitalist way of life. This struggle doubtless cut across every sector of society, but it also raged within the communist parties themselves. There was thus much settling of scores within the new forms of power. The word 'communism' therefore implied violence linked to a stable, united group's hold on power, and thus the chronic liquidation, known as purges, of real or imagined adversaries.

It can therefore be said that the word 'communism' has four different meanings related to violence: revolutionary violence, linked to the taking of power; dictatorial violence, linked to the destruction of the remnants of the old regime; transformative violence, linked to the more or less forced birth of new social relationships; and political violence, linked to conflicts within the party apparatus and the state.

In the real history of revolutions in the nineteenth and twentieth centuries, these four figures of violence are of course completely interwoven, overlapping, and almost indistinguishable from one another – something that has been the case from the French Revolution on. Consider, for example, the grisly episode known as the 'September Massacres'. A mob, led by radicals, slaughtered half of the Paris prison population. In a sense, this terrifying episode was like an episode in a bloody civil war. However, since the people who were massacred were prisoners, the revolutionary regime, the revolutionary state, was to blame. Furthermore, in order to prevent these 'spontaneous' tragic incidents from happening again, the regime itself would assume responsibility for an unprecedented intensification of repressive police and judicial measures. And that intensification would bring about typical, genuinely political violence, such as the execution of Hébert and Danton, and their respective parties. Thus, the September Massacres were no doubt a violent reaction dominated by the fear of treason, but the state was involved in both their causes and consequences. It can therefore be said that, in this case, dictatorial violence and bloody mob violence were interwoven, but that the revolutionary regime, revolutionary politics, attempted to have the last word.

On the other hand, the revolutionary state's violence may at first be selective, dominated by internal conflicts within the reigning parties and factions, and then later turn into uncontrolled mass violence. This is the impression we get from the history of the great Stalinist Terror that took place between 1936 and 1939. In the form of public show trials, this Terror staged the settling of scores between Stalin's group and well-known Bolshevik leaders such as Zinoviev, Kamenev, Bukharin and many others. But it eventually became one gigantic purge, throughout the country, involving hundreds of thousands of people who were executed or who died in the camps. This unprecedented purge would ultimately carry off most of those who were responsible for it – in particular Yezhov, the head of the repressive apparatus. In this case, the central state would appear to have launched a repressive process of the fourth type (political violence linked to conflicts within the central apparatus), which developed into a wholesale general purge that ended up resembling savage civil war–type extermination.

The distinction must nevertheless be maintained between, on the one hand, spontaneous mob violence, which was akin to acts of class vengeance, to brutal symbols of the new balance of power in civil society, and, on the other hand, state violence, discussed and deliberately organized by the leaders of the new regime, which affected both the body politic and society as a whole. It should be noted, moreover, that however barbaric the former may have been, it has always been the latter which, from Robespierre to Stalin, has served as a very effective argument to discredit revolutions.

So let us call 'Terror' that moment in revolutionary processes when the new regime takes police and judicial measures that are exceptional in terms of both their violence and their scope. And let us face up to the following problem: Is there a necessary relationship, in real history, between the communist Idea and Terror?

As we well know, this is an important issue, on which anti-communist propaganda depends almost entirely. In its usual connotation, the category of 'totalitarianism' designates Terror, precisely, as the inevitable outcome of revolutions whose manifest principle is communism. The underlying argument is that the construction of an egalitarian society is so unnatural an enterprise, so contrary to all the human animal's instincts, that advancing in that direction is impossible without appalling violence. Ultimately, the philosophy underpinning this propaganda goes back to Aristotle. Aristotle made a distinction between violent and natural movements in nature. Liberal propaganda extends this distinction to economics, politics, and history. With regard to human society, it makes a distinction between natural and violent movements. The private appropriation of resources and wealth, competition, and ultimately capitalism are considered natural phenomena, the adaptable, resilient products of individual nature. Collective action, the abolition of private property, and the construction of a centralized economy are viewed as purely ideological processes, abstractions that can only be imposed on people by the most extreme violence. And that violence itself can only exist because a state has been established that is itself somehow distinct from the real nature of society – an absolutely separate state, which can only be maintained by Terror, in fact.

We must give a clear response to this argument. We know that there are four means of refuting it with reference to the communist Idea and the importance of the political processes that subscribe to it. Either the scope and violence of repression, the very existence of Terror, can be denied, or its existence can be accepted in principle, and both its scope and necessity can be acknowledged. Or Terror can be regarded as having existed only owing to circumstances that have now disappeared, and as no longer having an organic connection with the communist Idea. Or, finally, we can regard the existence of Terror as a sign of a deviation, a practical error, of communist politics, and consider that it could have been, or, more to the point, *should* be, avoided. In short, either Terror is an invention of capitalist propaganda; or it is the price that must be paid for the triumph of the Idea; or it was justified by a sort of revolutionary prematurity, but is no longer relevant; or it has no necessary connection with the political process of the communist Idea, either in principle or owing to circumstances.

These different refutations of liberal propaganda are all supported by compelling arguments.

During the entire period when the Socialist states, and the USSR in particular, were in existence, the first two of these theories confronted each other. In the countries of the Atlantic Alliance, anti-communist propaganda made great use of what was known about repressive Stalinist methods. This propaganda equated Soviet power in the 1930s with the Moscow Trials, which served to liquidate the Bolshevik old guard. In the 1950s, it focused attention on the existence of concentration camps in Siberia. The communist parties, for their part, completely denied everything. And when the death sentences became only too obvious (as was the case with the Moscow Trials) they had no hesitation in insisting that it was only a matter of a handful of traitors and spies in the pay of foreign governments.

A very different process began at the end of the 1950s with Khrushchev's report to the Twentieth Congress of the Communist Party of the USSR. For one thing, to mark the beginning of a break with the Stalinist period, the Soviet leaders admitted that Terror had existed in the 1930s, though without acknowledging its mass scale. For another, democratic propaganda in the West gradually became focused on Terror as an immanent necessity of the Communist worldview – an exorbitant price to pay for a utopia with no basis in reality.

Remarkably, the Western interpretation, promoted by the clique of 'new philosophers' in France, actually became the consensus interpretation, especially during the last twenty years of the twentieth century. There was the dissolution of 'actually existing socialism', culminating, as we know, in a Russia embarking upon a version of state capitalism, and a rapidly developing China, under the paradoxical leadership of a party that is still called 'communist' – a ruthless capitalism very similar to that of the nineteenth century in England. These two countries, which are participating in a sort of global convergence around the most brutal capitalism, have no immediate reason to discuss anti-communist propaganda based on the evidence of Terror. As a result, the so-called 'anti-totalitarian' theory, which regards Terror as the inevitable outcome of the communist Idea's coming to power, has no opponents anymore in any countries, none of which defend the Idea any longer. It is as if the communist Idea, definitively associated with Terror, has very rapidly become no more than a dead planet in the historical universe.

The truth, in my opinion, is not at all that the revelation of Terror (Solzhenitsyn's books in particular) brought about the death of the communist Idea. *On the contrary, it was the continuous weakening of the communist Idea that made possible the anti-totalitarian consensus around the notion that there is a necessary link between that Idea and Terror.* The key moment in this temporary deadlock of the communist Idea was the failure of the Chinese Cultural Revolution, which had attempted to revive the communist Idea outside the confines of the party and the state through a general mobilization of the students and working-class youth. The restoration of state order under Deng Xiaoping sounded the death knell of a whole sequence of existence of the Idea – what can be called the party-state sequence.

The main task today is not so much to acknowledge the evidence of

Terror and its extraordinary violence. There has been much outstanding, incontrovertible work produced about it, in the first rank of which I would put Getty's great book, *The Road to Terror: Stalin and the Self-Destruction of the Bolsheviks 1932–1939*. Rather, the task is to examine, and possibly to interrogate or destroy, the consensus theory that places full responsibility for Terror on the communist Idea.

As a matter of fact, I propose the following method of thought: replacing the debate between theory 1 and theory 2 with a debate between theories 3 and 4. In other words: after a first historical sequence in which the communist Idea, on the side of bourgeois reaction, was said to be a criminal one, and the existence of any Terror whatsoever was, on the communist side, denied; after a second historical sequence in which anti-totalitarianism asserted that there was an organic link between the communist Idea, utopic and lethal, and state terror, a third sequence should now begin in which four things will be asserted simultaneously: 1. The absolute necessity for the communist Idea in opposition to the unbounded barbarism of capitalism; 2. The undeniably terroristic nature of the first effort to embody this Idea in a state; 3. The circumstantial origins of this Terror; and 4. The possibility of a political deployment of the communist Idea geared precisely towards a radical limitation of terrorist antagonism.

The heart of the whole matter, in my opinion, is that, although the revolutionary event does in fact lie, in a wide variety of forms, at *the origin* of any political incarnation of the communist Idea, it is nevertheless *not* its rule or its model. *I regard Terror as in fact the continuation of insurrection or war by state means.* But even if it has had to go through their vicissitudes, the politics of the communist Idea is not and must never be reducible to insurrection or war. For its true essence, the root of the new political time it constructs, has as its guiding principle not the destruction of an enemy, but the positive resolution of contradictions among the people – the political construction of a new collective configuration.

To establish this point more firmly, we must naturally start over again from the last two hypotheses concerning Terror. Even if the figures cited by the now consensual anti-communist propaganda are often absurd, we must fully recognize the violence and scope of Stalinist Terror. We must regard it as linked to the circumstances under which the historically unprecedented implementation of a regime inspired by the communist Idea, the regime of the socialist states, was undertaken. These circumstances were the worldwide slaughter of the inter-imperialistic wars, ferocious civil wars, and the aid given by foreign powers to the counter-revolutionary factions. They were the circumstances of an ongoing shortage of experienced, stoical political cadres, the best of whom were carried off early on in the whirlwind. All of this created a political subjectivity composed of a superego imperative and chronic anxiety. Uncertainty, ignorance, and fear of treason were decisive factors in what we now know about the climate in which the leaders made their decisions. This subjectivity in turn led to the main principle of action being to treat any contradiction as if it were antagonistic, as if it represented a mortal danger. The habit that developed in the civil war of killing anyone who was not with you became entrenched in a socialist state that was constantly amazed at having successfully prevailed.

All of this concerns not the communist Idea in itself, but rather the particular process of the first experiment with it in history. We must now start again from scratch, armed as we are with the knowledge of the potential outcome of that experiment. We must maintain that there is no relationship in principle between the communist Idea and state terror. I would even venture to make an analogy about this for which I will be criticized: Was the Christian Idea linked in principle to the Inquisition? Or was it instead linked in principle to Saint Francis of Assisi's vision? This issue can only be decided from within a real subjectivization of the Idea. Nevertheless, the only way we can break free from the circumstantial destiny of the communist Idea in its guise as the terrorism of the party-state, an organization whose vision was shaped by the metaphor of war, is by deploying this Idea again in today's circumstances.

There is nonetheless historical support for this undertaking that I would like to mention – that of the striking differences between the Soviet and Chinese experiments within the same model: the party-state.

The common features of these two experiments are obvious. In both cases, the victory of the revolution took place in an enormous country that was still largely rural, in which industrialization was only just beginning. It occurred under the conditions of a world war that had greatly weakened the reactionary state. In both cases, the responsibility for leading the process was assumed by a disciplined communist party that was linked to large military forces. In both cases the leadership of the party, and therefore of the entire process, was composed of intellectuals trained in dialectical materialism and the Marxist tradition.

The differences between them, however, are great. Firstly, the Bolsheviks' popular base consisted of factory workers and soldiers who had broken away from the official military apparatus. The Chinese Party's popular base certainly included workers, but it was dominated largely by peasants, especially in the military – the Red Army of which Mao strikingly remarked it was responsible for 'carrying out the political tasks of the revolution'. Secondly, the victory of the revolution in Russia took the form of a short insurrection focused on the capital and the cities, and was followed by a terrible, anarchic civil war in the provinces, with the intervention of foreign military forces. In China, on the other hand, there was first a bloody defeat of the urban insurrections based on the Soviet model, and later, under the conditions of the Japanese invasion, a very long sequence of people's war supported by remote provincial bastions in which new forms of power and organization were being tried out. It was only at the end that a short classical war, with huge battles in the open countryside, destroyed the reactionary party's military and governmental apparatus.

What I am particularly struck by is that the antagonistic confrontation with power and the political experimentation are not at all the same, and that the fundamental criterion of this difference is duration. Basically, the Soviet revolution was characterized by the conviction that all the problems were urgent, and that this urgency made violent, radical decisions necessary in every domain. The insurrection and the atrocities of the civil war controlled political time, even when the revolutionary state was no longer under any immediate threat. The Chinese revolution, on the contrary, was bound up with the concept of 'protracted war'. It was all about process, not sudden armed takeover. The most important thing to discern was long-range trends. And above all, the antagonism had to be calculated as precisely as possible. In the people's war, the preservation of one's forces would be preferred to glorious but useless attacks. And this preservation of forces also had to be able to be mobile if enemy pressure was too great. Here, in my opinion, we have a strategic vision: the event creates a new possibility, not a model for the real becoming of that possibility. There may well have been urgency and violence at the beginning, but the forces that resulted from this shock may have been dictated, on the contrary, by a sort of mobile patience – a long-term progress that could force a change of terrain without, however, reinstating the absolute rule of insurrectional urgency or relentless violence.

But what form, politically, does the preservation of forces opposed to domination take? Terror can certainly not resolve the problem. Of course, it imposes a certain type of unity, but a weak unity, a unity of passivity and fear. To preserve one's forces, and therefore the unity of those forces, is always in the final analysis to resolve internal problems within the political camp concerned. *And what experience shows is that, over the long term, neither antagonistic action, based on the military or police model, directed against enemies, nor Terror within your own camp can resolve the problems created by your own political existence.* These problems have to do with the methods linked to what Mao called 'the correct handling of contradictions among the people'. And throughout his life he insisted on the fact that these methods were absolutely different from those that concern antagonistic contradictions.

It is essential to maintain that communist-type politics seeks solutions to political problems. Communist-type politics is an immanent activity, an activity under the sign of a shared Idea, not an activity determined by external constraints such as the economy or the legal formalism of the state. Ultimately, every political problem boils down to a problem of the unity of orientation on an issue that is collectively defined as being the main issue of the moment or of the situation. Even a victory over the enemy depends on the subjective unity that was the victors'. Over the long run, the key to a victorious treatment of antagonisms lies in the correct handling of contradictions among the people—which also happens to be the real definition of democracy.

Terror asserts that only state coercion is equal to the threats to the people's unity in a revolutionary period. This idea naturally wins the subjective support of many people whenever the danger is enormous and treason widespread. But it should be understood that Terror is never the solution to a problem, because it is the problem's suppression. Terror is always far removed from the Idea, inasmuch as it replaces the discussion of a political problem, located at the border between the Idea and the situation, with a brutal forcing of the situation that swallows up the collective relation to the Idea along with the problem. Terror considers that, by its ostensibly shifting what it calls the 'balance of power', the parameters of the problem will also be shifted, making a solution possible. Ultimately, however, every problem suppressed by force, even the problem of traitors, is bound to return. Accustomed to solutions that are solutions in name only, the state officials themselves will reproduce internally the betrayal of the Idea that they have banished externally. This is because when the Idea, instead of lying in the problems posed by the situation, serves to justify the terrorist abolition of these problems, it is in a sense even more weakened than it would be by frontal attacks on the Idea itself.

It is easy to see, then, that everything hinges on the ability to give the formulation and resolution of problems the time required in order to avoid terrorist short-circuiting as much as possible. The main lesson learned from the last century's revolutions can be expressed as follows: the political time of the communist Idea must never compete with the established time of domination and its urgencies. Competing with the adversary always leads to the mere semblance, not the real, of force. For the communist Idea is not in competition with capitalism; it is in an absolutely asymmetric relationship with it. As the dramatic conditions that accompanied their implementation clearly showed, the Soviet five-year plans and Mao's 'Great Leap Forward' were forced constructs. Slogans like 'catch up with England in fifteen years' implied a forcing, a perversion of the Idea, and ultimately the obligation of implementing Terror. There is a necessary slowness, both democratic and popular in nature, which is particular to the time of the correct handling of contradictions among the people. That is why the fact that people worked slowly, and sometimes not very much, in socialist factories, just as people work slowly and often not very much in Cuba still today, is not in itself such a terrible thing. It was only – it is only – a form of protest in the eyes of the world of Capital. Work time cannot be measured in the same way when it is related to the production of surplus value – namely, the profits of the oligarchy – as when it seeks to accord with a new vision of what people's lives should be. Nothing is more important for communists than to declare that their time is not Capital's time.

In conclusion we can say: far from being a consequence of the communist Idea, Terror actually results from a fascination with the enemy, a mimetic rivalry with it. And this effect is twofold.

First, it confuses the conditions of the military confrontation with the enemy – insurrection or war – which are the conditions of the event of liberation, with the conditions of the affirmative construction of a new collective order under the sign of the power of the Idea. We can say that Terror is the effect of an equation of the event with the event's consequences, consequences which are the whole real of the process of a truth, a real oriented by a subjective body. In short, we will say that Terror is a fusion between event and subject in the state.

Second, the effect of competition with capitalism gradually leads to the Idea itself being purely and simply abandoned in favour of a sort of paradoxical violence that consists in wanting to achieve the same results as capitalism – whereas one actually wanted, and to a certain extent created all the conditions necessary, in order *not* to achieve the same results. What such violence especially destroys is the time of emancipation, which is on the scale of the life of humanity, not on that of the market's profit cycle. In the end, we wind up with people like Gorbachev or the current Chinese leaders, whose only aim is to be admitted into the little group that represents the international capitalist oligarchy. People who want more than anything to be *recognized* by their supposed adversaries. People for whom the Idea has no meaning anymore. People for whom the aim of all difference will have been to conquer power in identity. We can then see that Terror has only ended up being renunciation, precisely because it has not allowed for the preservation of forces and their shifting; because it has not devoted most of its time, as any political thought must, to that preservation; because it has not constantly *politicized* the people in the exercise of wide-ranging local and central powers, of efficient deliberation. Only the 'seize power' movement, or the 'occupations' movement in May '68 – as today in Egypt or on Wall Street – represent a first approximation of such politicization, which creates both its own places and its own time.

The renewal of the communist Idea, which is the task of the century now beginning, will be one in which revolutionary urgency will be replaced by what can be called its aesthetics, in the Kantian sense. It is not so much a change, even a violent one, which we will want to create in the status quo; rather, we will want everything existing to be somehow curved in a new space, with new dimensions. We will find for the Idea what it lacked – a lack for which the furious impatience of Terror was both the cause and the price: we will find the absolute independence of both its places and its time.

2 Communism as Commitment, Imagination, and Politics

Etienne Balibar

The first thing that I want to do is thank the organizers of the conference for their invitation. And in particular I want to express my deep gratitude to Alain Badiou: not only because he could not join us in person in this conference that he had entirely planned in close spiritual community with Slavoj Žižek, and is now experiencing hardship, but because it is entirely due to his repeated and personal insistence that I find myself tonight in your company. Alain and I are very old friends, going back almost to when I met him for the first time, although in those early years I was too impressed by his precocious philosophical mastery, and the age difference formed an unbreakable barrier, however small it may appear fifty years later. Soon after that he decided on a completely spontaneous and generous move to join the small group of young philosophers gathered around Althusser, and immediately brought to us a new impulse while displaying absolute egalitarianism. None of us could ever forget that. Alain and I over the years have had strong disagreements, both philosophical and political, leading sometimes to quite harsh exchanges (it was again the case recently when, after I had declined in somewhat aggressive terms his proposal to join the conference on the Idea of Communism held in Berlin in 2010, he wrote to me that I had managed never to find myself where 'things are really happening', after which each of us felt obliged to explain to the other why what he thought was not worth much). But we have succeeded in remaining faithful to one another; I have the fondest memory of his signals of solidarity and gestures of esteem, and I have found myself intellectually rewarded each time I have had to engage with his ideas or his arguments. I am sad that he is not here tonight, but I will try to act as if he were, and address him as if he could react or even respond.

The title that I had proposed with only a vague idea of how I would treat it in detail – 'Communism as Commitment, Imagination, and Politics' – has led me to build an argument in which I confront my own reflections with propositions from some of our contemporaries, indeed protagonists of the debate on the 'new communism', including Badiou and Žižek, which – as you could perhaps expect from a professional philosopher – follows a classical model. This is the Kantian model of the three transcendental (or perhaps only quasi-transcendental) questions, albeit in a non-classical order. The first question, corresponding to the issue of *commitment*, can be phrased like this: *Who are the communists? What are we communists hoping for?* In stronger terms, what do they/we desire? And the answer that I will propose, whose implications I will try to discuss as much as I can in such a short time span, is the following: the communists, we communists, desire to *change the world in order to become transformed ourselves*. As you notice, I use a floating designator for the subject of the proposition, this ambiguity being part of the problem which needs to be discussed. And I make use of formulae belonging to a well-known Marxian tradition, partially coinciding with our 'idea of communism', albeit somewhat modified. These two formal characteristics will reappear in the next questions. The second question, corresponding to the issue of *imagination*, is the following: *What are the/we communists thinking of?* – or, more precisely, what are they/we *thinking in advance*, in the sense of 'anticipations of the understanding'? And the answer is: they/we are *diversely interpreting the real movement which overcomes* ('aufhebt') *capitalism* and the capitalist society based on commodity production and exchange, or 'modelled' on this production and exchange. In other terms, they/we are diversely interpreting effective history in the making. Finally, the third quasi-transcendental question is the following: What are they/we *doing*, or better said – to retrieve diverse translations of the term *conatus* used by classical philosophers – what are they/we *endeavouring to do, striving at, fighting for*? And the answer could be, I will suggest: they/we are participating in various 'struggles' of emancipation, transformation, reform, revolution, civilization; but in doing that we are not so much 'organizing' as 'de-organizing' these struggles.

And now, without further ado, let us examine the first question, the question of communist commitment. The reason why I ask it in this form, related to hopes, desires (perhaps dreams), is that I want to explain right away in which sense I consider that a central proposition belonging to what Alain Badiou calls the 'communist hypothesis' is indisputable: namely, the primacy of the relationship between *idea* and *subjectivity*, and as a consequence the intrinsically 'idealistic' character of the communist discourse, however distorted or disavowed it becomes when it presents itself as a 'materialist' discourse (but I suspect that, in certain conditions, 'materialism' is but one of the names of idealism), is indisputable. But I want also to explain why I believe that some of the consequences of this indisputable fact are, to say the least, problematic. However, to say that they are problematic is not to reject the premise, it is only to ask for a philosophical disquisition of the consequences.

The truth of Badiou's central formula according to which communists 'live for an idea' (or answer the call of an idea, adapt their lives to the model provided by an idea) could be purely and simply inferred from the examples we know of subjects, both individuals and collectives, whom we consider to have been communists (since *there have been communists*, this is not an entirely new race on earth), including, I repeat, those among them who, for whatever reason, good or bad, rejected the term. They were all idealists, both in the ordinary and in the technical sense of the term: dreaming of another world and ready to sacrifice much of their lives, sometimes all of it, for their conviction, as Max Weber would say. This was indeed true of Marx, one of the clearest cases of practical idealism in the history of philosophy and politics. After decades of attempts on the part of some communists (not all of them, but among them some of the most authentic) to present the pursuit of communism as a process 'without a subject', it is high time to say that a rose is a rose, and not a bicycle, and that 'communism without a subject' involves a performative contradiction. But what makes the communist a subject different from others is primarily his or her commitment to a certain idea, which is also an ideal of course. But one can add an additional argument, more speculative: by definition, the ideal object or objective of the communist desire is not something that is part of the existing state of affairs. At the very least there is a *difference*, a distance that could become an abyss, between *what there is* and *what there will be*, or could be, and it is in this gap that the subject places his/her desire. To quote here the famous definition from Marx's *German Ideology* (to which I will return) – 'communism is the real movement overcoming the existing state of affairs' – changes nothing about the situation, because subjects can either resist the movement or contribute to it, and they contribute to it only if they desire it, whatever the conditions, material or spiritual, which can facilitate or even produce this subjective orientation. So idealism is the condition for the communist commitment, or, better, it is the philosophical name of that commitment. So far, so good; but now we have to carefully examine the implications of that ideological fact, one by one and step by step, and here perhaps we may find that the rigor of Badiou's insight, breaking with what I called the 'performative contradiction', is also accompanied by a certain blindness, or a certain refusal to envisage all the consequences. This will concern, I suggest, the place of communism in a 'world of ideas', the subjective consequences of idealistic convictions (*fidelities*, or *faithfulness*, in his terminology), or identification with the requisites and injunctions of an idea, and above all the modalities of the 'being in common' under the interpellation of that idea, which acquire a special importance in the case of the communist idea, because that idea happens to be precisely *the idea of the being in common* in its purest form. But let us be very careful about all this.

A quick word, to begin with, concerning the place of communism in the world of ideas. Communism is not the only idea, not even in the strong sense of an idea of the *non-existent which ought to exist*, after which the existing state of affairs could become different, overcome its limitations or contradictions, make life radically other, and so on, or can be represented as *becoming different*, following an anticipatory move to which I will return. And not even in the even stronger sense of an idea which possesses the ontological and epistemological character of the absolute – namely the coincidence of the mark of truth and the mark of goodness (and probably also, for that reason, the mark of beauty). I am not suggesting that there are infinitely many ideas of that kind in our intellectual world, but at least there are several, which we can try to enumerate: Justice, Liberty, Right, Love, Mankind, Nature, the Universal, Truth itself, Beauty, but also Democracy, Peace (but also War, in the form of the eternal *polemos* 'fathering everything'), the Market (as an ideal form of a universally beneficial and self-regulated system of exchanges, never realized in practice, but which can always be hoped for, and for which one can sacrifice certain interests), even the Nation (or rather the People). Even Property. It is important to notice that we receive all these ideas through signifiers, indeed master-signifiers: they place the desiring subject in a relationship of dependency with respect to this signifier, however freely chosen. There is nothing special about communism from this point of view, and this is an element that we will try to reflect on the *constitution of subjectivity* relative to ideas, inasmuch as they bear names, or pass through signifiers. What to do with this multiplicity? It might be tempting to explain (this is a certain form of simplified Platonism, with theological connotations) that all the ideas which are absolute, or eternal, as Badiou would say, are in fact identical, or form *different names* for the same absolute. But this is uninteresting in our case because it blurs the distinctions, even the *oppositions*, which give sense to the idea of communism, and account for the *kind of subjective desire* that it raises, or the kind of imperative that it 'enunciates'. The idea of communism becomes meaningless if it means the same as the idea of Property, or the idea of the Pure Market, which are nevertheless 'ideas' in the same ontological and epistemological sense. Badiou certainly has a tendency to suggest that communism *is the only Idea* in the true sense of the term, or the Idea of ideas (like Justice, the idea of the Good, in the philosophy of Plato), and conversely that *Idea* – or, for this purpose, rather, 'ideal' – and *communism* are synonymous terms. And as a consequence all the other ideas are either other names, perhaps partial names, for communism (such as Equality, or Justice, or the Universal) or *simulacra* of the communist idea (such as the Market) – the case of the idea of Democracy remains dubious . . . This could be a form of philosophical naivety, an expression of his personal commitment to communism, the passion that inhabits his own desire, and so on. But I believe there is a stronger reason, which is that Badiou does not want to expose the characteristics of communism from outside, in a distanciated or even relativistic manner, but from the inside, as a phenomenological elucidation of its intrinsic manifestation, or revelation. The idea reveals its true character only to the subject who desires its realization, and it is in this character that the 'communist subject' is interested. However, the problem will now become that it is impossible to analyze and to compare what differentiates a communist commitment from other commitments, which also can be rational or mystic, civilized or fanatic, and so on.

Let us suspend for a minute this comparison, and return to the *specificity* of the communist idea. I believe that we can express it by saying that what (we) the communists desire is *to change the world* (as Marx famously wrote, albeit that he did not invent this idea, which is typically post-Kantian, and also has precedents in the gnostic tradition). But, more precisely, they want to change the world – meaning, at least in a first approximation, the social and historical world, the 'ensemble of social relations' – *radically*, whereby (I keep following certain Marxian formulations) *humans themselves will be changed* (or a 'new man' will emerge, inasmuch as 'man' is nothing other than the immanent result of its own conditions or relations). Or *the life of the humans*, i.e. *our own life*, will be changed. It is important to underline this *telos*, implied in the combination of the two 'changes', because from the communist point of view, to change the world is uninteresting if it does not lead ultimately to a new form of life in which

the human qua *relational 'essence'* becomes different, reversing the characteristics of life under capitalism (particularly unlimited competition,
therefore permanent ranking of individuals according to their power or
their value, and in the limit cases elimination of useless or 'valueless' individuals); but changing the human involves changing the world, again if
by this term we understand the social world. Now there is a causal dissym-
metry in this articulation, which confers undoubtedly upon the communist
idea an *eschatological* character, but there is also a retroactive, or reflexive
effect, which allows it to mark the difference with a *religious eschatology*, in
spite of the obvious affinities, in particular with religions centred on the
perspective of *redemption* (I am not speaking of the historical legacies, but
of logical analogies). I will present this retroactive effect, or reflexive
dimension of the idea of communism, which is a *practical* dimension (and
here, again, the idealistic determination is obvious), in the following form:
although the emergence of the 'new men' (or the new human life) is possible only if the world is changed, the world can be changed only if the
subjects are extracting themselves, emancipating themselves from the
determinations of the existing world, or at least already engaged in a
process of self-emancipation. Otherwise, a redeemer of whatever kind
would be needed. Accordingly the practical, albeit subjective and reflexive, dimension we are talking about is also a 'secular' one, in a fairly simple
sense of the term. It corresponds to a *Verwirklichung* which is also a
Verweltlichung. It is *this world* which changes, and it changes into *this world*
– not an otherworldly realm – which is nevertheless becoming radically
different; and it changes through the immanent action of its 'men', its
'subjects' (we could also say, in a different terminology, more directly
political, its 'citizens'), who are already transforming themselves in order
to be able to change the world. Remember again Marx (in *Statutes of the
International Workingmen's Association*, 1864): 'the emancipation of the
working classes will be the work of the workers themselves'. He speaks of
workers, but clearly confers a universalistic dimension upon this name.
Now this could seem enigmatic, or perhaps tautological, but we can give
it another formulation, which is far from innocent (in particular because
it partially explains *a contrario* the failure of many 'communist attempts'):
the *commitment to the idea of communism* (or to the realization of the idea of
communism) is a commitment that *exists only in common*. Communist
'subjects' commit themselves (*negatively*, to begin with, in the form of the
elimination, the critique of their 'individualistic' self, their desire for
power, domination, inequality) in order to become the *agents* of a

collective transformation of the world whose immanent result will be a change of their own lives (whether necessary or contingent, transitory or lasting, is another matter, which I leave aside here with all questions of modalities and temporalities).

We are perhaps now, in spite of the brevity of this description, which remains partly allegoric, in a position to understand better what produces at the same time the strength and the problematic character of Badiou's understanding of the consequences of the idealism that he has rightly reaffirmed. There is something strange in the fact that Badiou frequently refers to a Lacanian heritage that he would preserve, whereas in fact he almost entirely reverses the articulation of subject-position and the action of the signifier as 'cause' of the subject that is so important for Lacan (and of course, a fortiori, behind Lacan, there remains, like it or not, a Freudian legacy of the analysis of the 'community effect' of the identification of subjects to a common ideal, or 'model' [*Vorbild*] from which they derive their shared ego-ideal).[1] It is as if, for Badiou, the communist subjects, or the subjects *in the absolute*, were also 'absolute' subjects, whose subjectivation is not *caused* by the signifier that they 'recognize' as a master-signifier, but on the contrary *detached* from its conflict with the real. The heterogeneity of the symbolic and the real becomes a pure possibility of liberation. Writes Badiou: 'it is in the operation of the Idea that the individual finds the capacity to consist "as a Subject"'.[2] This might provide a justification for the hypothesis that the communist idea is different from any other (and therefore a commitment, an identification with the communist ideal, works on its own subjects in a manner absolutely different from any other – for example the idea of the Republic, or the idea of the Law, or the idea of the Market), albeit that there is a great probability that the justification is tautological: all the other commitments would be heteronomous – they would involve a subjection to the master-signifiers on which they depend and after which they name themselves, whereas the communist commitment would be autonomous, or, if you prefer a less Kantian terminology, it would consist in a kind of *self-interpellation* of the individual as subject. But then we need to take into account what has emerged as the singular determination of the communist idea – namely the fact that its 'imperative' is a realization of 'being in common' in order to prepare for the world

---

1   To enter into that, we should discuss more precisely the differences between an *idea* and an *ideal*, and their differential relationship to the 'object' of desire.

2   *The Idea of Communism*, p. 239; see also the more explicit formulation in *L'idée du communisme*, Vol. II, Alain Badiou and Slavoj Žižek (eds) (Paris, Editions Lignes, 2011), p. 13.

of the common good. And the difficulty becomes redoubled – on the subjective plane as on the historical plane.

It is very striking here to see that Badiou has a marked preference for an adjective that is far from innocent to characterize the kind of 'community effect' that belongs to communism as a militant activity, as well as an ideal to become realized in the world: the adjective *intense*, leading to the notion of *intensity*. For example, 'We will call a site whose intensity of existence is maximal a *singularity*'.[3] It is *existence* whose 'intensity' is maximized, but it is maximized because it proves incompatible with a separation or an isolation of the subjects themselves. And here Badiou cannot but return to the concepts (perhaps the allegories) that had served in the theological tradition to describe, precisely, an 'intense' participation of subjects who transcend their own individuality as they transcend every form of power relation and hierarchic subordination, to become members of the 'glorious body' . . . which is that of a new collective Subject in politics.[4] And, not by chance, this is also where Badiou insists on the 'vital importance of proper names in all revolutionary politics'[5] and embarks on a provocative defence of the so-called 'cult of personality' of the charismatic leaders (Mao rather than Stalin, indeed) inasmuch as they represent an incarnated projection of the insurrectional powers of the people, and an 'ultra-political' function of the idea, which is to 'create the *we*' (we, the people; we, the revolutionaries; ultimately we, the communists). I do not say that this is either absurd or would have nothing to do with the idea of communism, in the name of what I called a moment ago its essentially 'secular' character (in the sense in which 'secular' refers to *thisworldlyness*); on the contrary. But I say that it reveals the problematic character of the notion of idealism that Badiou has a tendency to avoid discussing. The current return of the idea of communism, considered from the point of view of its consequences on the formation of a collective 'we' aiming at preparing the conditions of its own essential change, to a latent model of the church (even allegoric, and even or above all if it is not the model of an *institutional* church apparatus or *corpus juridicum*, but the model of what the theologians called the 'invisible church'), has not only symbolic determinations, but also strong historical reasons. They have to do with the awareness of the consequences of another model that had governed much of the political activity of the communists in the nineteenth and twentieth

---

3   Alain Badiou, *The Communist Hypothesis* (London, Verso, 2010), p. 215.
4   *The Communist Hypothesis*, pp. 244–5.
5   Ibid., p. 249.

centuries – namely the model of the *army* (with the very name 'militants', itself already used by the church), and more generally the model of the *state*, or the 'counter-state' so to speak. So, it performs a 'purifying' or 'cathartic' function. But it would be important, I believe, to recognize that it has its own ambivalent effects.

A simplified presentation of the whole story might go like this: given the fact that modern society, in other terms capitalism, has developed an *extreme form* of 'individualism', meaning in practice the disaffiliation of individuals and elimination of every protection against competition and solitude, but also the fact that it has 'compensated' for this 'dissolution' of solidarities and tried to 'control' the conflictual and violent effects of this dissolution (otherwise called 'class struggle' or 'social war') through the construction of powerful 'imagined communities' such as the *nation*, or even the *racial community*, the communist subjects have been engaged in the permanent quest for a form of community and community-feeling that is both *more intense* and *more disinterested* than any of these 'imagined communities' ('The Proletariat is the first class in history that does not seek to impose its particular interests', wrote Marx). The comparison with the nation is indeed the most important, both historically and analytically. Badiou's description of the becoming collective (therefore becoming revolutionary, on a given historical 'site', always largely unpredictable) of the commitment to the communist idea (which certainly owes much to various authors, from Saint Paul to Sartre, but interestingly neither to Hegel nor Freud) forms a sort of *reversal* of the argument that was famously developed by Carl Schmitt: the national myth is stronger than the communist myth in distinguishing the friend from the enemy, and maximizes the intensity of the community of friends. For Badiou it is the communist 'myth', or *collectivizing power of the idea*, which is always already more intense, more 'invisible', because it is based on love rather than hate (an argument strikingly similar to the discourse of Negri, with whom otherwise Badiou is in sharp disagreement; and at this conference we have heard that they now share the reference to Saint Francis of Assisi). But I wonder if this subtracts the constitutive relationship between subject and communist idea from every pattern of identification, representation, alienation or interpellation (whatever Freud, Hegel, Lacan, or Althusser would have called it), or on the contrary calls for an additional analysis of the dialectics of *subjection and subjectivation* that exists in communism as it exists in every commitment, albeit under forms which cannot become reduced to a single pre-existing model.

I will now have to be very schematic on my second question, because I want to keep some space for the third – although in a sense it is this second question that calls for the most detailed readings and comparisons. If another occasion provides me with an opportunity to continue along the same lines, I will try to be more explicit. So I will ask your permission to offer here a description of the argument and a statement of its intentions, rather than the argument itself. I formulated the second question in the form: What are the communists (what are we communists, constituted as a 'we' through our common commitment to what Badiou rightly calls an idea) *thinking in advance* concerning the history in the making, of which they/we are part – a resistant part or a subversive part, we might say, always located on what Foucault (who certainly was no communist) gave the Pascalian name of a *point of heresy*? And I tentatively answered: They/we are *diversely interpreting* the movement which overcomes capitalism (not to say *speculating* about it). I could have said: They are diversely *anticipating* the modalities of the 'crisis' of capitalism and the possibilities opened by that 'crisis', whose main characteristic is precisely to be unpredictable in its outcome. I am consciously playing on the terms of Marx's Eleventh Thesis on Feuerbach, to suggest that its first part, through a sort of historical nemesis, has reacted upon the second. 'Interpretation' was only repressed; it returned as soon as the 'revolutionary change', or the *change of the change* – which is perhaps the best possible description of a revolution, namely not a continuation of the orientation and the instruments of the spontaneous change of capitalism, but a discontinuity, a reorientation towards different goals, and a reversal of the 'means' of dialectical transformation (as Hegel would say), passing from states and leaders to masses and ordinary 'men without qualities' – as soon, I repeat, as this revolutionary change displayed its intrinsic equivocity or uncertainty or conflictuality. But this is not a negative fact, a catastrophic reversal; on the contrary, it is profoundly associated with two characteristics of *communist thinking* which call for a whole epistemological elaboration.

The first is that communist thinking, reflecting on the crisis of capitalism with the perspective of 'inserting' collective subjects into its development, can be described as a permanent exercise in projecting the political imagination into the rational exercise of the understanding, for which I try to use the Kantian category of the *anticipation* (I am not alone in doing that). An anticipation is not a *prediction*, in the sense in which positivist 'social science' tries to produce predictions, either on a grand historical scale, or within the limits of a carefully isolated model or system of methodological simplifications (most of the time implicitly governed by practical, therefore political, imperatives). It is also not a *prophetic* calling or announcement, whose characteristic is repetitive intemporality and historical indeterminacy (which, in fact, explains its irresistible power on a certain category of subjects). But it is an attempt at identifying within the present itself the limitations which are also 'limits of possible experience', where the reproduction of the existing structures, the continuous realization of the ongoing tendencies, or the applicability of the existing solutions to crises and contradictions, will prove impossible, and therefore call for heterogeneous actions. I find a beautiful formulation on this point by Slavoj Žižek in the volume from Berlin's Conference last year:

> a perception of historical reality not as a positive order, but as a 'non-all', an incomplete texture which tends towards its own future. It is this inclusion of the future into the present, its inclusion as a rupture within the order of the present, which makes the present an ontologically incomplete non-all and thus pulverises the evolutionary self-deployment of the process of historical development – in short, it is this rupture which distinguishes historicity proper from historicism.[6]

The second relevant characteristic of communist thinking is that tendencies are always accompanied by countertendencies, in thinking as in history, as Althusser was never tired of repeating – and probably the two are intrinsically linked: it is in the form of antithetic anticipations of the ongoing transformations of the present that the 'material' conflict of tendencies and counter-tendencies in history, or in society, becomes theoretically expressed, even if not directly or adequately. And therefore it is inasmuch as we carefully describe and discuss a pluralism of interpretations (of which we are always part ourselves) which tend to diverge rather than converge towards the same diagnoses, the same concepts, the same 'critiques', the same 'utopias', that we may have a chance to identify the play of tendencies and countertendencies, for example in the crisis of capitalism, which define our present – a present that is framed with incompleteness and non-contemporaneity. In short, there is 'anticipation',

---

6 *Idea of Communism*, II, p. 308. Incidentally, this formulation is not incompatible at all with much of what Negri – with whom Žižek has a fundamental philosophical disagreement, which I return to in a minute – writes on the issue of historical time; indeed both authors are continuing a line once opened by Ernst Bloch.

imagination working within the understanding, because there is neither necessity nor identity, but contingency and divergence. These are conceptual *determinations*, I insist, not impressionistic ruminations.

It has been my intention for some time now to address these issues through a confrontation of two authors who play a prominent role in contemporary debates about communism and defend strikingly opposite views of the revolution, or more generally the change, arising from opposite methodologies – namely Slavoj Žižek on one side and the twin authors Hardt and Negri on the other. One of them is here tonight, organizing this conference; the others are not, which is understandable for Antonio Negri because he is still banned from travelling to this country, but less so for Michael Hardt, whose absence, whatever its causes, I find quite regrettable. I will give a quick idea of what this confrontation should focus on in my view.

I have a formal, textual reason to set up this parallel, but I believe that it is not deprived of relevance even to the 'strategic' debates which concern the antagonistic relationship between capitalism and communism, because it regards their antithetic relationship to Marxism, and as a consequence to the 'concept of history' (or historical time, i.e. historicity) involved in Marxism. It is as if each of them had *dissociated* the elements of the Marxian conception, in particular the elements of the famous 'topography' (to borrow Althusser' s terminology) which allows Marx to explain the 'dialectics' of history and the 'inevitable' transformation of capitalism into communism, thus showing admittedly not that the unity of these elements was arbitrary in Marx, but that it was paradoxical, highly dependent on presuppositions that are not indefinitely tenable, and that arose from the intellectual and political conditions of a 'moment' which is no longer ours. It would be much too simple however to explain that, from this topography, Žižek retained only the *superstructure*, while Negri-Hardt retained the *base*. The situation is more complicated because in fact, as readers of the renowned Preface of the 1859 *Contribution to the Critique of Political Economy* will remember, the topography consists of not only two, but of *two times two*, or four distinct 'instances', between which a complex interplay becomes imagined or 'schematized' by Marx: the superstructure is divided into a juridical-political formalism and an ideological instance consisting of 'forms of social consciousness' within which the historical conflict becomes fought out (*ausfechten*), whereas the base is divided into a structure of 'relationships of production' which are essentially forms of property, and an autonomous movement of the productive forces

(*Produktivkräfte*) which, at some point, become incompatible with the existing relations of production. And it is in fact the paradoxical combination of the two 'extreme' instances, ideology and productive forces, which constitutes the essential movement or mobility 'negating' the stability, or rather the fixed order of Property and the State, in order to achieve, in a given conjuncture, a revolutionary change. This more complex pattern allows us to understand that what Žižek has essentially extracted from Marx is a dialectic of ideology (one is tempted again to write ideo-logy) against the apparatuses of State, Property, and Law; whereas Hardt and Negri have essentially extracted a conflictual relationship between productive forces and the same system of apparatuses (which they call the 'Republic of Property' in their newest volume, *Commonwealth*). Of course this leads each of them to reformulate and adapt quite substantially the terms which they isolate, and in particular the 'revolutionary' term, *ideology* in the case of Žižek, *productive forces* in the case of Hardt and Negri, combining philosophy, history, and political analysis. And, of course, for each of them the term that has been left aside and appropriated by the other represents essentially the germ of every misunderstanding of politics and the adversary of a genuine communist mode of anticipation of the future within the present: it is 'productive forces', for Žižek, that would be linked with vitalism, naturalism, evolutionism, progressivism, and the admiration for the creative capacities of capitalism as an economic system; and it is 'ideology', for Hardt and Negri, which would be linked with voluntarism, spiritualism, decisionism, terrorism, and the nostalgia for violent interventions to 'force' revolutionary changes from above, using the proletarian equivalent of the bourgeois state to undo its power.

But also, at the philosophical level, this accounts for the fact that they have an antithetic relationship to the Hegelian legacy in Marx, a legacy that is maximized or even entirely recreated by Žižek, whereas it is dismissed by Hardt and Negri (continuing ancient elaborations by Negri alone) as a pure expression of the 'modernist' trend in Marx, which emphasizes the importance of *mediations* to transform the 'constituent power' of the multitude into a legal 'constituted power' (against which Negri advocated the 'antimodernity' of Machiavelli and Spinoza, now rephrased as 'alternative modernity'). But again, let us not be too simple, because, just as in Žižek, there is no pure Hegelianism, but also a necessary intervention of a 'sublime' element of terror beyond or beneath the dialectic itself (which indeed owes much to an extreme interpretation of the Hegelian description of the Revolutionary 'terror', *das Schrecken*), and it accounts for the fact that, at some point, the 'real' in a Lacanian sense will intrude into the ideological realm and so to speak invert its function. Similarly in Hardt and Negri there is a sort of remaining dialectical element, or in any case a continuity with the idea that conflict, more precisely class struggle, generates the very development of the productive forces and the intrinsic relationship between a 'technical composition' and a 'political composition' of labour, at least until the point where the organicity of the system of productive forces becomes autonomized, or liberated (this is the legacy of Negri's intellectual and political formation within the ranks of Italian *operaismo*, for which he duly pays tribute to the path-breaking intervention of Mario Tronti). So we are led to understand that, in this confrontation, no less than a full radiography of the philosophical and political determinations of 'revolutionary' thought is involved, which pushes us to consider the *choices* that Marx did not want to make, but also that we would not have to make without Marx and the development of contradictions in the legacy of Marx and its practical implementation. This is not to say, of course, that other figures would be irrelevant to a complete examination of this 'heretical' pattern, in the sense of displaying the points of heresy of Marxism and showing their enormous relevance. But the Žižek-Negri confrontation has the enormous interest of illustrating a radical polarity.

Now, in order to name this polarity in the most eloquent possible manner, while remaining faithful to their terminology and their discourse, I will call the imaginative anticipation of the understanding of history *à la* Žižek 'divine violence' (following in the footsteps left by the afterword of his extraordinary book, *In Defense of Lost Causes*, where he appropriates the Benjaminian terminology); and I will call the imaginative anticipation *à la* Hardt-Negri, of course, 'exodus', following the direction of the already mentioned *Commonwealth* – the third volume in the trilogy that began with *Empire* (so Exodus is exodus from the domination of Empire that takes place inside the Imperial 'territory' itself; or, to put it in Deleuzian terms, it is the *line of escape* that appears possible, or virtually present, when the power of the multitude that Empire tried to control and territorialize becomes uncontrollable). And I will summarize in the following manner what seems to me to form, each time, the *relevant question*, even the *inescapable question* that they are asking, the *philosophical difficulty* that they are handling in a disputable manner, and the *determining problem* that they are thus opening, to be retained, as much as possible, in a 'synthetic' presentation of the anticipations of the revolutionary understanding (but a synthesis without synthesis, or one that remains 'disjunctive': being known for my eclectic capacity or temptation to occupy the mediating position, what is called in French the *juste milieu*, therefore I do my best to leave open what is, in fact, aporetic).

On the side of Žižek and 'divine violence', I believe that the absolutely correct question asked by him in *In Defense of Lost Causes* (particularly on p. 205) is the following one: 'How are we to revolutionize an order whose very principle is constant self-revolutionizing?' This is a question which is closely linked to the interpretation of the articulation between revolution and the developments of capitalism (its capacities of modernization), whereby what appears to have been the case in the last century was not the fact that revolutionary forces and class struggles represented modes of social organization *more advanced than capitalism*, but the fact that capitalism always retained or found the capacity to locate itself beyond the reach of these class struggles. But it is also linked to the interpretation of the new type of control that modern capitalism performs on subjectivities – in Freudian terms, the reversal of the function of the superego which leads not to suppressing the desire for enjoyment and affecting the murder of the father with inescapable guilt, but to locating guilt in the incapacity of the individual to liberate himself from constraints and immoderately seek the satisfaction of his demands on the market. And finally, most crucially, it is linked to the critique of *democracy* as a master-signifier used to produce voluntary servitude in our neoliberal societies, and a juridical-constitutional way to dismiss in advance, stigmatize, and expose to the brutal suppression of the global police any movement of rebellion, or transgression of the 'well-tempered' pluralistic order, that breaks with the standardized constitution of 'majorities' (often, in fact, due to the virtues of the parliamentary system combined with media distribution of information, these majorities are but oligarchic minorities).

But this is also where – in my opinion – the difficulties begin with the scenario of 'divine violence', politically and philosophically. There are at least two ways of understanding the normalizing function of democracy linked with the 'permanent revolution' of capitalism. One – which I would favour – is the idea that what currently counts as democracy is actually a process of 'de-democratization', so that there never exists anything like 'democracy' in a fixed and univocal sense, but only an endless conflict between processes of de-democratization and processes of the 'democratization of democracy', reclaiming equal rights and equal liberties for the citizens, which can take either a violent or a non-violent form, depending on circumstances and relationships of forces but always possesses an 'insurrectional' character. This is a certain form of 'negativity', but it is not the one that Žižek prefers, because it lacks the 'decisionist' (therefore in fact *sovereign*) element involved in the notions of 'divine violence', and a passage from the simple transgression of the law, or resistance to the oppressive order, into a 'terror' which he essentially defines in terms of the collective absence of fear of the consequences of an uncompromising *wager* on the possibility of equality and justice (therefore absence of the fear of death, both given and received: this is, incidentally, one of the important differences between Žižek and Badiou, the necessity or not of confronting death in the implementation of the communist idea, therefore also the existence of the death drive).

This is where, as we know, Žižek not only privileges the Leninist inter-pretation of Marxism – even the idea that revolution must be possible where its 'social' conditions of possibility are not given, because it *creates* retrospectively its own conditions or prerequisites in the course of its achievement, and in fact always represents a decision to try the 'impossi-ble', whose consequences are unknown, and probably fearful – but also returns from the Leninist concept of the dictatorship of the proletariat to its model or *Urbild* in the Jacobin terror, whose essential motto in his eyes is Robespierre's inverted tautology: 'Citizens, did you want a revolution without a revolution?' Although Žižek brilliantly manages to find a corre-spondence between this formula and the Hegelian notion of a 'revolution that includes within itself a reformation', or rather precisely because of this brilliant (*too brilliant*, in fact) demonstration, I believe that we face here a profound dilemma concerning the philosophical scheme of the 'negation of the negation' which affects every use that we can make of revolutionary schemes when we try to apply them to oppose the conserv-ative functions of democracy as a system of the disciplining of the exploited classes and the processes of de-democratization within the democratic form of the state. A 'revolution *not without revolution*' does not simply name the reiteration of the democratic idea; it names an *excess*, a decision, or even better – as Bruno Bosteels rightly suggests in his excellent discus-sion of Žižek (in *The Actuality of Communism*) – an *act* without which revolution returns to reform, and reform to reiteration of the status quo. So it is the perilous excess without which there is no difference between reformation and reform, and the internal, subjective reformation of the revolutionaries would become indiscernible from a subjection imposed from above. But it is also, for the same reason, a leap outside the dialectic of the institutions, or a sublime intrusion of the real into the symbolic, whereby, as Hegel perfectly knew and explained in the *Phenomenology*, the revolutionaries become subjectively unable to distinguish a destruction of the old order from their own self-destruction, inasmuch as they are themselves products and exemplars of the old order. This is the problem of the quality of the negation, the 'real negation', if I may say so (or the effective negativity), that Žižek profoundly works through, on the tracks of a re-Hegelianized Marxism; but it is also an extremist reading of Hegel that we can consider his contribution to the aporetic problem of the anticipations of communism, fully accepting his starting point in the critique of the inability of progressivist Marxism to cope with the transformative capacities of capitalism, but acknowledging that the distinction between an *internal* and an *external* negation, a *determinate* and *indeterminate* negativity, is extremely hard to find in history and open to unexpected returns of the death drive . . .

Let me now say something similar about Hardt and Negri. As I suggested briefly a moment ago, I take the *operaista* legacy to remain very important in their thinking; but this leads to another kind of difficulty, located in the immediate vicinity of what is probably their most interesting contribution to post-Marxist thought – namely their reformulation of the concept of the *productive forces* in 'biopolitical' terms, involving what they call a 'confusion' of the traditionally distinct processes of 'production' and 'reproduction' (in the sense of reproduction of the 'living capital', itself made of 'living individuals' who enter the labour process as producers under the control of capital). Finally it leads to the transformation of the category 'labour' as it was identified by industrial capitalism (all the way along from the industrial revolution to the transformations implemented by Fordism and welfare capitalism under the impact of workers' struggles inside and outside the factory, but also under the imaginary threat of the Bolshevik revolution, rightly identified by Negri in a brilliant essay from the 1970s as a decisive cause of the Keynesian reform), a more general, more diverse category of 'activity' that merges manual labour with intellectual labour, and combines the rational, utilitarian dimensions of exploitation with the 'affective' dimension of the reproduction of the labour force, which, in an ironic manner (since in other places they enthusiastically endorse a *queering* of the category of 'gender' amounting to a relativization of the distinctions inherited from the bourgeois family between the feminine and the masculine roles and identities), they do not hesitate to call a

'feminization of labour' – a feminization which is also a sort of natural-
istic de-naturation . . .

As we know, many things here are at the same time highly interesting
and also highly disputable, especially for Marxists, in terms of both
conceptual schematism and the interpretation of historical tendencies.
The discussion of the category 'labour' is especially fruitful because, while
it remains faithful to the idea that labour is centrally a political category
as much as an economic one, or the discussion of revolutionary politics
(which they also call 'insurrections' in the broad sense), it must remain
directly rooted in the activity of the 'producers', if not necessarily identified with a historical figure of the *worker* (*der Arbeiter*), at least with a
discussion of *what happens in*, and, so to speak, *to* the production process.
It also suggests that the transformation of the category 'labour' into a
multilateral activity of the individual – in fact only thinkable as a *transin-
dividual* activity, always already requiring the *various forms of cooperation*
between individuals – which for Marx (for example, in famous passages
of *The German Ideology*) formed the horizon of the 'communist' transformation of the productive forces when they have 'reached the stage of
forming a totality' at the global level, is now considered a *fait accompli*
under capitalism itself. Most readers of Negri and Hardt, except their
enthusiastic supporters, resist this idea, but I believe that it deserves a
careful discussion. There is a subtle, in fact conflictual relationship to the
utopian element in Marx involved here. On the one hand Hardt and Negri
tend to criticize an analysis of the tensions between a *narrow*, utilitarian
institution of wage labour dominated by the imperatives of capitalist
accumulation, and a wider notion of *activity* involving its multiple anthropological dimensions (manual and intellectual, rational and affective),
that would postpone it into the future, in the name of the critique of alienation. Instead, they want to project the utopia into the present, and make
it the permanent horizon of our understanding of contemporary capitalism. The great leap forward is accomplished when, as Marx explained
– in *Capital* – the process of production was not only a production of
goods, commodities, and new means of production, but also a *reproduction*
(even an *enlarged reproduction*) of the capitalist social relations themselves.
They now explain that the reproduction, in its most immediate and vital
aspects, has become so profoundly integrated into the production process
that it explodes the control of the existing forms of property, regulation
and disciplinary power, and gives rise, at least potentially – of course this
'potentiality' is the whole question – to an *autonomy* or an 'exodus' of the

living forces and their cooperation from the command of capital. Are we not here in the most blatant form of wishful thinking, in the name of historical materialism? In any case, we are certainly in a typical form of 'progressivism', in particular because Hardt and Negri have an avowed tendency to generalize what they present as the most 'advanced' and also 'subversive' forms of activity within contemporary capitalism, which shake the old territorialities and the old forms of the division of labour, as the already present image of the future that is awaiting every productive activity, especially in relation to the intellectualization and the feminization of labour.

My own critique of Hardt and Negri's grand narrative would focus on the following aspects of their argument, but also, for the same reasons, emphasize a *question* that, with their help, and qua communist subjects who are also thinking subjects, we cannot *not ask*, *not keep in mind* what we anticipate. First, I would say that they have a tendency to *ignore the counter-tendencies* in the developments that they describe (or imagine), therefore enhancing an evolutionist view of the development and transformations of capitalism. This is particularly true for their description of the intellectualization of labour, famously started long ago by Negri through his emphasis on the single page where Marx used the term 'general intellect' (in English), which plays a crucial role in their argument that the *law of value* linked to capitalist exploitation is transformed, because the profits of capital (or, as they prefer to say, the new *rent* extracted by capital) essentially derive from a cooperation among the producers, mediated by processes of communication and intellectual innovation whose result is not measurable: this would be the emergence of the 'new commons', which in turn anticipate (or already engage) a *new communism* (they fully endorse and extrapolate the theory and the practice of the 'creative commons'). But they ignore or minimize the counter-tendency – namely the gigantic forms of standardization, mechanization, and intensification of 'intellectual labour', especially in the fields of information technology, which through the use of iron discipline and savage constraints on a precarious workforce (corroborated in the new intensity of physical suffering in its computerized activities) forces cooperation to return under the law of value, and so to speak remakes 'physical labour' out of 'intellectual labour' (the category of biopolitics is misleading here, it seems to me). Similarly, on the side of the feminization of labour and the integration of the affective dimension of the reproduction of the living forces of production into the productive process itself, they ignore the counter-tendency which has been widely emphasized by recent debates on the uses of the newly fashionable category of the *care* to recreate forms of slavery, especially targeting the feminine workforce from the Global South (through the generalization of semi-controlled, criminalized migrations), but also the good old housewives and social workers of our 'developed' countries. Or perhaps *they do not ignore these counter-tendencies?* In that case they should develop their thinking concerning the *conflictual dimension* that, more than ever, affects the tensions between exploited labour and human activity in general, including its contradictory relationship with forms of coerced and autonomous cooperation, and they could thus contribute to a discussion of the extent to which 'real subsumption' of every aspect of the human life under the command of capital is in fact impossible, or *reaches a limit* within capitalism itself, which makes it impossible to create a 'pure' capitalism, or an 'absolute capitalism', even in the age of neoliberalism. Thus the outcome of capitalist development must remain suspended and uncertain. But this is in a sense a reverse reading of their notion of 'exodus'.

Second, I would say that the enormous interest of Hardt and Negri's discussion of the 'biopolitical' dimension of the transformations of labour and activity also lies in the fact of its imposing a fresh consideration of the relationship between Marxism and the issue of *anthropological differences* (of which the manual and the intellectual, the rational and the affective, but above all the sexual differences and the differences of gender-roles are typical examples). Again, they are perhaps suggesting a question that they too quickly resolve, or whose resolution in their terms is not the only possible one. This is because a notion of 'biopolitical reason' and the 'productivity of bodies' allows for the introduction into the 'political composition' of the multitude of all the differences without which there is no representation of the human, but which also can never become simply and forever encapsulated into administrative, sociological and psychological categories, beyond the simple model of the organization of industrial and commercial labour. But it also tends, paradoxically, to *homogenize* the multiplicity or diversity of social relations, subjective positions, conflicts between dominations and resistances, which it tries to articulate. I would suggest that the *order of multiplicity* that is involved in the consideration of all these anthropological differences (to which we should add others: ethnic and cultural differences, normality and abnormality, adulthood and childhood, and so on) is in fact greater than such concepts as 'productive forces' or 'biopolitics' allow us to think. This is not to say that, each time, a problematic of the 'common' or 'commonality' is not involved, especially in the form of collective struggles against the use of differences to isolate and oppose individuals, and attempts at basing solidarities on relations and interdependencies. But there is nothing that guarantees that these *diverse types of difference* will contribute to the same, or to a single, total idea of communism – or only in the most abstract form (for example, claiming equality), however important it is politically. Once again, this is a problem that we may want to inscribe in the aporetic column of communist thinking, as a diverse interpretation of the transformation of the world, rather than a universally agreed element of the history that 'we' are making. But, again, as in the case of Žižek, there would be no way to ascertain the diversity of the interpretations and ask about the real contradiction that they reveal if nobody had actually taken the risk of boldly choosing one of the branches of a conceptual antinomy.

I realize now that I have exhausted my time, so I will not actually present my third point in detail. I will only indicate, in the most telegraphic manner, which aspects I would try to articulate (and I will do it more effectively as soon as there is time, space, or another opportunity for that).

I would start with the simple consideration that we can know only *after the event* what the 'communists' do – how they act, which struggles they endorse, which concrete causes they fight for – when they are confronted not only with their own desire, but with existing social conditions and already given political alternatives, which is always the case in practice. However, at the same time (and this is part of both the subjective logic of commitment and the intellectual structure of anticipation), they can never, by definition, observe a quietist attitude or a position of 'wait and see'. What they need to do is find an angle, or a viewpoint, from which the contradictions of emancipatory, transformative – and, I would add, also civilizing – political movements, for example against forms of extreme social and political cruelty, can become radicalized and, as Badiou would say, intensified. From this point of view, the final page of Marx's *Communist Manifesto* is extraordinarily interesting and revealing, because it simultaneously affirms two things that are in fact interdependent and remain, in my opinion, completely actual (or perhaps have become actual again). One is that the communists do not form a *special party*; or the 'party' that they form is nothing else than the 'general interest' and the 'general movement' of the existing parties (perhaps we could say, in generic terms, *organizations*) pursuing emancipatory objectives and seeking to transform the world. The second is that the convergence of this 'general movement' is guaranteed in Marx by the fact that the 'proletarians', a paradoxical 'class' as we know, different from any other social class (in fact it is a non-class according to the terms that define social classes in past and present societies), combine a rejection of *private property* with a rejection of nationalist prejudices, or let's simply say *the national idea*. This is what allows Marx to declare, in a manner at the same time historical and prophetic, that the communists and the proletarians, 'uniting' at the level of the whole world, are but two names for the same collective subject, at least *in potential*. As I have argued on a previous occasion,[7] we have lost this conviction. But we did not lose the awareness, even the acute awareness, of the importance of the problem. The tentative conclusion I draw from this is a radicalization of the idea that the communists 'do not form a specific party'. I give it the form, intentionally provocative: the communists as such are certainly participating in organizations, and in the organization of movements, campaigns, or struggles, because there is no effective politics without organizations, however diverse their figure can and must be, depending on the concrete objectives. But they are not building any organization of their own, not even an 'invisible' one – they are, rather, *de-organizing the existing organizations*, the very organizations in which they participate: not in the sense of undermining them from the inside, or betraying their friends and comrades in the middle of the battles, but in the sense of questioning the validity of the distances and incompatibilities (very real, most of the time) between different types of struggles and movements. In that sense they essentially perform a 'negative' function in the form of a very positive commitment.

For that function, I was always tempted to borrow, once again, and as others already have done here, the famous name of the 'Vanishing Mediator' invented by our friend Fredric Jameson in his extraordinary essay comparing the function of the Jacobins in Marx's theory of the constitution of the bourgeois state, and the function of Calvinist Protestantism in the transition towards modern entrepreneurial capitalism as seen by Max Weber.[8] This was because a 'mediator' can be interpreted as a figure of temporality or historicity, but also as a figure of spatiality, translation, and heterotopy: a Vanishing Mediator is a vanish-

---

7   See 'Occasional Notes on Communism', available at krisis.eu.
8   See Fredric Jameson, 'The Vanishing Mediator, or Max Weber as Storyteller', in *The Ideologies of Theory*, vol. 2, Routledge 1988, 3–34.

ing traveller across borders that can be geographic, but also cultural and political; he can be a translator between incompatible idioms and organizational logics – and in order to do that he may have to *change name*, which is an important idea to discuss with respect to 'communist politics' today, and its being located sometimes, perhaps most of the time, where we do not see it. However, without losing the benefits of this crucial allegory, another reference comes to my mind, with which I want to conclude provisionally, and which has affinities with the allegory of the Vanishing Mediator although, in a sense, it reflects a different logic. This is Althusser's idea, repeated several times, that 'philosophers' (but in fact he was thinking of 'communist philosophers', and I submit that we can readily extend this consideration to 'communists' in general) are those who 'disappear in their own intervention' (vanish, if you like). This is what, according to him, demonstrates as much as possible that this intervention was *effective*. This is, of course, a very different idea from the one proposed by Badiou that communists display their fidelity to an idea whose consequences they enact: not so much perhaps because the practice, in the end, would be different – this is of course, as always in politics, a matter of the circumstances, the conditions and the forces – but because the philosophical reference is antithetic: not Saint Paul or Plato, but Spinoza, and possibly Machiavelli. I am not asking you to choose, I am just suggesting, once again, that we reflect on the diversity of the interpretations.

3 On the Christian Question

Bruno Bosteels

We think the 'political' like Romans, i.e., imperially.
— Martin Heidegger, *Parmenides*

Rome conquered Christianity by becoming Christendom ... Thus twenty Christian centuries were necessary to give the ancient and naked Roman idea a tunic with which to cover up its shameful parts and a conscience for its base moments. And now that idea is here, perfect and equipped with all the forces of the soul. Who will destroy it? Is it precisely its ruins that humanity has conquered with thousand-fold efforts?
— Elias Canetti, *The Human Province*

I would like to preface the remarks that follow by invoking the memory of two prior meetings at the Cooper Union in New York City. Certainly, both of these meetings were missed opportunities, or failed encounters: promises of things that could have been but never were. Yet they also eloquently speak to the legacy of a strong socialist and communist tradition that all too often tends to be forgotten in this country, due to the lasting effects of anti-communist propaganda during and after the Cold War.

The first meeting I want to bring to bear on this discussion is the Socialist Scholars Conference that took place at the Cooper Union on 1–2 April 1983. In a recent book, titled *Radical-in-Chief: Barack Obama and the Untold Story of American Socialism*, this meeting is described as a 'transformational moment' for Obama, the moment when he allegedly firmed up his decision to bring socialism to the United States. This is why the author of the book feels the need to warn his readers: 'Over the long term, Obama's plans are designed to ensnare the country in a new socialism, stealth socialism that masquerades as a traditional American sense of fair play, a soft but pernicious socialism similar to that currently [in 2010] is strangling the economies of Europe'.¹ In fact, according to the same author, the likelihood of such plans becoming a reality is much greater than the naive and uninformed reader might think:

> The idea that America might inadvertently and incrementally fall into socialism is a great deal closer to the strategies of 'actual existing socialists' than textbook definitions of economies nationalized at a single revolutionary blow. The reason Americans don't understand this is that the universe of post-sixties socialism has remained largely hidden from public view. Yet this is Obama's world. It's time we got to know it.²

Now I think we can all agree that this is not, or no longer, the world of President Obama, if it ever was – except in the eyes of Tea Partiers. But it is nonetheless true that, with the worldwide crisis of capitalism, ironically, the promise of some return of true socialism, or rather a new beginning for communism, is discussed as being closer than even a year or two ago.

The Socialist Scholars Conference of 1983 was also a commemorative event, celebrating the centennial of the famous meeting held in the Great Hall of the Cooper Union on 19 March 1883 in honour of Karl Marx, who had died five days earlier. This meeting was attended – or at least so his chronicle gives us reason to believe – by the Cuban writer José Martí, who at the time resided in New York City and worked as a foreign correspondent for the Argentine newspaper *La Nación*. Martí's chronicle about the meeting at the Cooper Union has been acknowledged as being 'a first pillar in the reception of Marxism in the strict philosophical sense in Latin America'.³ And yet, this too in some sense was a missed opportunity, since Martí's chronicle never ceases to respond adversely to the great labour of Marx as a militant political organizer.

Up to half a dozen times, Martí repeats the reproach that Marx and his followers from the first International sought to accomplish their noble ends with wrong or misguided means. 'Karl Marx studied the means of establishing the world on new bases; he awoke the sleepers and showed

---

1   Stanley Kurtz, *Radical-in-Chief: Barack Obama and the Untold Story of American Socialism* (New York: Threshold Editions, 2010), p. viii.
2   Ibid., p. 60.
3   Raúl Fornet-Betancourt, *Transformaciones del marxismo: Historia del marxismo en América Latina* (Mexico City: Plaza y Valdés/Universidad Autónoma de Nuevo León, 2001), p. 28.

them how to cast down the cracked pillars', writes Martí. 'But he went very fast and sometimes in darkness; he did not see that without a natural and laborious gestation, children are not born viable, from a nation in history or from a woman in the home'.[4]

For Martí, this mistake has to do with the differences between the Old and the New Worlds. According to him, Marx's German, French or Russian followers in the United States bring the gospel of class hatred and violent warfare to a country that has enough republican ideals to be able to do without such violent solutions:

> The future must be conquered with clean hands. The workmen of the United States would be more prudent if the most aggrieved and enraged workmen of Europe were not emptying the dregs of their hatred into their ears. Germans, Frenchmen, and Russians guide these discussions. The Americans tend to resolve the concrete matter at hand in their meetings, while those from abroad raise it to an abstract plane. Good sense and the fact of having been born into a free cradle make the men of this place slow to wrath. The rage of those from abroad is roiling and explosive because their prolonged enslavement has repressed and concentrated it. But the rotten apple must not be allowed to spoil the whole healthy barrel – though it could! The excrescences of monarchy, which rot and gnaw at Liberty's bosom like a poison, cannot match Liberty's power![5]

It would take Martí several more years, until after the execution of the Haymarket anarchists, to turn around this verdict. In November 1887, he thus is able to completely revise his earlier distinction between the tactics and strategies to be used in Europe and the New World. 'This republic, in its excessive worship of wealth, has fallen, without any of the restraints of tradition, into the inequality, injustice, and violence of the monarchies', Martí now observes about his host country. And later in his chronicle about the Chicago anarchists, he is even more direct: 'America, then, is the same as Europe!' – so that the use of violence as an inevitable last resort may now seem justified: 'Once the

---

4   José Martí, 'Tributes to Karl Marx, Who Has Died', in *Selected Writings*, ed. and trans. Esther Allen (New York: Penguin, 2002), p. 131. For a more detailed reading, see Chapter 1 of Bruno Bosteels, *Marx and Freud in Latin America: Politics, Religion, and Psychoanalysis in Times of Terror* (London: Verso, 2012).

5   Martí, 'Tributes to Karl Marx', p. 131.

disease is recognized, the generous spirit goes forth in search of a remedy; once all peaceful measures have been exhausted, the generous spirit, upon which the pain of others works like a worm in an open wound, turns to the remedy of violence.'[6]

These meetings from 1883 and 1983 also prove something that decades of anti-communist and anti-anarchist propaganda have nearly obliterated – namely, the proud internationalist tradition that stands behind the communist idea even in the United States. This is a tradition of internationalism that I would like to extend by paying homage to the work of the Argentine philosopher León Rozitchner, who passed away on 4 September 2011 after spending the last months of his life working on a painstaking rereading of Marx's 'On the Jewish Question'.[7] For Rozitchner, this question of religion is not a secondary issue compared to, say, the urgency of the economic crisis or the groping efforts to invent new political forms on the part of the left. To the contrary, there are several reasons for returning to the critique of religious ideology in the present. Not only is the current war on terror legitimized in terms of a civilizational clash among the three so-called 'religions of the book'. But numerous leftists also have recourse to religion in their efforts to interrogate the limits of political sovereignty or to define forms of militancy of a new type. Witness the place of messianic, eschatological or apocalyptical modes of thought in the thinking of authors such as Jacob Taubes or Jacques Derrida, as well as the ubiquitous invocation of saintly figures, from Saint Augustine for Jean-François Lyotard, to Saint Paul for Alain Badiou and Slavoj Žižek, to Saint Francis for Toni Negri and Michael Hardt. It is in this context that I want to revisit what Rozitchner calls 'the Christian question', starting with a critical reflection on Marx's 'On the Jewish Question'. Ultimately, this is a question about the kind of subject that might be called communist today, and whether, or to what extent, the religious matrix is helpful in grasping how communism can become subjectivized.

That the Christian matrix of subjectivity, unravelled by Marx, continues to play a pivotal role in our current political situation – crises and revolts included – can be gauged from the following response to the protests by secularists in Spain against the official visit of (then still) Pope

---

6   José Martí, 'Class War in Chicago: A Terrible Drama', *Selected Writings*, pp. 199–200.
7   León Rozitchner, 'La cuestión judía', in Daniel Bensaïd, Karl Marx, Bruno Bauer and Roman Rosdolski, *Volver a 'La cuestión judía'*, ed. Esteban Vernik (Barcelona: Gedisa, 2011), pp. 193–253. Unless otherwise indicated, all translations are my own. For a more detailed discussion of Rozitchner's work, see Chapters 4 and 5 of my *Marx and Freud in Latin America*.

Benedict XVI to the Jornada Mundial de la Juventud (World Youth Day) in July 2011. The speaker is Esperanza Aguirre, president of the Community of Madrid, from the right-wing Partido Popular, who at the time had already been facing several weeks of protests from the so-called *indignados* in the Puerta del Sol in Madrid:

> These gentlemen who march in protest should know that the values that Christianity has brought to the West and to the world – the equality of human beings, the dignity of persons, liberty, piety, sacrifice, the concern for others – are all positive. All this has been brought about by Christianity. Don't believe it when they say that Marx has brought this.

Except for the positive evaluation of said values, Marx of course would have agreed with every word of this assessment. But to understand this requires that we focus on Marx's treatment of the Christian rather than only the Jewish question.

'On the Jewish Question', Marx's text from 1843 published the following year in the *Deutsch-Französische Jahrbücher* that he co-edited with Arnold Ruge, is one of those texts that we may have 'understood' all too well. Not only has this text been buried under a mountain of accusations against its author, ranging from charges of Jewish self-hatred to outright anti-Semitism, but even authors such as Daniel Bensaïd, who are otherwise wholly sympathetic to Marx's arguments, often see no need to go beyond the plea for a complete secularization of all theological arguments over and against the current 'religious turn' among radical thinkers of the left and right alike.

Marx himself, admittedly, may seem to be arguing along these lines. Indeed, does he too not propose to bring heaven down to earth, to put the spiritual back on its material base, and to reduce the infinite to the strictly finite? As he writes: 'We do not turn secular questions into theological questions. We turn theological questions into secular ones. History has long enough been merged in superstition, we now merge superstition in history.'[8] However, merely to argue for the secularization of theology misses the whole point of 'On the Jewish Question'. Worse, it confuses Marx's argument with that of its principal interlocutor, Bruno Bauer, in the original text called 'The Jewish Question', *Die Judenfrage* – a title that

---

8   Karl Marx, 'On the Jewish Question', in Karl Marx and Friedrich Engels, *Collected Works* (New York: International Publishers, 1975), vol. 3, p. 151.

incidentally we ought perhaps to consider translating as 'The Jewish Demand' or 'The Demand of the Jews'.

It is Bauer, not Marx, who reasons that Jews in Germany cannot be emancipated so long as they do not emancipate themselves from being Jewish. 'Bauer therefore demands', to quote Marx's paraphrase, 'on the one hand, that the Jew should renounce Judaism, and that mankind in general should renounce religion, in order to achieve *civic* emancipation. On the other hand, he quite consistently regards the *political* abolition of religion as the abolition of religion as such'.[9] Marx is still paraphrasing Bauer when he later writes: 'The *political* emancipation of the Jew, the Christian, and in general of *religious* man is the *emancipation of* the state from Judaism, from Christianity, from *religion* in general'.[10] Clearly, even for the future author of *Das Kapital* who will delight in signalling all the 'theological niceties' involved in 'commodity fetishism', the argument for the political emancipation from religion cannot suffice. In fact, the abolition of religion risks leaving intact the religious – and more properly Christian – core of the dominant form of modern politics; that is to say, it fails to touch upon the Christian core of the modern state as propounded even by Bauer and other Young Hegelians such as Ruge, Marx's friend and co-editor, with whom he will promptly break both personally and ideologically.

In his recent extended reinterpretation of 'On the Jewish Question', written on the occasion of the Spanish translation of Bensaïd's presentation of Marx's text, Rozitchner draws attention to our continuing inability to come to terms with the complexities of this text, blinded as most contemporary readers undoubtedly continue to be by Marx's constant use of ironic, not to say sarcastic language that seems all the more disturbing in the wake of the Holocaust. For Rozitchner, the point is not to secularize religion and spirituality in the name of materialism, but rather to travel down the road genealogically to the religious alienation that lies at the root of political and economical alienation.

Why else would Marx see the need to pick up the question of religion again, if already in the so-called Kreuznach manuscript from the beginning of 1843, in a summary settling of accounts with his own Hegelianism, he had written that 'the criticism of religion is in the main complete'?[11] Why else would he return to religiosity when in this same pivotal year he

---

9   Ibid., p. 149. All emphases in original, unless otherwise indicated.
10   Ibid., p. 151.
11   Marx, 'Contribution to the Critique of Hegel's Philosophy of Law', *Complete Works*, vol. 3, p. 175.

is already moving away from humanist themes like the freedom of the press in favour of the critique of political economy and other topics of historical materialism, such as the polemics unleashed by the question of the theft of wood?[12]

It should not come as a surprise that Marx is especially sensitive to the call for religious self-sacrifice that Bauer proposes to the Jews as the solution to their demand for political emancipation in Germany. This call must have awakened painful personal memories in the young Marx. Upon the recommendation of his father Heinrich, Karl after all had been christened at the age of six. As a Jew turned into a socially acceptable Christian, Marx thus already had travelled half the road towards complete political emancipation proposed by Bauer. In Marx himself, this experience seems to have left deep psychic scars.

In a long letter to his father written when he was nineteen years old, shortly after arriving at the University of Berlin, young Karl would justify his career choice by explaining why he had abandoned the study of law in favour of philosophy, first idealist and then materialist. 'From the idealism which, by the way, I had compared and nourished with the idealism of Kant and Fichte, I arrived at the point of seeking the idea in reality itself. If previously the gods had dwelt above the earth, now they became its centre', as Marx puts it. '[L]ike a vigorous traveller I set about the task itself, a philosophical-dialectical account of divinity, as it manifests itself as the idea-in-itself, as religion, as nature, and as history'.[13] And yet, even through such a near-materialist working-through of religion as nature and as history, this loving son never seems to have fully healed from the trauma of his formal conversion to Christianity decided upon by his father. He thus writes in the same letter from November 1837 to Heinrich Marx: 'A curtain had fallen, my holy of holies was rent asunder, and new gods had to be installed.'[14]

When Marx returns to the relation of politics and religion in 'On the Jewish Question', he is thus speaking partly from the painful memory traces left in him by his forced christening. What this experience allows Marx to see, perhaps in a sadly privileged way, is the extent to which there is a Christian foundation that lives on, hidden at the very heart of the supposedly secular modern state. This is because the logic of

---

12   See Daniel Bensaïd, *Les Dépossédés: Karl Marx, les voleurs de bois et le droit des pauvres* (Paris: La Fabrique, 2007).
13   Marx, 'Letter from Marx to His Father in Trier', *Collected Works*, vol. 1, p. 18.
14   Ibid.

secularization, as in the separation of church and state so often invoked – whether with pride or nowadays with increasing regret – in North America, presupposes a prior separation of the private and the public, symbolized in the split nature of the human being as 'man', on one hand, and 'citizen', on the other – as in the different Declarations of the Rights of Man and the Citizen that accompanied the French and American Revolutions.

The real question, then, does not pertain to the difference between two religions, Jewish and Christian, according to what Bauer, in the second text to which Marx responds, calls their respective capacities for being free. Instead, for Marx, this religious difference is itself a displaced version of the division between the private realm, in which there exists freedom of religious belief, and the public sphere, which is supposed to be the realm of politics proper and in which, as a consequence, religion should no longer have any place. But then, Marx adds, this last division in turn does nothing more than prolong the Christian division between the heavenly and the earthly, the infinite and the finite. 'Where the political state has attained to its full development, man leads, not only in thought, in consciousness, but in *reality*, in *life*, a double existence – celestial and terrestrial', Marx writes with great sarcasm. 'He lives in the *political community*, where he regards himself as *communal being*, and in *civil society* where he acts simply as a *private individual*, treats other men as means, degrades himself to the role of a mere means, and becomes the plaything of alien powers. The political state, in relation to civil society, is just as spiritual as is heaven in relation to earth'.[15] What this means is that modern politics, embodied in the so-called rational secular state, continues to be built on the permanence of a form of subjectivity that is profoundly Christian. Or, as Rozitchner concludes: 'The Christian subjective scission becomes objective and unfolds itself in that scission within the State', and this is all the more so, not less, when the latter proclaims itself to be secular: 'The Christian spirit, subjective, infinite and immanent, which had become objective, finite and transcendent in the theological Christian State, has constituted itself into the secular and political basis of the perfect rational secular State'.[16]

Marx blames Bauer, in short, for failing to see the extent to which the Jewish question cannot be answered without addressing the Christian question: 'The division of man into a *public man* and a *private man*, the

---

15   Marx, 'On the Jewish Question', *Collected Works*, vol. 3, p. 154.
16   Rozitchner, 'La cuestión judía', p. 200.

displacement of religion from the state into civil society, this is not a stage in political emancipation but its *completion*; this emancipation therefore neither abolishes the *real* religiousness of man, nor strives to do so'.[17] The Christian state, which still leaves Christianity in existence as an explicit creed, as in the case of Prussia at the time of Marx, has not yet fully perfected the transubstantiation of religion into politics. Paradoxically, this level of perfection is achieved only in the so-called secular democratic state, which Marx associates with the United States of America:

> In the perfect democracy, the religious and theological consciousness itself is in its own eyes the more religious and the more theological because it is apparently without political significance, without worldly aims, an affair of the heart withdrawn from the world, the expression of the limitations of reason, the product of arbitrariness and fantasy, and because it is a life that is really of the other world. Christianity attains here the *practical* expression of its universal-religious significance in that the most diverse world outlooks are grouped together alongside one another in the form of Christianity, and still more because it does not ask that anyone should profess Christianity, but simply that he should have some kind of religion.[18]

What Marx proposes to do in 'On the Jewish Question', then, is at least theoretically to retrace some of the steps that led up to the paradoxical accomplishment of the Christian spirit in the modern secular state. The political timeliness of this proposal for the present moment should be obvious enough for everyone to see, provided that we are not seduced by the secularization thesis nor misled by the accusations of anti-Semitism. But theoretically, too, there are important lessons to be learned from Marx's youthful text. To do so would require not just developing a materialist theory of the genesis of subjectivity out of substance, of spirit out of nature, or of form out of matter, but also delving deeper into the genealogy of different forms or types of subjectivity. In terms of politics, this perhaps means moving away from philosophy, with its inherent propensity for always asking the transcendental question, towards a dialectical articulation of history and theory. In addition to developing a Marxist theory of the subject, a contemporary reading of 'On the Jewish Question' thus requires that we also reconstruct a history of modern capitalist as

---

17   Marx, 'On the Jewish Question', p. 155.
18   Ibid., p. 159 (translation modified).

well as pre-capitalist forms of subjectivity, along the lines of what Rozitchner himself does in *La Cosa y la Cruz* ('The Thing and the Cross'), a book which offers a close textual reading of Saint Augustine's *Confessions* as the quintessential manual of subjection of the individual to both the Christian religion and the power of command of the Roman Empire.

In retrospect, this is an agenda for theoretical work that, following Rozitchner, we may already find in Marx's text from the *Deutsch-Französiche Jahrbücher*, perhaps because Marx derives the task of historical genealogy from his own autobiographical trajectory. Rozitchner is quick to add that Marx himself, even later in his mature work, did not bring to fruition the agenda of such a combined history and theory of political subjectivity:

> It is true, Marx does not analyze in detail the historical conditions, the 'social relationships' that from historical religious Judaism and in a determinate context produced the metamorphosis operated in the ancient popular pagan imaginary by the new Christian myth so dear to Constantine, with whom religion at its origin appears as a new technology of domination in the production of subjects appropriate for the subsistence of the Roman Empire. But contemporary Marxists will not be able to ignore this, as can be deduced from their analysis, when they pretend to transform the consciousness of alienated political subjects by modifying only the economic relations of production, without putting into play the mythical determinations of Christianity.[19]

Today, there are those, like my friend Slavoj Žižek, who manage to defend Christianity as a legacy still worth fighting for, or a lost cause worth defending. For them, such endeavours require a materialist reversal whereby what otherwise appears to bask in the light of dogmatic truth all of a sudden shines forth as a fragile absolute, summed up in Christ's exclamation on the Cross: 'Oh Father, why hast Thou forsaken me?' What this cry symbolizes is precisely that which resists symbolization absolutely – that is, the fact that the order of the universe is inherently incomplete, dysfunctional, not-all. 'In short, with this "Father, hast thou forsaken me?", it is God who actually dies, revealing His utter impotence, and thereupon rises from the dead in the guise of the Holy Spirit.'[20] Far

---

19   Rozitchner, 'La cuestión judía', p. 204.
20   Slavoj Žižek, *For They Know Not What They Do: Enjoyment as a Political Factor*, second edn (New York: Verso, 2002), p. liii.

from simply betraying a momentary lack of faith, Jesus's cry highlights the properly revolutionary nature of Christianity in the eyes of Žižek, who is a strict follower in this regard of Chesterton when he wrote in his *Orthodoxy*: 'Christianity is the only religion on earth that has felt that omnipotence made God incomplete. Christianity alone has felt that God, to be wholly God, must have been a rebel as well as a king.'[21]

No matter how much we may spice them up with examples from Hegel to Hollywood, though, all such dialectical reformulations and reversals of Christianity – including Žižek's bold reformulations of the passage from Judaism to Christianity – in the name of a newborn materialism remain, strictly speaking, at the level of a structural or transcendental discussion of the conditions of possibility of subjectivity as such. At a time when wars continue to be waged, and people continue to be murdered, in the name of the so-called civilizational values embodied in the Christian faith, these arguments fail to take account of such profound complicities as the one that, according to Marx, links the rational democratic form of the state to the essence of Christianity. Nor does it suffice merely to abandon the vocabulary of the religious turn, if at the same time the very religious – and more properly Christian – foundations of the modern theory of the subject are not only left untouched, but not even explicitly admitted anymore.

For all my deep affinity and personal affection for the thoughts presented by thinkers such as Žižek and Cornel West, I believe that proposals for a revolutionary or prophetic Christianity to break with the rule of capital amount to attempts to fight fire with fire. What would be needed to break this circle is a long-term genealogy of the history and politics of capitalist subjectivity, as well as of the difficulty of formulating a communist alternative that would not remain trapped in more of the same. 'We therefore must reach back from political to religious alienation in order to understand the persistence of the religious within the political', as Rozitchner also writes in his commentary about 'On the Jewish Question'. 'We must show that the Christian essence, which "critical criticism" claims to have overcome, remains and is objectified in the material social relations of the democratic secular State whose terminal form, as

21   Gilbert Keith Chesterton, *Orthodoxy* (New York: John Lane, 1908), p. 256. See Žižek, 'A Modest Plea for the Hegelian Reading of Christianity', in Slavoj Žižek and John Milbank, *The Monstrosity of Christ: Paradox or Dialectic?*, ed. Creston Davis (Cambridge, MA: MIT Press, 2009), p. 48. For a discussion, see Bruno Bosteels, 'Žižek and Christianity, or, the Critique of Religion after Marx and Freud', in Jamil Khader and Molly Anne Rothenberg, eds, *Žižek Now: Current Perspectives in Žižek Studies* (London: Polity, 2013).

Marx demonstrates, is the United States of America. And to show, let us add, how it persists to this very day'.[22] Precisely such a genealogical task is taken up in Rozitchner's formidable book, *The Thing and the Cross: Christianity and Capitalism (About Saint Augustine's* Confessions).[23]

A good vantage point from where to approach this book would be based on a comparison between the respective readings of Augustine's *Confessions* found in Lyotard and Rozitchner: the first, offering a posthumous and unfinished, almost hagiographic testament; and the second, a painfully dense, frequently repetitive, and occasionally vicious attack. For Lyotard, Saint Augustine's *Confessions* seem to provide the occasion for an experience of near-sublime joy: 'The ability to feel and to take pleasure unencumbered, raised to an unknown power—this is saintly joy. Rarely did grace take a less dialectical turn, less negativist and less repressive. In Augustine, flesh bestowed with grace fulfills its desire, in innocence.'[24] Despite sharing an interest in the relation between grace and the flesh, Rozitchner would have had to reject this interpretation almost word for word. Beyond the appearance of sheer innocence and sensuous joy, nothing could in fact be more repressive or more negative than the dialectic between death and salvation, or between grace and terror, which Rozitchner uncovers in the *Confessions*.

Rather than serving as a substitute love letter, in which the divine 'Thou' comes to stand in effortlessly for the beloved, as is the case for Lyotard, Augustine's text in Rozitchner's hands thus becomes the target of an incursion into hostile territory where a declining Roman Empire, making a common front with the Christian church in a world-historical juncture best depicted in Augustine's own subsequent elaboration in *City of God*, gives rise to a sinister subject formation that prepares the onslaught of capitalism several hundred years later. Saint Augustine, then, is not a model; he is the enemy, the one who serves as an anti-model. 'In his

22   Rozitchner, 'La cuestión judía', p. 199.

23   León Rozitchner, *La Cosa y la Cruz: Cristianismo y Capitalismo (En torno a las* Confesiones *de san Agustín)* (Buenos Aires: Losada, 1997).

24   Jean-François Lyotard, *The Confession of Augustine*, trans. Richard Beardsworth (Stanford: Stanford University Press, 2000), p. 12 (translation modified). Compare with the tone of Hardt and Negri's last page in *Empire* (Cambridge, MA: Harvard University Press, 2000):

here is an ancient legend that might serve to illuminate the future life of communist militancy: that of Saint Francis of Assisi . . . Once again in postmodernity we find ourselves in Francis's situation, posing against the misery of power the joy of being. This is a revolution that no power will control – because biopower and communism, cooperation and revolution remain together, in love, simplicity, and also innocence. This is the irrepressible lightness and joy of being communist. (p. 413) theological libidinal economy the saint proposed to us, from the oldest times, the most productive originary investment to accumulate sacred capital', Rozitchner writes, before summing up the bold hypothesis behind his reading of the *Confessions*: 'The Christian Spirit and Capital have complementary metaphysical premises'.[25] Following this hypothesis, we slowly delve into the visceral depths of the subject so as to locate the place where terror and the fear of death, from the earliest experiences of the child onward, become ingrained into the material soul. In fact, without this inscription – for which we can find the user's manual on page after page of Augustine's *Confessions* – Rozitchner claims that capitalism would not have been possible. Finally, the theoretical core of this argument is twofold, combining as it does a thorough investigation into the roots of power and subjection in terror, on the one hand, with a wilful retrieval of the collective potential for rebellion and subjectivization, on the other.

The first theoretical strand allows us in hindsight to posit that terror and grace are actually twin developments, which the critique of subjection therefore cannot treat as separate or mutually exclusive phenomena. For Rozitchner, terror derives from the anxiety of death installed in the innermost core of the subject due to the guilt felt over killing or wanting to kill the primordial father. Grace, however, is merely a false solution, or a defence formation in which the origin of power and its extension into the subject's life are covered up, or, precisely, promised an imaginary solution.

It is not just that terror and grace are said to correspond to two forms of fundamentalism, one supposedly Islamic and the other Christian, competing on the stage of world history today. In fact, Rozitchner's investigations into the place of terror in any theory of subjection, as well as his interest in the Christian model of grace, precede by many years the events of the American 9/11 and the ensuing war on terror. But it is also not just a matter, as it seems to be for Badiou and Žižek, of re-establishing the original link between (good) terror and revolution, from the Jacobins to Hegel. Rather, the unenviable epistemological privilege of Rozitchner's viewpoint stems from the insight that the regime of terror that is the military dictatorship in Argentina extends its reign well beyond the so-called Process of National Reorganization. The 'view from the South' thus opens up a completely different perspective on the

---

25   Rozitchner, *La Cosa y la Cruz*, p. 12.

war on terror that was to be unleashed with particular violence in March 2003, during the 'Shock and Awe' operation in Iraq. In fact the other, Chilean 9/11 – that is, Pinochet's 1973 military coup and the spectacular bombing of the presidential palace of La Moneda in the nation's capital – in this sense would be instructive for the logic of events surrounding 9/11 in the United States.

We must come to think through the sinister dialectical link between grace and terror, without placing the former as the gift of peace or democracy or civilization that would come *after*, and *in response to*, civil war or dictatorship or barbarism. 'To understand the pacification we must first start from the terror that grounds it', Rozitchner writes. 'War and the dictatorship are terror; but democracy is a grace that the power of terror concedes to us as a truce. Both, democracy and dictatorship, are two modalities of politics, and they constitute the alternating domain in which social contradictions are fought out.'[26] Such would be the sad lesson to be learned from the experience of the military dictatorships, which we now know amounted to the violent imposition of the reign of neoliberalism. The transition to democracy, however, did not mark a break with the underlying logic of terror. To the contrary, the democratic process continues to be grounded in this very logic, only now it is hidden or disavowed: 'The dictatorship from which we come, then, is not an *accident* nor an *abnormal* fact in our political development: military terror, on the contrary, is part of the same system together with the implicit limits of democracy itself. It constitutes its founding and persistent violence.'[27] Much less obvious is the answer to the question of what is to be done once the founding violence behind the current political order is exposed.

The difficulty in question stems from the play of dissimulation through which democracy appears as the epitome of liberty and peace, only temporarily interrupted by the abnormality of civil war and dictatorship. Insofar as this game of hide-and-seek is not accidental but constitutive of the democratic order, the first step necessarily requires an effort of undoing the logic of dissimulation. As Rozitchner writes: 'Terror represses the personal place that feeds the impulses for resistance: the collective drives. Because of this it is necessary to undo this subjective trap: to keep present, in order to conjure it, the mortal threat that will emerge again when resistance appears.'[28]

---

26   Rozitchner, *El terror y la gracia*, ed. Rubén H. Ríos (Buenos Aires: Norma, 2003), pp. 26–7.
27   Ibid., p. 121.
28   Ibid., p. 122.

Rozitchner goes so far as to suggest that capitalism imposes a diffused 'Shock and Awe' operation on each and every subject, in the civilized West no less than in the rest of the world – as witnessed, by way of a dark precursor, under the military regimes in the Southern Cone:

> Terror, denied in political society but always threatening, corrodes human subjectivity from within. This unconscious fear that runs through society – the terror of death in religion, which it enlivens in the face of rebellion; the terror of unemployment, of bankruptcy or of poverty in the economy; the terror of the armed forces of repression; the terror of the covering-up of those forms of knowledge that might be able to unravel this domination – is the ground on the basis of which the system negates, within each one, the very thing that it animates.[29]

Here, however, we also already begin to grasp the other, rebellious strand in Rozitchner's overarching theoretical proposal. In effect, his aim is never merely to uncover the originary violence of the political field per se, but rather to retrieve the potential for rebellion and resistance with which this violence always has had to come to terms in the first place, from time immemorial until today.

This originary rebellion, for instance, of the child against the father, is precisely the moment that Rozitchner seeks to bring to the foreground in his pivotal rereading of the myth of the killing of the primordial father in Freud's so-called 'collective' writings, particularly *Totem and Taboo* and *Civilization and Its Discontents*. Unlike what happens in certain texts by Agamben or even Žižek, the killing of the primordial father upon this reading is not meant to produce a radical metaphysics of the state of exception or of the death drive. Beyond the unmasking of originary violence, the aim is above all to put force into the collective subject. In other words, if there is a constant effort to reach back and delve into the roots of subjection, the purpose of this return is to enable a collective form of emancipatory subjectivization. The real task, then, consists first and foremost in the ongoing effort to reactivate a possible return to this forgotten origin of subjectivity in rebellion. This is an effort at *desfatalización* or 'defatalization' – that is, an effort to restore the force of historical possibility by reanimating the event-like structure of the process of subjectivization, whose archaic persistence does not preclude the option of reaching out for its effective supersession.

---

29   Ibid., pp. 128–9.

Such an effort continues even in Rozitchner's book on Augustine, published when the author had already reached the mature age of seventy-three, in an astonishing feat that combines a painstaking and sustained close reading with a series of wild theoretical speculations about a saint who may actually have been the first modern subject.

Now why would an incredulous Jew want to write, Rozitchner himself asks from the beginning, about the *Confessions* of a Christian saint? And I might second this by asking: Why would communism today, in the midst of worldwide crises and uprisings, be able to take on a new beginning by addressing the Christian question? Among the various answers, the most audacious one – certainly out-daring Max Weber's hypothesis about the ideological affinity between capitalism and Protestantism – holds that capitalism simply would not have been possible without Christianity: 'Triumphant capitalism, the quantitative and *infinite* accumulation of wealth in the abstract monetary form, would not have been possible without the human model of religious infinity promoted by Christianity, without the imaginary and symbolical reorganization operated in subjectivity by the new religion of the Roman Empire.'[30] Augustine is the pre-eminent model of these profound transformations in the psychic economy – and his *Confessions* a user's manual for subjection and servitude. The complete devalorization of the flesh, of pleasure, and of the social in general, together with the newly constituted subject's submission to the rule of law and imperial order, constitutes the lasting religious premises of the political sphere.

Rozitchner's project, however, does not amount to a reconstruction of the possible transpositions and systematic analogies between the political and the theological. Unlike Carl Schmitt, he does not propose a political theology. He also does not focus on *City of God*, as a student of political theology might, not even in order to invert its hierarchy in favour of the 'earthly city', as Hardt and Negri propose to do in *Empire*. Rather, he chooses to concentrate on the personal itinerary in the *Confessions* that, according to him, lays the subjective foundation for *City of God* as Augustine's grand politico-theological synthesis, written years later. Finally, the main discourse of reference for Rozitchner is not juridical but psychoanalytical – Freud being a more useful reference than Schmitt for understanding the subjective stakes of politics.

Rozitchner's work, then, seeks to uncover the material, bodily and

---

30   Rozitchner, *La Cosa y la Cruz*, p. 9.

affective parts of the subject that had to be subdued in the name of either a transcendent religion or a purely immanent reason – but only after the power of authority, of the law and of empire had already been able to impose itself in these very same recesses that were subsequently to have been denied:

> Augustine interests me only for the apparatus of domination and war with which he constructed human subjectivity under the sign of law and truth. This is what continues to be relevant today. Augustine knew how to find the intimate place where power enlivens and incites the emotions and fires up the most sinister fantasies in order to put the body in action and, at this terrible hour when the old world collapses, to yoke it to the war chariots of political and economical power.[31]

Tracing the path of this investigation, we obtain not only a detailed picture of how the subject, prior to becoming the flesh and fodder of capitalist accumulation, first had to become the subject of law following the Western Roman Empire's collapse around the time of the sack of Rome in 410 AD, which will mark the immediate reference point for Saint Augustine in *City of God*, but also a daring series of comparisons between Christianity and Judaism – as well as a powerful suggestion to supplement Freud's own doctrine of Oedipal guilt and the superego law (including its origin in the killing of the primordial father, which takes its cues mainly from the Jewish God) with an interpretation of the theory of the subject derived from Christianity. Here is how Rozitchner retrospectively describes the challenge faced by his reading of the *Confessions*:

> If we take this human model, considered to be the most sublime, and if we show that there, in the exaltation of the most sacred, the commitment to what is most sinister also finds a niche, will we not also, in doing so, have uncovered the obscene mechanism of the Christian process of religious production? This is the challenge: to understand a model of being human that has produced sixteen centuries of subtle and refined, brutal and merciless subjection.[32]

Compared with the current rush to retrieve the figure of saintliness as a future model for political militancy, Rozitchner's book on Augustine has

---

31   Ibid., p. 16.
32   Ibid., p. 10.

the enormous virtue of exposing the extent to which the notion of political subjectivity continues to be contaminated by Christian theology:

> This is why we were interested in finding the ground of the political in what is most specifically religious. And we asked ourselves if it is possible that each believer, with the content of the Christian imaginary, and despite the best of intentions, and even if he or she subscribes to the Theology of Liberation, can have a political experience that is *essentially* different from the politics it is fighting against. We ask if the fundamental ground of Christian religion is not *necessarily* the fundament of domination precisely in what is religious in it.[33]

The examples of Badiou, Negri, and Žižek reveal the real difficulty there is in answering the demand for a political experience, including on a subjective level, that would be *essentially* different from the one it combats. All of these thinkers, in fact, remain deeply entangled in the political theology of Christianity – unable to illustrate the militant communist subject except through the figure of the saint.

What, then, is the task of theory or philosophy in the face of this persistence of the Christian matrix of terror and grace? How can we reconcile the pursuit of philosophy when it would not be difficult to show that, at the foundation of every mastered truth, there lies the beaten flesh of a repressed body, terrorized in the name of the spirit?

When the world's military powers cease to hide the kernel of terror and the anxiety of death that underlies every principle of authority, the task of theory or philosophy can only consist in seeking out and undoing the spaces within thought where this kernel finds a way to nest itself: 'At times when the contradictions and crisis deepen, as it occurs now among us, we must ask ourselves about the essence of reflection and, thus, about the essence of philosophy that terror, by opposing it in its answer, seeks to cut short. Once again: it is war that nests itself within truth, and whoever pronounces truth is, in his or her own way, a combatant.'[34] Rozitchner, in a near-Adornian style, will use the powers of reflection to undo the ties that in principle bind all reflection to power and terror: 'To think the conditions of truth in philosophy means to reach out within the thinking human beings for the foundation where the core of terror takes refuges

---

33   Ibid., 11.
34   Rozitchner, 'Filosofía y terror', in *Freud y el problema del poder* (Buenos Aires: Losada, 2003), pp. 245–6.

within them, as their own limit.'[35] To think against this limit means abandoning neither the subject nor the concept, but rather turning the power
of the subject against the domination of constituted subjectivity, as well as
opening up the concept to that which cannot but remain unconceptual-
ized. Such would be the possible role of theory or philosophy in the face
of terror – even, or especially, when this terror seeks refuge within the
hearts of combatants who are called upon to fight against it in the name
of freedom and grace as Christianity's lasting gifts to the West.

---

35   Ibid., p. 250.

u

4   A Comm onist Ethics

Susan Buck-Morss

I

The first point: politics is not an ontology. The claim that the political is always ontological needs to be challenged.[1] It is not merely that the negative is the case – that the political is never ontological[2] (as Badiou points out, a simple negation leaves everything in place[3]). Instead, what is called for is a reversal of the negation: the ontological is never political.

It follows that the move from *la politique* (everyday politics) to *le politique* (the very meaning of the political) is a one-way street. With all due respect to Marcel Gauchet, Chantal Mouffe, Giorgio Agamben, and a whole slew of others, the attempt to discover within empirical political life (*la politique*) the ontological essence of the political (*le politique*) leads theory into a dead end from which there is no return to actual, political practice. There is nothing gained by this move from the feminine to the masculine form. The post-metaphysical project of discovering ontological truth within lived existence fails politically. It fails in the socially disengaged Husserlian–Heideggerian mode of bracketing the *existenziell* to discover the essential nature of what 'the political' is. And it fails in the socially critical, post-Foucauldian mode of historicized ontology, disclosing the multiple ways of political being-in-the-world within particular cultural and temporal configurations.

---

1   Bruno Bosteels cites Mouffe in 'The Ontological Turn', in his informative new book, *The Actuality of Communism* (London/New York: Verso, 2011), pp. 40–1. Mouffe: '[I]t is the lack of understanding of "the political" in its ontological dimension which is at the origin of our current incapacity to think in a political way.' (Chantal Mouffe, *On the Political* [New York: Routledge, 2005], p. 8). Also Negri: 'Here is where communism is in need of Marx: to install itself in the common, in ontology, and vice versa: without historical ontology there is no communism.' (Antonio Negri, 'Est-il possible d'être communiste sans Marx?' cited in Bosteels, 'Ontological Turn', p. 49.)
2   For a critical discussion of a leftist ontology, see Carsten Strathausen, ed., *A Leftist Ontology: Beyond Relativism and Identity Politics* (Minneapolis: University of Minnesota Press, 2009), particularly the concluding 'Afterword' by Bruno Bosteels (reprinted as 'The Ontological Turn', cited above).
3   'On Evil: An Interview with Alain Badiou,' *Cabinet* 5 (2001/02), at cabinetmagazine.org.

This is not news. From the mid 1930s it was Adorno's obsessive concern, in the context of the rise of fascism, to demonstrate the failure of the ontological attempt to ground a philosophy of Being by starting from the given world – or, in Heideggerian language, to move from the *ontic*, that is, being (*seind*) in the sense of that which is empirically given, to the ontological, that which is essentially true of existence (*Dasein* as the 'a priori structure' of 'existentiality'[4]). Adorno argued that any ontology derived (or reduced[5]) from the ontic turns the philosophical project into one big tautology.[6] He has a point, and the political implications are serious.

Ontology identifies. Identity was anathema to Adorno, and nowhere more so than in its political implications – the identity between ruler and ruled that fascism affirmed. Indeed, even parliamentary rule can be seen to presuppose a striving for identity, whereby consensus becomes an end in itself regardless of the truth content of that consensus.[7] It is not that Heidegger's philosophy (or any existential ontology) is in itself fascist (that would be an ontological claim). Rather, by a resolution of the question of Being *before* subsequent political analyses, the latter have no philosophical traction. They are subsumed under the ontological a prioris that themselves must remain indifferent to their content.[8]

---

4   For post-metaphysical ontology, essence cannot be a transcendent category but must remain immanent to existence. As Heidegger writes: 'the "essence" [*Wesen*] of this entity lies in its "to be"' (Martin Heidegger, *Being and Time*, trans. John Macquarrie and Edward Robinson, [New York: Harper & Row, 1962], p. 67; German original, p. 42). The being referred to here (being with a small 'b') is the 'given' world, the world which *es gibt* (which 'there is'), while conscious, human being is ontologically understood as *Dasein* ('being-there').

5   Compare Husserl's method of phenomenological reduction that influenced Adorno as a student.

6   At the level of the ontic, the verb 'is' is used descriptively, and truth is a matter of accurate perception, hence basically an epistemological problem. But it is quite another thing to suppose, by delving into the structures of the ontic, that they themselves are capable of disclosing a deeper, ontological truth. If such an 'ontological difference' is impossible, as Adorno claimed, then the whole procedure is a sham.

7   Adorno criticized the liberal-parliamentarian notion of compromise, as did Schmitt, but precisely for the opposed reason – that the differences in positions were not great enough. Adorno's principle of non-identity – his claim that the truth is not the safe middle; that, rather, *les extrêmes se touchent* – could be interpreted politically as an uncompromising means to this democratic end.

8   '[T]he existential analytic of *Dasein* [Being with a capital B] comes *before* any psychology or anthropology, and certainly before any biology' – i.e. before the material bodies of actual human beings! (Heidegger, *Being and Time*, p. 71; German, p. 45). Or, in another example, tools are mere 'beings-at-hand', and his example is the pen with which he writes. If ontological analysis precedes ontic knowledge, there is no way that the ontological description can differentiate between the philosopher's tools-at-hand and those of a worker on an assembly line (ibid., pp. 95–102; German, pp. 67–72). Or, on the relationship between philosophy and the social sciences: 'We must always bear in mind that the ontological foundations can never be disclosed by subsequent hypotheses derived from empirical material, but that they are always 'there' already, even when that empirical material simply gets *collected*.' (ibid., p. 75; German, p. 50).

Existential ontology is mistaken in assuming that, once 'the character of being' (Heidegger) is conceptually grasped, it will return us to the material, empirical world and allow us to gather its diversities and multiplicities under philosophy's own pre-understandings in ways adequate to the exigencies of collective action, the demands of actual political life. In fact, the ontological is never political. A commonist (or communist) ontology is a contradiction in terms.

But, you may ask, did not Marx himself outline in his early writings a full ontology based on the classical, Aristotelian claim that man is by nature a social animal? Are not the 1844 manuscripts an elaboration of that claim, mediated by a historically specific critique, hence an extended *social* ontology of man's alienation from nature (including his own) and from his fellow man? Yes, but in actual, political life, this ontological 'man' does not exist.

Instead, we existing creatures are men and women, black and brown, capitalists and workers, gay and straight, and the meaning of these categories of being is in no way stable. Moreover, these differences matter less than whether we are unemployed, have prison records, or are in danger of being deported. And no matter what we are in these ontic ways, our beings do not fit neatly into our politics as conservatives, anarchists, evangelicals, Tea Party supporters, Zionists, Islamists, and (a few) communists. We are social animals, yes, but we are also anti-social, and our animal natures are thoroughly mediated by society's contingent forms. Yes, the early Marx developed a philosophical ontology. Nothing follows from this politically. Proletarian dictatorship is not thereby legitimated, and the whole thorny issue of false consciousness (empirical vs. imputed/ ascribed [*zugerechnectes*] consciousness) is not thereby resolved. At the same time, philosophical thought has every right – and obligation – to intervene actively in political life. Here is Marx on the subject of intellectual practice, including philosophizing:

> But again when I am active scientifically, etc. — when I am engaged in activity which I can seldom perform in direct community with others – then I am social, because I am active as a man [human being]. Not only is the material of my activity given to me as a social product (as is even the language in which the thinker is active): my own existence is social activity, and therefore that which I make of myself, I make of

myself for society and with the consciousness of myself as a social being[9]

Again, no matter how deeply one thinks one's way into this ontological generalization, no specific political orientation follows as a consequence. It describes the intellectual work of Heidegger and Schmitt every bit as much as it does that of Marx or our own.

For Marx, ontological philosophy was only the starting point in a lifelong practice of scientific thinking that developed in response to the historical events surrounding him. Through the trajectory of his work, the entire tradition of Western *political* philosophy took a left turn away from metaphysics and towards an engagement with the emerging social sciences – economics, anthropology, sociology, psychology – understood not in their positivist, data-gathering or abstract mathematical forms, but as sciences of history – not historicality, historicity, historicism and the like, but concrete, material *history*. With this hard-left turn (which is an orientation that may or may not involve elements from the 'linguistic turn,' the 'ethical turn,' the 'aesthetic turn'), political philosophy morphs into social theory done reflectively – that is, critically. It becomes critical theory.

When Marx said thinking was itself a practice, he meant it in this sense. He did not then ask: What is the ontological meaning of the *being of practice*? Instead, he tried to find out as much as he could about the socio-historical practices of actual human beings in his time.

So the question Marx's early writings leaves us with is this: How do we turn this social – we could say, in a descriptive way, social*ist* – fact of our work, and our consciousness of this work as social beings, into a communist practice? How are we to conceive of a commonist ethics? Not by the phenomenological reduction to some essence of what it is to be a social being: i.e., a caring being, a being-to-death, a being-with, and so on, as Heidegger proposed – but rather by an analysis, a becoming-conscious, of the specific society, the specific cares, the specific deaths that are

---

9   Robert C. Tucker, *The Marx-Engels Reader*, second edn (New York: W.W. Norton & Co., 1978), p. 86. The original German is:

Allein auch wenn ich *wissenschaftlich* etc. tätig bin, eine Tätigkeit, die ich selten in unmittelbarer Gemeinschaft mit andern ausführen kann, so bin ich *gesellschaftlich*, weil als *Mensch* [ital. mine] tätig. Nicht nur das Material meiner Tätigkeit ist mir – wie selbst die Sprache, in der der Denker tätig ist – als gesellschaftliches Produkt gegeben, mein *eignes* Dasein *ist* gesellschaftliche Tätigkeit; darum das, was ich aus mir mache, ich aus mir für die Gesellschaft mache und mit dem Bewußtsein meiner als eines gesellschaftlichen Wesens.

simultaneous with our own; not common in the sense of the same as ours (experiences are very unequal in today's society), but of happening to others who share, in common, *this* time and *this* space – a space as big as the globe and a time as actual as now.

II

Marx changed the relationship between politics and philosophy by creating a hinge out of the social sciences. This hinge has worn thin. Today's philosophically naive social sciences purport to be objective as they splinter reality into self-referential academic disciplines that argue from present-day 'givens' as a quasi-natural base (rather than from dynamic, unstable structures that depend on human action). For its part, philosophy, going it alone, retreats to the humanities – to normative thinking, an analysis of reason and the Kantian world of moral oughts, or, alternatively, to a Nietzschean-inspired anti-rationalism, the celebration of affect, cultural relativism, literary narrativity, hermeneutic contingency. Even *critical* philosophy shares with the positivist sciences from which it has cut itself off the presumption that it can know reality on its own. Both approaches – thought without empirical understanding and empirical understanding without thought, without critical reflection – are extremely susceptible to reification.

Meanwhile, Marxism, orphaned by both sides of the academic project, the sciences and the humanities, risks dogmatism if it claims to provide knowledge beforehand (a priori) of the political meaning of events on the basis of century-old texts, fitting every empirical factoid into its pre-existing interpretive frame. As the master-code of history, Marxism grants to an anthropomorphized capitalist system all-powerful agency. Capitalism masterminds events, exploits voraciously for private gain, delights in crisis, all the while thwarting our best moral intentions, determining historical outcomes with a cleverness far greater than any Hegelian cunning of reason could provide.

Marx, as everyone knows, used the term capitalism only a handful of times. The big book is called *Capital*. And it is a critical exposure of the economic practices of his time, including the processes of fetishism and reification that make it appear that the laws of capital are our necessary fate.

Now I am going to make a tedious point: due to the epistemological consequences, we need to reject creating an -ism out of any political or theoretical orientation – no commun*ism*, no capital*ism*, no Marx*ism*, no totalitarian*ism*, no imperial*ism* – no -isms at all.[10] These are cosmological systems, economies of belief that resemble the medieval Christological economy (*oikonomia*) in that all their elements are internally consistent and logically satisfying, as long as there is no contamination by facts or events that, like illegal aliens of some sort, enter from the outside. The simple words – communist or socialist, capitalist or Marxist, and so on – are a different story. If they are used merely as descriptive adjectives, they refer to qualities (determinations) of objects in the world, which they define – objects that, if we are to be consequent materialists, must have priority over the concepts we use to name them.[11]

Political practice, too, is vulnerable to seduction by the -ism. It is a mistake to adopt anarch*ism* or social*ism*, Trotsky*ism* or Islam*ism*, radica-*ism* or parliamentarian*ism*, as a system of belief determining one's actions in advance. Conditions change, and practice needs to respond to new situations. Seize state power so as to control its ideological apparatuses? Yes, but what if, after the global transformation of capital, the state itself has become an ideological apparatus? Base one's politics on an anarchist respect for democratic agency? Absolutely. But not if that means yielding to the manipulative tactics of right-wing populism in its increasingly widespread forms.

To say, with Althusser, that Marx abandoned his early humanism for a 'science of history' implies that Marxist science is trans-historical and eternal, an ontological first principle immune to precisely the historical specificity on which it insists – as if science were not itself historical. (We have only to think of the historical limits of the science of Ricardo or Malthus, or, given the present crisis, of the Chicago School of economics, to make that point clear.) To argue, with Negri, for a 'historical ontology' based on a scientific understanding of the process of capitalist class strug-gle is a dubious alternative. Negri wants to add historical contingency to the mix, at the same time counting on an ontological fix to avoid the dangers of relativism that contingency implies. He does not let go of the class struggle as the *prima philosophia*, the philosophic first principle, on which the whole political project is grounded. But if, *pace* Negri, there can be no ontology of history, it is because history is the realm of human free-dom, and *therefore* the realm of the unpredictable – in thought as well as in

---

10   I am grateful to Ahmad Jalali of Iran for gently questioning my choice of the title for my book, *Thinking Past Terror: Islamism and Critical Theory on the Left*, on precisely these grounds.

11   Compare Adorno's insistence on the priority of the object (*Vorrang des Objekts*).

practice. At this point, rather than trying to develop an ontology of freedom, we need to recognize freedom's surprising, and fleeting, appearance in the world.

I am showing my true colours. I am an incorrigible pragmatist when it comes to critical theory. But that is not pragmat*ism*, in Rorty's or even Dewey's sense (and it has nothing to do with being an American). It is closer to what Bert Brecht described (and admired) as *plumpes Denken* – non-elegant thinking. So, for example, where the elegant philosopher would discover a concept by searching for the classical Greek meaning of a term, I take my lead from modern Greek, *demotiki*, the street language of the people (*demos*), that, along with the so-called fiscal irresponsibility of the Greeks themselves, is largely disdained by the European intelligentsia. *Ta pragmata* in modern Greek refers to the practical things that you use in daily existence. In German: *die Klamotten*, in the sense of the stuff that – though it might look like junk to others – you need and use every day.

Deployed in this sense, a pragmatic approach to doing theory bears a resemblance to the point that the Nigerian novelist Wole Soyinka made when he criticized the understanding of *négritude* as ontology by saying: 'A tiger does not proclaim its tigritude, he pounces.' He later clarified: 'a tiger does not stand in the forest and say "I am a tiger." When you pass where the tiger has walked before, you see the skeleton of a duiker, you know that some tigritude has emanated there.'[12]

Soyinka abandons ontology for something close to what I mean by a theoretical pragmatics.[13] It is a practice of theorizing whereby things acquire meaning because of their practical, pragmatic relationship with other things, and these relationships are constantly open, constantly precarious. Their future cannot be predicted in advance.

Now if we were interested only in the empirical science of tiger practice, we would be behaviourists, observing from a safe distance what a tiger does. But as political actors in the midst of things, we are duikers, and duikers need to know the latest news.

---

12   Soyinka, cited in Michael Richardson, ed., *Refusal of the Shadow: Surrealism and the Caribbean* (London: Verso, 1996), p. 10.

13   Of course, Achille Mbembe is absolutely right to point out that *négritude* was not a philosophy of first principles but a fully engaged political practice. We have to acknowledge that the writers who theorized *négritude* were engaged in a pragmatics of counter-hegemony with real institutional and political effects (Achille Mbembe, seminar, Committee on Globalization and Social Theory, CUNY Graduate Center, September, 2011). See also Ngugi wa Thiong'o, *Globalectics: Theory and the Politics of Knowing* (New York: Columbia University Press, 2012), p. 23.

Can we imagine Lenin without a newspaper? Or Marx, or Hegel, for that matter? Marx wrote for newspapers about events far away from Europe – colonialism in India, China trade, the US Civil War. And Hegel was formulating the dialectic of master and slave because of the Haitian Revolution that he read about in successive issues of the political periodical, *Minerva*.

Lenin, let us remember, did not expect the revolution would happen a) in Russia at all, or b) in the summer, or even fall, of 1917. But he allowed his theory to yield to historical developments as they actually occurred.[14] The historical event that surprises – this is the 'radical reality' to which Lenin remained open.[15] Here I am in total agreement with Badiou regarding the political centrality of the event, and on the same page as he, when he stresses 'the absolute unpredictability of the event' that 'can be the source of the emergence of the radically new'.[16] But I would take liberties with Lacan's formulation in ways that Badiou does not. It is not 'truth' that 'punches a hole in knowledge'. Rather, it is social action. And the truth that such action reveals is the possibility of human freedom. So, if we put together the idea of pragmatics and the idea of the event, we get: *a pragmatics of the suddenly possible* as an expression of human freedom. And that is not a bad definition of what a commonist ethics would imply.

Spoken in the inelegant language of *plumpes Denken*, then, the philosophically infused questions that a pragmatics of the suddenly possible would need to ask are these:

1. What's happening? (The pragmatic alternative to 'historical ontology'.)
2. What's new? (Is there an 'event' going on here?)

---

14   See Lars T. Lih, *Lenin Rediscovered: What is to Be Done? In Context* (Chicago: Haymarket Books, 2008), on his trust of the workers, especially German Social Democrats, when he wrote this pamphlet. Many argue that the Russian Revolution came too early, and *therefore* failed. Perhaps, instead, the too-early years of the Bolshevik revolution are the most relevant, in that their practices have never ceased to inspire: the aesthetic avant-garde; the street theatre; agitprop trains; the worldwide general strike of 1919 that was one of the earliest, largely spontaneous acts of global solidarity. In the US, Eugene V. Debs responded to Lenin's victory by exclaiming: 'From the top of my head to the bottom of my shoes, I am a Bolshevik, and proud of it!' In 1920 he ran for president from jail as the Socialist Party candidate, and won a million votes. The journalist Victor Berger posted on billboards: 'War is Hell Caused by Capitalism' – and was the first Socialist candidate elected to US Congress. Convicted, like Debs, under the Espionage Act, he was denied the Congressional seat into which he was twice voted by the electorate.

15   V. I. Lenin, cited in Robin Blackburn, ed., *After the Fall: The Failure of Communism and the Future of Socialism* (New York: Verso, 1991), p. 167.

16   Alain Badiou, *Being and Event*, trans. Oliver Feltham (New York: Continuum, 2005).

3. What gives? (What structures of power are suddenly yielding to the actors in the event?)

4. What's going on? (Are certain structures *not* in the process of change?)

And only then do we get to the Big Question:

5. *What to do?* ('What is to be done?' is the wrong translation of *Chto delat?*).

We might tarry over these questions for a while to view them in a commonist mode.

III

The event is not a miracle that overcomes us with awe and strikes us down. It lifts us, precisely because it is accomplished by ordinary people who interrupt business as usual in order to act collectively, empowering not only those who are present, but those who, in watching, feel a tremendous surge of solidarity and sense of human togetherness – even (dare I say it?) universality. We witness the actuality of human beings joining together to overcome barriers, to initiate change. This capacity to act in common is the real possibility of a commonist ethics.

The solidarity produced in the spectator, made famous by Kant in the case of the French Revolution, has become intense in the electronic age. Unlike in Kant's time, and also Lenin's, it was television's live coverage of political action that tipped the balance in favour of non-violent resistance. (Terror may be a political tool [Badiou], but it is a very blunt instrument, as historically dated, perhaps, as the hydrogen bomb).[17] In recent years, in the Iranian election protests of 2009–10, and throughout the Jasmine revolutions of the Arab Spring, the power of non-violent protest has multiplied exponentially.

For Kant, because of the bloodiness of French Revolutionary events, it

---

17   Badiou on what is to be done:

[T]he use of terror in revolutionary circumstances or civil war does not at all mean that the leaders and militants are insane, or that they express the possibility of internal Evil. Terror is a political tool that has been in use as long as human societies have existed. It should therefore be judged as a political tool, and not submitted to infantilizing moral judgment. It should be added that there are different types of terror. Our liberal countries know how to use it perfectly.

See the video of this lecture ('Alain Badiou. Philosophy: What Is to Be Done? 2010) at youtube.com. (His paper for this conference clarifies that violence is not a necessary condition of the communist idea.)

was only the idea that garnered enthusiasm. On Tahrir Square it was the reality of peaceful force[18] – the force of non-violence in the face of violence, articulating a meaning of martyrdom that has universal human implications. The technological revolution of hand-held internet devices has enabled an explosion in possibilities for eye-witness reporting of events. In live time, the reporting itself becomes a weapon of resistance. No doubt, the way in which the new technologies are used depends on the hands that hold them. But what is remarkable is how reliable such information-sharing has been. Human actors have taken responsibility for others in ways that risk their own personal safety, releasing what has all the appearance of a pent-up desire for non-commercial, non-self-interested information-exchange, and trusting the international community of viewers to respond in solidarity – and they do.[19] (Perhaps we are by nature social*ist* animals after all.)

On the first level, then, 'What's happening?' is an empirical question. Approached from the mandate of a commonist ethics, answering this question requires first and foremost the full freedom of communication, by anyone who has knowledge to share, with anyone who has the desire to know. Here the reporting of independent media, the reliable collection of news, and its unfiltered, unblocked dissemination, are political projects of the highest import.[20] The more dispersed the points of observation, the fuller the picture of events will be.[21]

Incidentally, the life of Steve Jobs *is* about the US benefitting from immigration (his father was a Syrian Muslim, his mother was of German ancestry). While he is praised as a hero of free enterprise, his crucial *political* contribution is the fact that in developing the personal computer, he gave people control over the means of production of the global

---

18   Not violence [*Gewalt*] but force [*Kraft*], as the term is used by Hegel in the *Encyclopedia Logic* (paragraph 136).

19   In contrast, in the Iranian case, the (Finnish–German) corporation of Nokia put political conscience aside to work with the Iranian government in blocking the demonstrators' internet communication.

20   The effects of government regulation have already been felt in China, where the government blocked Facebook and Twitter as detrimental to 'Chinese national interest'. Google refused to comply, and moved its towers to Hong Kong, leaving the Chinese domestic search engine (Baidu) space to expand. Regulation of virtual national borders produces a global trade war on information.

21   I am not impressed with the idolization of figures like Julian Paul Assange, who has gained celebrity status and perhaps other narcissistic pleasures from his simple leaking of a mass of private documents. To say that his dumping of Pentagon papers sparked the Tunisian revolution is a bit like crediting Ronald Reagan for the fall of the Berlin Wall. Such acts are far more likely to be politically useful as an excuse for self-named democratic governments to implement control of the internet (which means that, regardless of his personal motives, Assange needs to be defended in this case).

economy – a commonist act if there ever was one. Cell-phone videos keep citizen protest and state violence in view. But Apple takes away citizen power when it designs the iPhone and iPad as platforms for profits from rent, and when these forms diminish the usability of the keyboard, emphasizing instead the internet as a place of consumption, where users' actions are monitored and sold as information.

On the second level, what's happening is an act of interpretation. To know what is happening, beyond the virtually mediated sense-perception (which, when it means seeing videos of brutality towards unarmed protesters, is the most unanimously and universally opposed moment in the event), is to name the action and place it in context. It is here that the difficult, often contentious work of political analysis begins, and this on the most basic level. What are we to call this moment of citizen action? Is it democracy that we are witnessing? Yes, surely. But by calling it this, we already seem to suggest the trajectory of events: success then means founding political parties, holding elections, and declaring loyalty to a secular nation-state that plays by the predetermined rules of the given world order. In other words, that which is suddenly possible in an event is to follow the lead of the self-proclaimed democracies that are already established. But none of those steps necessarily follows from what has happened, which, for the old, self-proclaimed democracies is a cause for alarm. The known steps, the ones they have taken, reduce the meaning of the suddenly possible to a pre-written script. If we then revisit the question, 'What's new?', the answer ends up being: not much.

But what if the truly eventful social action initiated in Tunis, Cairo and elsewhere is a previously unimagined structure of politics – not the universal one-size-fits-all relevance of nation-state democracy that, even allowing for the difference of culturally pluralistic contexts, presumes an eternal verity for two-century-old, Euro-American forms (which at present are responding badly to the global economic crises that their economic institutions caused), but a glimpse of global solidarity wherein national and cultural identities are suspended, and unity is the consequence, not of who you are but, rather, what you do? Let us call this a commonist practice.[22] The whole process of the act of protest and its

---

22   If we are to find a precedent in Hegel, it would be his comment in the *Encyclopedia Logic* that people are to be judged not by their motives, but by their actions: '[H]ere, too, the essential unity of inward and outward generally holds good; and hence it must be said that a person *is* what he *does*'. In this same section, he criticizes what was then called 'pragmatic historiography', referring (in contrast to our use here of 'pragmatic') to those who debunk the whole idea that historical actors are motivated by anything other than personal vanity, foibles, and so on. Hegel maintains that, as one's inner

virtual dissemination is, in its non-exclusionary, horizontal organizational forms, a brilliant manifestation of a qualitatively different, commonist ethic, pointing to the suddenly possible power of global solidarity. This is the new that reveals itself in this event – an event that is less a rupture than an opening for alternatives to the given state of things.

The idea here would be to oppose Schmitt's and Agamben's definition of the sovereign as he who decides in a state of emergency, turning its temporality and its agency inside-out, and we can do this by returning to the sixteenth-century meaning of the English word, 'emergency,' as the condition of emergence.[23] The state of emergency that produces a crisis for the sovereign is a liberating possibility for the sovereign's subjects – a moment for the 'emergency' of a new situation, a possibility that subjectivity itself can be transformed.

Finally, on 28 September 2011 the *New York Times* brought to mainstream media the biggest political story of the year, officially acknowledging what has been happening all along. A front-page story[24] put together the global pieces: the Arab Spring, India's support for Anna Hazare's hunger strike, Israeli citizens' pro-justice protests, days of rioting in Athens and London, the Indignados de la Republica in Spain – as well as citizen sleep-ins of the 'excluded' that are ongoing in civic spaces from Tahrir Square to the Plaza del Sol to Zuccotti Park. We need to add: the amazing bravery of citizens in Syria, Yemen and Bahrain who, with no help from NATO, persist in the face of violent repression by governments, the legitimacy of which they steadfastly refuse to recognize.

Arab Spring, European Summer, Wall Street Fall. We are witnessing a global social movement that affirms diversity and universality, both at

---

essence appears in one's actions, 'it must be recognized that the great men willed what they did and did what they willed'. One does not need to adopt his Great Man theory of history to argue, nonetheless, that self-conscious, collective action inspires us precisely because it evinces the human possibility of personal interests being sublated within the collective good. Indeed, critical reflection tells us that what society claims is in our self-interest is in fact always mediated by the interests of others – and in its present, individualist form, is deeply alienating. See Hegel, *Encyclopedia Logic*, paragraph 140.

23   This linguistic connection does not work in German (emergence = *Entstehung*), but another connection does. What for the sovereign is a sudden state of emergency (in German, *Notstand*), is, for the subjects, a rupture of their everyday experience of existential precariousness and poverty (in German, *Not*). Whereas the sovereign reacts to crisis with lightning speed and dictatorial power – there is no time for legal niceties – the sovereign's subjects have no need to move quickly; they demand time for change to emerge. To use Walter Benjamin's image, perhaps revolution is not, *pace* Marx, the locomotive of history, but the reaching by humanity riding in that train for the emergency brake (*Notbremse*).

24   By Nicholas Kulish (with networked colleagues Ethan Bronner in Tel Aviv and Jim Yardley in New Delhi). Chinese protests in Lufeng is from a later article by Andrew Jacobs, with Ia Li contributing (24 September 2011).

once. Clearly, it is radical, refusing to accept the given rules of the game. Is it a turn to the left? Perhaps this nomenclature can no longer be used – and this fact, too, is what's new. In our cyber-geographic situation, left-turns are positioned differently on the ground. They are local in orientation and necessarily plural. This, among many things, separates global, commonist action from right-wing populism. Where the latter marshals anger at the global disorder to support rigid ideologies of neo-national-ism, free-market privatization, and anti-immigration, thereby co-opting grassroots movements for the benefit of existing political parties, the trans-local constellation of forces refuses to be nationally or politically contained. For 'left' and 'right' to make any political sense, there have to be borders – territorial borders between nations, and partisan borders within them. The new activists are unwilling to be seduced by the rhetoric of divide-and-rule. Are they impractically naive? Is this an event at all?

IV

What gives? Walls fall, tyrants fall, an African-American immigrant's son is elected president of the United States. But what goes on? What contin-ues through all these transformations? Marxists will tell you: the global capitalist system – and the answer is not wrong. When Warren Buffett proclaimed (speaking the truth *from* power): 'there's class warfare alright, and we are winning', he could have added: 'worldwide'. At a time like ours today, when we are considering a new political beginning, the 600-pound gorilla in the room is radical politics' past, its debt to Marx's analysis of capital that dealt intensely with economic inequality, outlining a theory of global exploitation of land and labour, a dialectical history of class struggle, and a rationale for the necessity of political revolution in order for human society to move forward.

Never, in my lifetime, has the Marxist critique of capital and its global dynamics seemed more accurate. And never has it seemed more wrong to go back to Marx*ism* in its historical forms. At least through the 1960s, Marxist theory was the lingua franca of activists globally, no matter how much they disagreed on the proper interpretation (Soviet, Trotskyist, Maoist, humanist). The fall of the Soviet Union and the adoption of capi-talist elements by the Republic of China dealt a fatal blow to this commonality. At the same time, Marxist theory could not withstand the scrutiny of feminist, post-colonial, critical race, and other theorists, and others who extended the meaning of oppression and exploitation far beyond what happens on the factory floor. In its definition of human universality, Marxism was provincial at best. And its logic, often determinist, was firmly lodged in a theory of historical stages that has been shown to be simply inaccurate – by Samir Amin, Janet Abu-Lughod and Dipesh Chakrabarty, to name a few.

And the idea of the revolutionary proletariat? Is the working class as political vanguard still the relevant organizational form? Official unions – not all of them, but too many and too often – have acted as groups that do not rise above economist concerns. Clearly, labour protests continue to matter in innovative ways. From Suez, Egypt, where non-official unions played a crucial role in empowering the Tahrir activists by their own power to block the Suez Canal, to Xintang, China, where migrant workers took to the streets to protest against being denied access to basic citizen rights, to Madison, Wisconsin, where the very right to collective bargaining was under attack, to the workers' councils and other labour groups that have come to Occupy Wall Street in support, labour organizing remains a crucially important location of struggle.[25] But not only are most jobs in most places in the world today non-union. The reasons Marx argued for the pivotal importance of the organized working class may no longer hold. The wage rate, as 'variable capital', was supposed to be the part of the cost equation in the production process that lent itself to downward pressure (as opposed to the fixed capital of machines), but, as we have seen, it functions by a different logic when productivity eliminates jobs completely. The International Labour Organization estimates that the number of unemployed workers worldwide is 200 million.[26] A January 2011 Gallup poll put world unemployment at 7 per cent of the workforce.[27] The young generation is particularly hard-hit. Unemployed youth

---

25   It was striking that those in power were aware of the connections between trans-local protests of 2011:

> Wisconsin Rep. Paul Ryan, a rising star in the Republican Party, on Thursday equated the protests against his home-state Gov. Scott Walker's (R) budget plan to the world-historic demonstrations in Egypt that last week led to the fall of President Hosni Mubarak. 'He's getting riots. It's like Cairo's moved to Madison these days,' Ryan said on MSNBC's *Morning Joe*.

Available at rawstory.com. In the case of Xintang: 'The security clampdown this year is also generally attributed to the protests roiling the Middle East and North Africa, which Chinese authorities don't want to see imitated in their country.' Available at pbs.org. For the significance of the unofficial Suez unions in Egypt's spring, see 'Striking Suez Unions Fuel the Uprising after 10 Years of Labor Organizing,' at democracynow.org.

26   See the UN News Story on unemployment at un.org.

27   This according to the Los Angeles Times, 19 January 2011, 'Worldwide unemployment is about 7%, new Gallup survey finds', at latimesblogs.latimes.com.

today, worldwide, fear less the status of an economically necessary labour reserve army than being economically *un*necessary – a superfluous population of permanently excluded, expendable human beings. And that is a really frightening (but at the same time, dialectically powerful[28]) answer to the question: What's new?

As the mega-cities of the globe make evident, massive proletarianization of the workforce has indeed taken place. But factories have left the cities and moved to enclaves. It is striking that the migrant workforces they employ have shown themselves to be remarkably capable of collective action, despite their precarious position, and despite ethnic and linguistic differences.[29] And yet their own cosmopolitan consciousness remains far in advance of what has been achieved by nationally organized political parties.

Where is the revolutionary class? This may be the wrong question to ask. Perhaps neither category – neither revolution *nor* class – has the necessary traction in our time. First: Is societal transformation any longer about revolution in the classical-modern sense? It has long been my suspicion that the Iranian Revolution of 1979 was the last in a long tradition that has run its course, whether in pro-nationalist, anti-colonial, Marxist or theocratic form. Khomeini's political institution of sovereign power, *Wilayat al-Faqih*, was a personal invention, foreign not only to Western traditions but also to Sunni Islam and even Shiite political thought. And yet, his triumph in a violent civil war has affinities with the French Revolutionary prototype in many of its distinguishing characteristics: prolonged fratricide; tens of thousands of political executions, including the ritualistic beheadings of political enemies before the public; a trajectory of increasing radicalism; a reign of virtue; a Thermidorian reaction of authoritarian centralization; and, finally, a Girondist foreign policy of revolutionary expansion. But if you can spread revolution by twittering your triumph to the world, why choose the path of a foreign invasion?

Today, the videotaped beheadings of random victims does not have the same effect as regicide on the crowd of citizens at the Place de la Révolution. It is not felt by the global public as justified revenge. Like the bombing of civilians, the bulldozing of houses, and the torturing and

---

28   Žižek is absolutely correct in pointing this out: 'As this logic reaches its extreme, would it not be reasonable to bring it to its self-negation: is not a system which renders 80 per cent of people irrelevant and useless *itself irrelevant and of no use?*' Slavoj Žižek, *First as Tragedy, Then as Farce* (London: Verso, 2009), p. 103.
29   See Paul Apostolidis, *Breaks in the Chain: What Immigrant Workers Can Teach America about Democracy* (Minneapolis: University of Minnesota Press, 2010).

humiliation of prisoners, it is perceived as inhuman and wrong. Abstraction here works dialectically: without the legitimating language of the perpetrators, without the contextual pre-given meanings, the viewing of violence towards the powerless evokes an affective, visceral reaction from global observers who, precisely because the scene is taken out of context, respond concretely, and with empathy. Fratricide, the bloody struggle of civil war as the means of social transformation, is short-sighted, as the truth and reconciliation process that must follow proves enormously difficult. And as Thermidorian reactions make clear, it is far easier to smash the old order than to construct the new.

So much for violent revolution. But are we really done with class? The 600-pound gorilla is still with us: the fact that, in this global capitalist world, virtually across the board geopolitically, the rich keep getting richer and the poor poorer – and those in power, far from protesting, tell us that this system needs greater, special protection, far greater than that given to the citizens themselves. Free markets (uncontrolled capitalist accumulation) and free societies (Western-style democracies) have joined hands, and the end-product is global oligarchy. The so-called community of nations protects a global system of enclosures, which works to appropriate every use value that can be turned into a profit-making endeavour. Nothing – not schools, not prisons, not human genes, not wild plants, not the national army, not foreign governments – nothing is exempt from this process of privatization.

So, there *is* class warfare being waged, from the top down. But is there class war? Only if the rest of the world, the 99 per cent of us, responds in kind. (Even Warren Buffett is not happy with the role he is supposed to play.) I want to oppose the idea that the whole point of politics is to name the enemy (Schmitt's friend/enemy distinction) and to structure one's political organizing in an instrumental way in order to defeat that enemy.

Agonistic politics is a mutually dependent social relationship. Both sides must play the game. Perhaps nothing would play into conservative hands more surely than identifying our resistance to the neoliberal, capitalist order in the limited and traditional terms of class war. Perhaps nothing would make the authorities more relieved than if Occupy Wall Street became a violent movement, because the state could then justify using police violence to put it down. But the vast majority, the 99 per cent, have the force they need in sheer numbers, and do not require armed struggle to prove their point. And that point is: the system upon which we depend, the system that is incorporating more and more of our world, is not only out of control; it is punishing, irrational, and immoral – or, in Badiou's words, brutal and barbaric.

A world community of democratic and sovereign nation-states was supposed to be the end of history, not the end of humanity. But what are we to make of our world, based on absurd contradictions, in which the democratically elected parliament of Greece taxes the people into destitution in order to save the nation? Or the nation of Iraq is liberated by the destruction of its infrastructure and the death or displacement of 20 per cent of the population? The logic has indeed something fundamental in common with that of the Cold War, when the capacity to destroy life on the planet was the gold standard of military security, and when post-colonial villages in Vietnam were bombed into oblivion in order to save their inhabitants from communism.

This is acceptable social behaviour, and it's crazy! A commonist ethics requires us to say so. The so-called free choice of citizen voters is not freedom, and it is not a choice.[30] Weber's thesis is distorted into a tautology: the capitalist state produces the objectivized spirit of capitalism, which reproduces the capitalist ethic, in an eternal return of the same.

V

The glow of optimism felt worldwide when Barak Obama won the US presidency in 2008 was a last (and lost) chance to believe that the system was capable of righting itself. In Obama's loyalty to the two pillars of the world order – capitalist economics and national self-interest – his presidency has demonstrated the bankruptcy of both. Given that free markets in a free society have failed to deliver basic human needs, can the world's citizens be asked to hope again? Of course the analogy is exaggerated, and the political emergency is qualitatively different – Obama is, happily, not a fascist, and, sadly, not socialist enough – but one is reminded of an exchange between Albert Speer and Adolf Hitler in March 1945, as the Soviet army closed in on Berlin. Hitler was enraged to discover Speer had blocked his orders, but then calmed down and said 'in a relaxed tone':

'Speer, if you can convince yourself that the war is not lost, you can continue to run your office . . .'
'You know I cannot be convinced of that,' I replied sincerely but without defiance. 'The war is lost.'

---

30   Hegel's criticism of liberal democracy's understanding of free choice as formal freedom, hence 'not freedom itself at all', is pertinent here (See Hegel, *Logic*, paragraph 145).

Hitler launched into his reflections . . . of other difficult situations in his life, situations in which all had seemed lost but which he had mastered . . . [H]e surprisingly lowered his demand: 'If you would believe that the war can still be won, if you could at least have faith in that, all would be well . . .'

Agitated . . . I said: 'I cannot, with the best will in the world . . .' Once again Hitler reduced his demand to a formal profession of faith: 'If you could at least hope that we have not lost! You must certainly be able to hope . . . that would be enough to satisfy me.'

I did not answer.

There was a long, awkward pause. At last Hitler stood up abruptly . . . 'You have twenty-four hours to think over your answer! Tomorrow let me know whether you hope that the war can still be won.' Without shaking hands, he dismissed me.[31]

Again, the point of comparison is not one of leadership. It is only to point out that hope, too, can be an ideology. I cannot help feeling that Obama himself is aware of this danger, surely having believed in the democratic process that brought him to electoral victory such a short time ago. Obama was fond of repeating, 'This is not about me.' And he was precisely correct. It was not. But he himself lacked faith in the people who had elected him. Obama is proud to call himself a pragmatist. He just forgot one thing: in attempting to be realistic within the confines of the crazy status quo, he betrayed the pragmatics of the suddenly possible, which is, after all, the force that elected him in the first place. It is a global force, and it desperately wants change. It is the only sane politics the world now has.

At this moment, being pragmatic in the sense of being cautious, proceeding reasonably within the irrational whole, is the truly risky path. Will the world's leaders recognize this? Will they wake up to the fact that the system they rely on is bankrupt, and that their power rests on air?

As the Egyptian Feminist Nawal Sadaawi urged last spring: make your own revolution. The ways forward will be as varied as the people of this world. Feminists globally have taught us the need for such variety.[32] All

---

31   Albert Speer cited in Nicholas H. Smith, 'Peter Dews, *The Idea of Evil*' book review in *Critical Horizons* 9: 1 (2008), p. 13.
32   See Zillah Eisenstein and Chandra Mohanty, 'In Support of Occupy Wall Street,' *Feminist Wire*, posted 14 October 2011, at thefeministwire.com.

of these ways forward deserve our solidarity and support. We, the 99 per cent, must refuse to become invisible to each other. The experiments that are going on now in thousands of locations need space, the space that Walter Benjamin called a *Spielraum* ('space of play') to try doing things differently. And they need time, the slowing of time, the pulling of the emergency brake, so that something new can emerge. This is time that state power wants to cut short, and space that old-style political parties want to foreclose.

There is no rush. The slowing of time is itself the new beginning.[33] Every day that this event continues, it performs the possibility that the world can be otherwise. Against the hegemony of the present world order that passes itself off as natural and necessary, global actors are tearing a hole in knowledge. New forms emerge. They nourish our imagination, the most radical power that we as humans have.

---

33 Badiou's critique of capitalist time in Chapter 1, above, is right to the point here.

5 Communist Desire

Jodi Dean

I

In a widely cited essay published in 1999, Wendy Brown uses Walter Benjamin's term, 'left melancholy', to diagnose a melancholia of the contemporary left.[1] Her concern in the essay, which closely tracks Stuart Hall's discussion of the rise of Thatcherism, is to analyze the fears and anxieties of a left in decline, a left that is backwards-looking, self-punishing, attached to its own failure, and seemingly incapable of envisioning an emancipatory, egalitarian future. Timely and evocative, Brown's essay, for many, seemed to capture a truth about the end of a certain sequence of the North American, British and European left. Attuned to the ends and loss occasioned by the disintegration of the 'we' previously held in common by the discourse of communism – in her words, to the 'unaccountable loss' and 'unavowedly crushed ideal, contemporarily signified by the terms *left, socialism, Marx*, or *movement*' – Brown provided an opportunity to reflect on the failures and continuities in left projects in terms of the desires that sustain them.[2] Her treatment of a 'lost historical movement' thus suggested a kind of left 'coming to grips' with or facing of reality: the reality of neoliberal capitalism and the defeat of the welfare state.

Read from the vantage point afforded by more than a decade, however, Brown's essay is less convincing, for now it appears to err in its basic account of what was lost and why. Her discussion of Benjamin is misleading. Her treatment of Freud is one-sided. Nonetheless, by analyzing the left in terms of a general structure of desire establishing the contours of a key mode of left theorizing, Brown opens up possibilities for re-conceiving communist desire, possibilities I try to extend in this essay.

'Left-Wing Melancholy' is the title of Benjamin's 1931 review of the

---

1 Wendy Brown, 'Resisting Left Melancholy', *Boundary 2* 26: 3 (Autumn 1999), pp. 19–27.
2 Ibid., p. 22.

poetry of Erich Kästner.[3] Kästner was a well-regarded poet, novelist and journalist during the Weimar period. Kästner's sobering satire appealed to middle-brow readers attracted by its seemingly unadorned and honest portrayal of a stark reality. Benjamin himself disparages Kästner's poetry. He describes it as giving way to the complacency and fatalism of 'those who are most remote from the processes of production and whose obscure courting of the state of the market is comparable to the attitude of a man who yields himself up entirely to the inscrutable accidents of his digestion'.[4]

In a further essay, 'The Author as Producer', Benjamin uses Kästner as the exemplar of the 'new objectivity' – a literary movement that Benjamin argues 'has made *the struggle against poverty* an object of consumption'.[5] Citing 'a perceptive critic' – in fact himself, writing in 'Left-Wing Melancholy' – Benjamin quotes his earlier piece:

> With the workers movement, this left-wing radical intelligentsia has nothing in common. It is, rather, a phenomenon of bourgeois decomposition . . . The radical-left publicists of the stamp of Kästner, Mehring, or Tucholsky are the proletarian mimicry of decayed bourgeois strata. Their function is to produce, from the political standpoint, not parties but cliques; from the economic standpoint, not producers but agents – agents or hacks who make a great display of their poverty, and a banquet out of yawning emptiness.[6]

As far as Benjamin is concerned, left-wing writers such as Kästner have no social function other than rendering the political situation into amusing content for public consumption. They transmit the apparatus of production rather than transform it, assimilating revolutionary themes into the bourgeois apparatus of production and publication while in no way placing in question the existence of the bourgeois class. Benjamin writes, 'I define a hack as a writer who abstains in principle from alienating the productive apparatus from the ruling class by improving it in ways

---

3   Walter Benjamin, 'Left-Wing Melancholy', trans. by Ben Brewster, in Michael W. Jennings, Howard Eiland, and Gary Smith, eds, *Walter Benjamin, Selected Writings: 1931–1934*, vol. 2, part 2 (Cambridge, MA: Harvard University Press, 1999), pp. 423–7.
4   Ibid., p. 426.
5   Walter Benjamin, 'The Author as Producer', trans. Edmund Jephcott, in ibid., pp. 768–82. All emphases in original unless otherwise indicated.
6   Ibid, p. 776.

serving the interests of socialism'.[7] Most generally put, Benjamin's critique in both 'Left-Wing Melancholy' and 'The Author as Producer' targets intellectual compromise, adaptation to the market, and the betrayal of the workers' movement, particularly insofar as this compromise, adaptation, and betrayal banks on and cans authentic revolutionary impulses already part of everyday proletarian life.

Brown claims that 'left melancholy is Benjamin's unambivalent epithet for the revolutionary hack who is, finally, attached more to a particular political analysis or ideal – even to the failure of that ideal – than to seizing possibilities for radical change in the present'.[8] I disagree. Nowhere in his review of Kästner does Benjamin fault him for a lingering attachment to political ideals. Benjamin in fact makes the opposite point, condemning Kästner for writing poems that are blind to action because 'their beat very precisely follows the notes according to which poor rich folks play the blues'. Benjamin describes Kästner's lyricism as protecting 'above all the status interests of the middle stratum – agents, journalists, heads of departments . . . it noticeably abandons any striking power against the big bourgeoisie, and betrays its yearning for patronage with a heartfelt sigh: "If only there were a dozen wise men with a great deal of money"'.[9] Kästner's melancholy is a pose, a fashion trend, a commodity. He is not attached to an ideal; he has compromised revolutionary ideals by reducing them to consumer products.

Perhaps because her preoccupation is more with the inadequacies of the contemporary left than with Benjamin's discussion of what the service intellectuals do to the bourgeoisie when they turn revolutionary themes into consumer contents, Brown does not emphasize the compromise of the left melancholic. Instead she reads Benjamin's critique of Kästner as suggesting that 'sentiments themselves become things for the left melancholic who "takes as much pride in the traces of former spiritual goods as the bourgeois do in their material goods"'. Brown locates in this reified loss a point of contact with the contemporary left: 'We come to love our left passions and reasons, our left analyses and convictions, more than we love the existing world that we presumably seek to alter with these terms or the future that would be aligned with them.'[10]

It is important to note that Brown's continuation differs from

7   Ibid., pp. 776, 774.
8   Brown, 'Resisting Left Melancholy', p. 20.
9   Ibid., pp. 426, 424.
10 Ibid., p. 21.

Benjamin's. Benjamin is not criticizing a left for its attachment to left passions, reasons, analyses and convictions. Rather, he is calling out Kästner and the 'new objectivity' trend for their compromise and the resulting 'metamorphosis of political struggle from a compulsory decision into an object of pleasure, from a means of production into an article of consumption'.[11] He derides Kästner and other 'left-radical publicists' as compromised intellectuals who turn revolutionary reflexes into 'objects of distraction, of amusement, which can be supplied for consumption' and readily purchased at the 'intelligentsia's department store'.[12] Unlike Brown's, Benjamin's left melancholic sublimates left commitment to revolution and the proletariat. A new objectivist, he fatalistically gives way to the bourgeois vision of the existing world instead of holding fast to the revolutionary struggle of the proletariat to reorganize and transform production.

Brown argues:

> If the contemporary Left often clings to the formations and formulations of another epoch, one in which the notion of unified movements, social totalities, and class-based politics appeared to be viable categories of political and theoretical analysis, this means that it literally renders itself a conservative force in history – one that not only misreads the present but installs traditionalism in the very heart of its praxis, in the place where commitment to risk and upheaval belongs.[13]

In our present of undeniable inequality, class war and ongoing capitalist crisis, the relevance, indeed the necessity, of unified movements and class-based analysis is undeniable in a way that it perhaps was not when Brown was writing at the end of the nineties. This clarity helps illuminate Benjamin's own position as opposite to the one Brown takes. That is, his concern is not with a traditionalism at the heart of praxis but rather with the sublimation of left ideals in market-oriented writing and publishing.

In 'Left-Wing Melancholy', the author Benjamin admires is Brecht – the Brecht fully committed to communist revolution, the Brecht Badiou describes as making 'Marxism or communism into a condition for the question of the being of art'.[14] In contrast to Brecht's poems, Kästner's,

---

11   Benjamin, 'Left-Wing Melancholy', p. 425.
12   Ibid., p. 424.
13   Brown, 'Resisting Left Melancholy', p. 25.
14   Alain Badiou, *The Century*, trans. Alberto Toscano (Cambridge, UK: Polity, 2007), p. 42.

Benjamin writes, are removed from the process of production, detached from the labour movement, and at a distance from unemployment. They are for 'people in the higher income bracket, those mournful, melancholic dummies who trample anything and anyone in their path'.[15] Kästner's poems, and similar such writings, participate in the transmission and production of the class power of the bourgeoisie. They are ultimately a conservative social force. Commitment to Marxist ideals, to unified movements and class-based politics, is not. Benjamin sees Kästner as complicit with the sublimation of revolutionary desire in intellectual booms; his poems have 'more to do with flatulence than with subversion'. Unlike Brown's, Benjamin's left melancholic is the one who gives way to 'complacency and fatalism', ceding desire like the 'satiated man who can no longer devote all his money to his stomach'.[16]

What, then, of melancholia? The most valuable aspect of Brown's analysis comes from her turn to Freud's 1917 paper on melancholia to provide an account of a particularly left structure of desire. As is well known, Freud distinguishes melancholia from mourning. Mourning responds to the loss of an object of love, whether that object is a person, a country, freedom or an ideal.[17] Over the time of mourning, the subject painfully and piecemeal confronts the reality of her loss. Slowly she withdraws her attachment from the lost object. The work of mourning is complete when the subject is again free, uninhibited and capable of love. As in mourning, the melancholic subject presents an absence of interest in the outside world and a general inhibition of activity. The crucial difference is that the melancholic's lowering of self-regard is manifest in a self-reproach and self-reviling that exceeds self-punishment and extends to the very 'overcoming of the instinct which compels every living thing to cling to life'. The death drive, the force of loss, reformats the structure of drive itself:

> The melancholic displays something else besides which is lacking in mourning – an extraordinary diminution in his self-regard, an impoverishment of his ego on a grand scale. In mourning it is the world which has become poor and empty; in melancholia it is the ego itself. The

---

15   Benjamin, 'Left-Wing Melancholy', p. 426.

16   Ibid.

17   Sigmund Freud, 'Mourning and Melancholia', *The Standard Edition of the Complete Psychological Works of Sigmund Freud, Volume XIV (1914–1916): On the History of the Psycho-Analytic Movement, Papers on Metapsychology and Other Works*, pp. 237–58, ed. J. Strachey (London: The Hogarth Press and the Institute of Psycho-analysis, 1957).

patient represents his ego to us as worthless, incapable of any achieve-ment and morally despicable; he reproaches himself, vilifies himself and expects to be cast out and punished. He abases himself before everyone and commiserates with his own relatives for being connected with anyone so unworthy.[18]

To account for this difference in self-regard, Freud distinguishes between mourning's consciousness of loss and the unknown and unconscious dimension of object loss in melancholia. Something about the melanchol-ic's loss remains unconscious. Even when the melancholic knows *that* he lost, he does not know *what* he has lost, in what his loss consists for him. Psychoanalysis addresses this unconscious element of melancholic loss.

Freud accepts the melancholic subject's self-accusation – the subject really is weak, dishonest, petty, egoistic. Yet he notes that most of us, with our reasonably healthy neuroses, don't acknowledge these limita-tions. We actually are at pains to hide these weaknesses from ourselves and others. The accuracy of the melancholic's self-description, then, isn't at issue. It's basically correct, and Freud accepts it: 'He [the subject] has lost his self-respect and he must have good reason for this.'[19] The real question is why the subject has lost his self-respect, what the 'good reason' for this loss is.

Answering, Freud notes how, in melancholia, a critical agency splits off from the ego, a voice of conscience that criticizes the poor ego for all its moral failings. He explains that clinical experience reveals that the specific criticisms the melancholic levels against himself correspond most fully not to the melancholic subject, but to one whom the subject loves or should love: 'the self-reproaches are reproaches against a loved object which have been shifted away from it on to the patient's own ego.'[20] What the patient seems to be saying about himself is really about someone else. The melancholic subject thus is one who has narcissistically identified himself with and attached himself to someone else, his loved object, now lost. Rather than acknowledging the loss, narcissistic identification protects the subject from it, bringing the object into the subject and enabling him to keep it as part of himself. This identification is fraught insofar as there is much about the loved object that the subject does not love, that the subject hates. To deal with this unavowable hatred, a 'special

18   Ibid., p. 245.
19   Ibid., p. 246.
20   Ibid., p. 247.

agency' of the ego splits off to judge and condemn the loved object, now part of the subject himself. Freud explains: 'In this way an object loss was transformed into an ego-loss and the conflict between the ego and the loved person into a cleavage between the critical activity of the ego and the ego as altered by identification.'[21] The answer to the question of the subject's loss of self-respect turns on the object: it is the internalized object who is judged, criticized and condemned, not the subject at all. I return to this point below.

Brown uses Freud's account of melancholia to understand the fears and anxieties preventing the left from revising its anachronistic habits of thought. She highlights the persistence of melancholic attachment to a lost object, a persistence that, in superseding conscious desires to recover, to move on, renders 'melancholia a structure of desire, rather than a transient response'. She also emphasizes the unconscious, 'unavowed and unavowable' nature of melancholic loss. And she notes the shift of the 'reproach of the loved object' onto the left subject, a shift that preserves 'the love or idealization of the object even as the loss of this love is experienced in the suffering of the melancholic'. Recounting some of the many losses on the left – of local and international community, of a moral and political vision capable of sustaining political work, of a historical moment – Brown asks whether there might also be a still unconscious, unavowed loss, namely, of 'the promise that left analysis and left commitment would supply its adherents a clear and certain path toward the good, the right, and the true'.[22] She suggests that this promise formed the basis for left self-love and fellow feeling. So long as it remains foundational, unavowed and untransformed, it will doom the left to self-destruction.

Freud's study of melancholia enables Brown to bring to light the disavowed attachment underlying the fierce debates over poststructuralism and the status of the subject characteristic of a particular mode of left theory. She asks: 'What do we hate that we might preserve the idealization of that romantic left promise? What do we punish that we might save the old guarantees of the Left from our wrathful disappointment?'[23] The answer, she suggests, is that hatred and punishment are symptoms, strikes we wage upon ourselves so as to preserve the promises and guarantees of left analysis itself. Scorn for identity politics and disparagement of discourse analysis, postmodernism and 'trendy literary theory' is the

---

21   Ibid., p. 248.
22   Brown, 'Resisting Left Melancholy', pp. 20, 21, 22.
23   Ibid., p. 22.

displaced form of narcissistic attachment to Marxist orthodoxy. It is an attack aimed at an interiorized object, the loved and lost object that promised unity, certainty, clarity and political relevance.

A benefit of Brown's discussion is its illumination of a certain fantasy in left desire: left melancholia extracts historical experiences of division, contestation and betrayal from the Marxist tradition in theory and socialist states in practice. In their place it leaves an invincible, reified figure of the Master, one that is itself split between its authoritative and its obscene enactments. When leftists, stuck in their failure, blame this failure on poststructuralist theory and identity politics, Brown suggests, they disavow the nonexistence of such a Master. Clinging to an impossible, fantastic Marxism that never existed, they protect themselves from confronting the loss of its historical time – the end of the sequence beginning in 1917, or perhaps 1789. They shield themselves from the passing away of a time when it made sense to think in terms of the determinism of capital and the primacy of class.

Is Brown right? Having diagnosed left immobility and self-loathing as melancholic, does she correctly identify what was lost and what is retained, what is displaced and what is disavowed? And does her account of melancholia as a structure of desire exhaust the potential of her move to Freud, or might additional elements of his analysis also prove helpful for coming to grips with the left and the force of loss?

Benjamin's own account of left-wing melancholy suggests a loss of a different sort than Brown's – the betrayal of revolutionary ideals, of the proletariat. He criticizes Kästner and other new objectivists not only for clinging to a form marked by the depiction of the brutalities of everyday life, but for commodifying this form, for packaging up the traces of spiritual goods as so much commercial content to be marketed and sold to the bourgeoisie. As Benjamin argues in 'The Author as Producer', however revolutionary the political tendency associated with the 'new objectivity' may appear, it 'has a counterrevolutionary function so long as the writer feels his solidarity with the proletariat only in his attitudes, not as a producer'.[24] Attached to an ideological experience of solidarity, the left melancholic disavows his practice – the practical effect of his journalistic activities. What Brown construes as a real loss of socialist ideals for which the left compensates through an obstinate and narcissistic attachment, Benjamin presents as compromise and betrayal, a compromise and

---

24   Benjamin, 'The Author as Producer', p. 772.

betrayal that ideological identification with the proletariat attempts to displace. Brown suggests a left defeated and abandoned in the wake of historical changes. Benjamin compels us to consider a left that gave in, sold out.

Freud's gesture to the melancholic's loss of self-respect points in a similar direction. To be sure, he is not explicit here. His discussion somewhat evades the reason for the loss of self-respect (to which I said I would return). Nonetheless, the example he takes from the clinic hints at why the subject loses self-respect. Describing a woman who 'loudly pities her husband for being tied to such an incapable wife', Freud observes that she is really accusing her husband of incapacity. Her self-reproaches, some of which are genuine, 'are allowed to obtrude themselves, since they help to mask the others and make recognition of the true state of affairs impossible'. These reproaches, Freud writes, 'derive from the pros and cons of the conflict of love that has led to the loss of love'.[25] Might it not be the case, then, that the woman is quite rightly recognizing her own incapacity in finding a capable husband, one capable of sustaining her desire? Might she not be punishing herself for compromising, for making due, for allowing the pros and cons of the conflict of love to constrain her desire as she acquiesces to a reality of acceptance and moderation to which there seems to be no alternative? If the answer to these questions is 'yes', then the woman's loss of self-respect is an indication of the guilt she feels at having ceded her desire. To use the terms given to us by Lacan, 'the only thing one can be guilty of is giving ground relative to one's desire'.[26] The woman's identification with her husband is a compromise by means of which she sublimates her desire so as to make him the object of it. The ferocity of her super-ego and the unrelenting punishment to which it subjects her indicate that she has given up on the impossibility of desire, desire's own constitutive dissatisfaction, to accommodate herself to everyday life.

Freud notes the delight the super-ego takes in torment, as well as the fact that the subject enjoys it:

> If the love for the object – a love which cannot be given up though the object itself is given up – takes refuge in narcissistic identification, then the hate comes into operation on this substitutive object, abusing it,

---

25   Freud, 'Mourning and Melancholia', p. 247.

26   Jacques Lacan, *The Ethics of Psychoanalysis: The Seminar of Jacques Lacan, Book VII*, ed. Jacques-Alain Miller, trans. Dennis Porter (New York: Norton, 1997), p. 321.

debasing it, making it suffer and deriving sadistic satisfaction from its suffering. The self-tormenting in melancholia, which is without doubt enjoyable, signifies, just like the corresponding phenomenon in obsessional neurosis, a satisfaction of trends of sadism and hate which relate to an object, and which have been turned round upon the subject's own self . . . [27]

His analysis here uses the terminology of the drives set out in 'Instincts and Their Vicissitudes'. In that essay, Freud says that the drives undergo the following vicissitudes: reversal into their opposite, turning round upon the subject's own self, repression, and sublimation.[28] As Lacan makes clear, what is crucial in the Freudian account of the drives is the way drive provides the subject with another way to enjoy. The enjoyment, *jouissance*, that desire cannot attain, drive cannot avoid. Unable to satisfy or maintain desire, the subject enjoys in another way – the way of the drive.

If desire is always a desire to desire, a desire that can never be filled, a desire for a *jouissance* or enjoyment that can never be attained, drive functions as a way to enjoy through failure. In drive, one does not have to reach the goal to enjoy. The activities one undertakes to achieve a goal become satisfying on their own. Because they provide a little kick of enjoyment, they come themselves to take the place of the goal. Attaching to the process, enjoyment captures the subject.

Further, as Slavoj Žižek argues, the shift from desire to drive effects a change in the status of the object. Whereas the object of desire is originally lost, 'which emerges as lost', in drive loss itself is an object.[29] In other words, drive is not a quest for a lost object; it is the enactment of loss or the force loss exerts on the field of desire. Drives do not circulate around a space that was once occupied by an ideal, impossible object. Rather, drive is the sublimation of desire as it turns back in on itself, this turning thereby producing the loop of drive and providing its own special charge.

An emphasis on the drive dimension of melancholia, on Freud's attention to the way sadism in melancholia is 'turned round upon the subject's own self', leads to an interpretation of the general contours shaping the

---

27   Freud, 'Mourning and Melancholia', p. 250.
28   Sigmund Freud, 'Instincts and Their Vicissitudes', *Standard Edition of the Complete Psychological Works of Sigmund Freud, Volume XIV*, p. 126.
29   Slavoj Žižek, *In Defense of Lost Causes* (London: Verso, 2008), p. 328.

left that differs from Brown's. Instead of a left attached to an unacknowl-
edged orthodoxy, we have one that has given way on the desire for
communism, betrayed its historical commitment to the proletariat, and
sublimated revolutionary energies into restorationist practices that
strengthen the hold of capitalism. This left has replaced commitments to
the emancipatory, egalitarian struggles of working people against capitalism – commitments that were never fully orthodox, but always ruptured,
conflicted and contested – with incessant activity (not unlike the mania
Freud also associates with melancholia), and so now satisfies itself with
criticism and interpretation, small projects and local actions, particular
issues and legislative victories, art, technology, procedures, and process.
It sublimates revolutionary desire to democratic drive, to the repetitious
practices offered up as democracy (whether representative, deliberative
or radical). Having already conceded to the inevitably of capitalism, it
noticeably abandons 'any striking power against the big bourgeoisie', to
return to Benjamin's language. For such a left, enjoyment comes from its
withdrawal from responsibility, its sublimation of goals and responsibili-
ties into the branching, fragmented practices of micro-politics, self-care,
and issue awareness. Perpetually slighted, harmed and undone, this left
remains stuck in repetition, unable to break out of the circuits of drive in
which it is caught – unable because it enjoys.

Might this not explain why such a left confuses discipline with domination, why it forfeits collectivity in the name of an illusory, individualist
freedom that continuously seeks to fragment and disrupt any assertion of
a collective or a common? The watchwords of critique within this structure of left desire are moralism, dogmatism, authoritarianism and
utopianism – watchwords enacting a perpetual self-surveillance: has an
argument, position or view inadvertently *risked* one of these errors? Even
some of its militants reject party and state, division and decision, securing
in advance an inefficacy sure to guarantee it the nuggets of satisfaction
drive provides.

If this left is rightly described as melancholic, and I agree with Brown
that it is, then its melancholia derives from the real existing compromises
and betrayals inextricable from its history – its accommodations with
reality, whether of nationalist war, capitalist encirclement, or so-called
market demands. Lacan teaches that, like Kant's categorical imperative,
the super-ego refuses to accept reality as an explanation for failure.
Impossible is no excuse – desire is always impossible to satisfy. A wide
spectrum of the contemporary left has either accommodated itself, in one

way or another, to an inevitable capitalism or taken the practical failures of Marxism-Leninism to require the abandonment of antagonism, class, and revolutionary commitment to overturning capitalist arrangements of property and production. Melancholic fantasy (the communist Master, authoritarian and obscene) as well as sublimated, melancholic practices (there was no alternative) shield this left, shield *us*, from confrontation with guilt over such betrayal as they capture us in activities that feel productive, important, radical.

Perhaps I should use the past tense here and say 'shielded', because it now seems, more and more, that the left has worked or is working through its melancholia. While acknowledging the incompleteness of psychoanalysis's understanding of melancholia, Freud notes nonetheless that the unconscious work of melancholia comes to an end:

> Just as mourning impels the ego to give up the object by declaring the object to be dead and offering the ego the inducement of continuing to live, so does each single struggle of ambivalence loosen the fixation of the libido to the object by disparaging, denigrating it, and even as it were killing it. It is possible for the process in the [unconscious] to come to an end, either after the fury has spent itself or after the object has been abandoned as useless.[30]

Freud's reference to 'each single struggle of ambivalence' suggests that the repetitive activities I have associated with drive and sublimation might be understood more dialectically – that is, not merely as the form of accommodation but also as substantive practices of dis- and reattachment, unmaking and making. Together with Mladen Dolar, Žižek also emphasizes this destructive dimension of the drive, the way its repetitions result in a clearing away of the old so as to make a space for the new.[31]

In a setting marked by a general acceptance of the end of communism and of particular political-theoretical pursuits in ethics, affect, culture and ontology, it may now be less accurate to describe the left in terms of a melancholic structure of desire than to point to the fragmentation or even nonexistence of a left as such. Brown's essay might then be thought of as a moment in and contribution to the working through and dismantling of left melancholia. In its place, there are multiple practices and patterns which circulate within the larger academic-theoretical enterprise that has

---

30   Freud, 'Mourning and Melancholia', p. 255.
31   Mladen Dolar, 'Freud and the Political', *Theory and Event* 12: 3 (2009).

itself already been subsumed within communicative capitalism. Some of the watchwords of anti-dogmatism remain, but their charge is diminished, replaced by more energetic attachment to new objects of inquiry and interest. The drive shaping melancholia, in other words, is a force of loss as it turns round, fragments, and branches. Over time, as its process – its failure to hit its goal – is repeated, satisfaction attains to this repetition and the prior object, the lost object of desire, is abandoned, useless. So, for example, some theorists today find the analytic category of the subject theoretically uninteresting, essentially useless; they have turned instead to objects, finding in them new kinds of agency, creativity, vitality, and even politics.

The recent reactivation of communism also bears witness to the end of melancholia as a structure of left desire. Describing the massive outpouring of enthusiasm for the 2009 London conference on the idea of communism, Costas Douzinas and Slavoj Žižek note that even the question and answer sessions were 'good-humoured and non-sectarian' – a clear indication 'that the period of guilt is over'.[32] Similarly, in his own contribution to the communist turn, Bruno Bosteels glosses the idea of the communist horizon as invoked by Álvaro García Linera. In contrast to melancholia's self-absorption, the communist horizon effects 'a complete shift in perspective, or a radical ideological turnabout, as a result of which capitalism no longer appears as the only game in town and we no longer have to be ashamed to set our expecting and desiring eyes on a different organization of social relationships'.[33]

Is it possible to understand this reactivation of communism in terms of desire, and if so in what sense? I think that it is. In the next section, I offer a provisional sketch of what such a communist desire might look like. I have two theses: first, communist desire designates the subjectification of the gap necessary for politics, the division within the people; second, this subjectification is collective – our desire and our collective desire for us.

II

The contemporary rethinking of communism provides at least two paths towards a concept of communist desire: the desire of the multitude and the desire of the philosopher. The first comes from Antonio Negri's

32 Costas Douzinas and Slavoj Žižek, eds, 'Introduction: The Idea of Communism', in Douzinas and Žižek, *The Idea of Communism* (London: Verso, 2010), p. ix.
33 Bruno Bosteels, *The Actuality of Communism* (London: Verso, 2011), p. 228.

Spinoza- and Deleuze-inspired emphasis on the productive desire of the multitude of singularities. Negri emphasizes that 'the multitude is a totality of desires and trajectories of resistance, struggle, and constituent power'.[34] The second, the desire of the philosopher (an expression provided by Alessandro Russo), tags Badiou's emphasis on the eternity of communism.[35] In a text from 1991, Badiou argues that the so-called death of communism was not an event. The political sequence associated with October 1917 was already long dead. Communism as a political truth names an eternity, not a historical state formation, so it cannot die – it necessarily exceeds any particular instantiation.[36] Badiou gives further expression to the philosophical idea of an eternal communism with his 'communist invariants' – 'the egalitarian passion, the Idea of justice, the will to end the compromises with the service of goods, the eradication of egoism, the intolerance towards oppression, the desire for the cessation of the State'.[37] So, to reiterate, there is Negri, who writes, 'Communism is possible because it already exists in this transition, not as an end, but as a condition; it is development of singularities, the experimentation of this construction and – in the constant wave of power relations – its tension, tendency, and metamorphosis.'[38] And there is Badiou, who treats communism as a trans-historical truth, a regulative ideal capable of grounding (Badiou uses the word 'incorporating') a subject in history. In one version, communism is already immanent in the world. In the other, communism is the real of a truth that introduces the impossible into the world.

These two seemingly opposed approaches to communist desire operate similarly. Each points, in its own way, to an underlying communist necessity or unavoidability – a kind of communist absolute. Whether as the real existing power of the multitude or the real of a truth procedure in the symbolic narrative of history (via an individual subjectification), communist desire is a given. What Negri positions within the totality of capitalist

34   Antonio Negri, 'Communism: Some Thoughts on the Concept and Practice', in Douzinas and Žižek, The Idea of Communism, p. 163.

35   Alessandro Russo, 'Did the Cultural Revolution End Communism', in Douzinas and Žižek, Idea of Communism, p. 190.

36   Badiou writes, '"Communism", having named this eternity, cannot anymore adequately name a death'. Alain Badiou, Of an Obscure Disaster, trans. Barbara Fulks, Alberto Toscano, Nina Power and Ozren Pupovac (Maastricht, NL: Jan van Eyck Academie, 2009), p. 19.

37   Badiou, Of an Obscure Disaster, p. 17. Bruno Bosteels emphasizes that these invariants are 'the work of the masses in a broad sense' and 'the immediate popular substance of all great revolts'. Bosteels, Badiou and Politics (Durham, NC: Duke University Press, 2011), pp. 277–8.

38   Negri, 'Communism', p. 163.

production in the present, Badiou positions within the eternity of the philosophical idea.

Negri and Badiou are reassuring. For those committed to egalitarian universalism and unwilling to accommodate themselves to the era's dominant capitalist realism, they establish places to stand, sites from which to think and act and understand thinking and acting. As communism, socialism, the working class and the social welfare state have all been vilified and dismantled, both as utopian ideals and as post-war compromise, this reassurance has been essential to the maintenance of courage, confidence, and even knowledge of revolutionary theory and practice. At the same time, as Brown's discussion highlights, such reassurance can and sometimes does become an object of fetishistic attachment. It provides a guarantee as if the time for guarantees had not passed, something to hold on to in a setting of absence, a setting where loss itself operates as a force.

The reassuring promise from Negri is that communism has already arrived; it needs only to be released from its capitalist constraints. Rather than a political-economic system ruptured by division and antagonism, one where the desires and activities of producers conflict with themselves and with each other, the desire of the multitude appears as an already given convergence, abundance and wholeness, shielding us from confrontation with the gap within and between us. The reassurance from Badiou is not only that there are truths, but that these truths are from time to time incorporated in the world. The implicit promise is thus that the political truth of the idea of communism will again be incorporated in new subjects. Rather than a conviction forcing the divisions of enactment by a party and a state, the desire of the philosopher appears as a form of thought that may guide or direct the affective attachments of those who contemplate it. Rather than a ruptured field of practical and theoretical knowledge and will, this desire manifests itself as a form that sees and impresses itself on history's varying rebellious subjectivities.[39]

These approaches to communist desire (particularly in the reductive descriptions I have provided here) rub uneasily against the grain of the last thirty years or so of critical theory, especially against those strands of poststructuralist and post-colonial theory to which Brown gestures in her essay. While the refusal to give way on desire and wallow in melancholia is vital to the power of these approaches, something can nonetheless be learned from those who compromised. First, not all political struggles

---

39   See Bosteels, *Badiou and Politics*, p. 277.

present or past are communist (just as, contra Rancière, not all political struggles are democratic). The subsumption of all *ongoing* political struggles into the multitude (even if the multitude is one of singularities) disavows the tensions and oppositions among them, as well as the ways that these tensions are and can be manipulated in the interests of capital. The absorption of all *past* popular struggles into a content unchanging over the course of millennia discounts the impacts of prior struggles on later ones, as well as the material and technological determinations of forces, capacities and interests.[40] One does not have to embrace the historicist's happy positivism to argue that the communist combination of emancipation and egalitarianism is unique. It is informed by multiple other struggles – as Marx already makes clear in distinguishing, for example, between bourgeois and proletarian revolutions, and as is attested by both twentieth-century struggles for civil and women's rights and twenty-first-century struggles for gay and trans rights. But it is not the same as these struggles. Second, and consequently, communism is informed by its own failures and mistakes – an informing repressed by reassuring appeals to a communist entirety or invariance.[41] This is why there is an endeavour to rethink communism today, to interrogate and learn from the past in order to instantiate something better this time. There are specific histories and struggles whose successes and failures can continue to inspire, that can – but may not – incite a desire to look at our present differently, to see it in light of the communist horizon.[42]

What interest is served in disavowing knowledge of the differences among struggles beneath the expanse of an eternal communist substance? If there was a left structure of desire appropriately understood as melancholic, and if that structure no longer holds, then some sort of work or working-through has taken place. Such a work would have already called into question all-encompassing visions of a communism persisting apart from rather than through centuries of struggles and the signifying stresses they leave behind, a communism seemingly incapable of learning and adaptation, as well as of a communism uniting multiple struggles that patently refuse its terms.[43] Whereas some might treat this work as

---

40   I rely here on ibid., p. 278.

41   My view here is informed by conversations with James Martel, as well as by his compelling argument in his *Textual Conspiracies* (Ann Arbor, MI: University of Michigan Press, 2011), pp. 147–9.

42   See also Bosteels's dialectical approach to 'concrete history and the ahistorical kernel of emancipatory politics', in Bosteels, *Actuality of Communism*, pp. 275–83.

43   I take the term 'signifying stress' from Eric Santner, 'Miracles Happen', in Slavoj Žižek, Eric Santner and Kenneth Reinhard, *The Neighbor: Three Inquiries in Political Theology* (Chicago: University

'traversing the fantasy' or moving from the desire to the drive, I have argued that the sublimation of the drive captures the subject in the repetitive circuits of communicative capitalism.[44] What's left? A new, shifted desire, one that recognizes the impossibility of reaching or achieving its object and holds on, refusing to cede it.[45] Žižek links this new desire to Lacan's notion of the 'desire of the analyst'.[46] Such a desire is collective, sustaining a community even as it has moved past the need for some kind of phantasmic support. Collectivity, built around a lack, provides a common desire capable of breaking through the self-enclosed circuit of drive without reinstalling a new authority or certainty.[47]

Even as they take communist desire as a kind of given, Negri and Badiou also contribute to this other thinking of communist desire – one that, with Lacan, associates desire with the constitutive role of lack. Desire depends on a gap, a question, a missingness, and an irreducible non-satisfaction. In this vein (and in contrast to his usual approach to desire), Negri writes, 'communist imagination is exalted in the moment of rupture'.[48] Badiou, too, albeit differently, emphasizes rupture, the rupture of the event 'in the normal order of bodies and languages as it exists for any particular situation'. Each thereby links communism to a gap or a break (although, again, they differ in their theorization of the time and place of such a gap). Badiou expresses it well in his earlier writing: a militant obstinacy, a certain subjective form, 'has always and forever accompanied the great popular uprisings, not when they are captive and opaque (like everything we see today: nationalisms, market fascination, Mafiosi and demagogues, raised on a pedestal of parliamentarianism), but rather in free rupture with being-in-situation, or counted-being which keeps them in check'.[49]

These emphases on rupture resonate with Rancière's emphasis on the

---

of Chicago Press, 2005). Bosteels writes that 'the communist invariants are the work of the masses in a broad sense. There is as yet no specific class determination to the logic of revolt in which slaves, plebeians, serfs, peasants, or workers rise up against the powers that be'. Bosteels, *Badiou and Politics*, p. 277. Further, in delineating three basic factors of ideological content, Bosteels notes the '*unchanged content* of the communist program, that is, the immediate popular substance of all great revolts, from Spartacus to Mao'. My criticism of Badiou addresses the claim of 'unchanged'. I am arguing against the idea that there is an unchanged and immediate popular substance to all great revolts. There are different kinds of revolts; not all mass or popular revolts have a communist 'substance'.

44   See Martel, *Textual Conspiracies*, for an overview of these debates.
45   Martel develops this idea via a reading of Poe's metaphor of the maelstrom.
46   Slavoj Žižek, *The Ticklish Subject* (London: Verso, 1999), p. 296.
47   That is, without reverting to what Martel theorizes as idolatry.
48   Negri, 'Communism', p. 161.
49   Badiou, *Of an Obscure Disaster*, pp. 6, 17–18.

division within politics between politics and the police.[50] For Rancière, politics is the clash of two heterogeneous processes – the process of the police and the process of equality. He views the police as 'an order of bodies that defines the allocation of ways of doing, ways of being, and ways of saying . . . it is an order of the visible and the sayable'. He then uses 'politics' to designate 'whatever breaks with the tangible configuration whereby parties and parts or lack of them are defined by a presupposition that, by definition, has no place in that configuration – that of the part of those who have no part'.[51] Politics inscribes a gap within an existing order of appearance. The 'part of those who have no part' is this gap in the existing order of appearance between that order and other possible arrangements, this space between and within worlds. The part-of-no-part does not designate a subset of persons, a 'we' or a 'concrete identity' that can be empirically indicated. It names the gap, division or antagonism that marks the non-identity of any ordering with its own components. The Lacanian term for the part-of-no-part would then be *objet petit a*, an impossible, formal object produced as the excess of a process or relation, a kind of gap that incites or annoys, the missingness or not-quite-rightness that calls out to us. It is the gap, the non-identity between something simply present and something desired, the object-cause of desire, or, returning to the political field, the gap between a politicized people and a population or set of persons.

Rancière notes that political subjectification is itself a disidentification and registration of a gap.[52] He explains that there are 'political modes of subjectification only in the set or relationships that the *we* and the *name* maintain with the set of "persons", the concrete play of identities and alterities implicated in the demonstration and the worlds – common or separate – where these are defined'.[53] So we have a rupture or a gap and the subjectification of this gap. But subjectification in what sense? There are various politicizations, various mobilizations and subjectifications that call out to and organize different convictions and interests.

The gap necessary for *communist* desire is manifest in the *non-coincidence* of communism with its setting, the gap that is within and part of the setting, as Marxist themes of negation and the communist legacy of

---

50   See my discussion of Rancière in 'Politics without Politics', *Parallax* 15: 3 (2009).
51   Jacques Rancière, *Disagreement*, trans. Julie Rose (Minneapolis: University of Minnesota Press, 2004), pp. 29–30.
52   Ibid., p. 36.
53   Ibid., p. 59.

revolution both affirm. Communism is of course not the only political ideology that mobilizes negation and revolution – there are and have been liberal-democratic, bourgeois revolutions. Moreover, communism shares with capitalism a revolutionary mobilization of negation – hence communism as the negation of the negation. The difference in the ways they subjectify the gap, then, is crucial. Capitalist subjectification, the desire it structures and incites, is individual (even as it tends to sublimate desire in drive, or, in other words, even as individuated desires get caught up in and give way to drive's powerfully repetitive circuits). To invert Althusser, capitalism interpellates subjects as individuals. A communism that does likewise fails to effect a rupture or install a gap. Communist desire can only be collective: a common relation to a common condition of division.

Rancière's connecting of political subjectification with the gap between 'we' and the set of persons points in this direction: it describes a common relation to a common condition of division that is subjectified as the 'we' of a collective subject. Negri directly and explicitly emphasizes *collective* desire. Badiou, in his writing on the 'death of communism', invokes a collective subject, albeit one that at the time of the collapse of the Soviet party-state 'has been inoperative for more than twenty years'. Badiou observes that 'it was the phrase "we communists", a nominal precision added to "we revolutionaries", which in turn gave political and subjective force to this "we" construed as an ultimate reference – the "we" of the class, the "we" proletarians, which was never articulated, but which every ideal community posited as its source as a historical axiom. Or in other words: we, faithful to the event of October 1917'. Badiou tells us that such a sense of 'we' informed his adolescent understanding of Sartre's phrase 'Every anti-communist is a dog' – because, he explains, 'every anti-communist thereby manifested his hatred towards the "we", his determination to exist solely within the limits of the possession of himself – which is always the possession of some properties or goods'.[54] A constitutive component of the communist subjectification of the gap between what exists and what could be, between working and capitalist classes, between revolutionaries faithful to October 1917 and other political subjectifications, is the opposition between a collective 'we' and an individual determined in and by his singular self-possession. The communist subject is not an ensemble or assemblage of individuals, but a force opposed to such an individualism and its attachments. Badiou qualifies

---

54   Badiou, *Of an Obscure Disaster*, pp. 11–12.

this view today. Even as he insists that 'every truth procedure prescribes a Subject of this truth, a Subject who – even empirically – cannot be reduced to an individual', he nonetheless highlights the subjectification of individuals: 'What is at issue is the possibility for any individual, defined as a mere human animal, and clearly distinct from a Subject, to decide to become part of a political truth procedure.' The individual decides. Badiou construes this decision of the individual as an 'incorporation' into the 'body-of-truth'. The individual materializes truth in the world; he or she serves as the site of the synthesis of politics, ideology and history: '[W]e will say that an Idea is the possibility for an individual to understand that his or her participation in a singular political process (his or her entry into a body-of-truth) is also, in a certain way, a *historical* decision'.[55] Describing a conversion markedly similar to the Christian's participation in the Holy Spirit, Badiou maintains:

> This is the moment when an individual declares that he or she can go beyond the bounds (of selfishness, competition, finitude . . .) set by individualism (or animality – they're one and the same thing). He or she can do so to the extent that, while remaining the individual that he or she is, he or she can also become, through incorporation, an active part of a new Subject. I call this decision, this will, a subjectivation. More generally speaking, a subjectivation is always the process whereby an individual determines the place of a truth with respect to his or her own vital existence and to the world in which this existence is lived out.[56]

Insofar as Badiou argues that 'communist' can no longer 'qualify a politics' or function as an adjective for a party or a state, it makes sense that he has to find another locus for communism's incorporation – that is, for an operation capable of connecting truth to history. Likewise, insofar as our contemporary setting is not one wherein the story of the historical mission of the industrial working class to usher in communism remains compelling, the question of the subject of communism remains open and pressing. Yet Badiou's choice of the individual as the locus of such a subject effaces the difference that matters in communist desire: it is and has to be collective, the common action and will of those who have undergone a certain proletarianization or destitution, of those who relinquish

55   Ibid., p. 3.
56   Badiou, 'The Idea of Communism', pp. 2–3.

their attachment to an imaginary individuality. If communism means anything at all, it means collective action, determination and will.

Under conditions of capitalism's cult of individualism, to emphasize acts of individual decision and will reduces communism to one among any number of possible choices. Such an emphasis thereby assents to capitalist form, rendering communism as just another content, an object of individual desire rather than the desire of a collective subject. In Badiou's version the individual's active participation in a new subject does not even require any radical change on the part of the individual – he or she can remain 'the individual that he or she is'. What gets lost is the common that gives communism its force, the loss that drives capitalism. Communism is subordinated to an individual's decision for it. Desire remains individual, not communist; nothing happens to its basic structure. In effect, desire is sublimated within the larger circuits of drive which perpetually offer different objects, different nuggets to enjoy, different opportunities to get off on failure, repetition and the immediate movement from one thing to another. Social, economic and political conditions may well contribute to a setting wherein the choice for communism becomes more compelling to more individuals, but the constitution of these individuals as something more, as a 'we', has fallen out of the picture.

Although our political problem differs in a fundamental way from that of communists at the beginning of the twentieth century – we have to organize individuals; they had to organize masses – Georg Lukács's insight into individualism as a barrier to the formation of collective will is crucial to the theorizing of communist desire as collective desire. Lukács notes that the 'freedom' of those of us brought up under capitalism is 'the freedom of the individual isolated by the fact of property', a freedom over and against other, isolated individuals, 'a freedom of the egoist, of the man who cuts himself off from others, a freedom for which solidarity and community exist at best only as ineffectual "regulative ideas"'.[57] He argues that 'the *conscious* desire for the realm of freedom can only mean consciously taking the steps that will really lead to it'. In a setting of capitalism's distractions and compulsions, one may very well feel like something is wrong, something is missing, something is deeply unfair. Then one might complicate this idea, or contextualize it, or forget about it and check email. Or one might try to make a difference – signing petitions, blogging, voting, doing one's own part as an individual. And here is

---

57 Georg Lukács, *History and Class Consciousness*, trans. Rodney Livingstone (Cambridge, MA: MIT Press, 1985), p. 315.

the problem: one continues to think and act individualistically. Under capitalist conditions, communist desire entails 'the renunciation of individual freedom', the deliberate and practical subordination of self in and to a collective communist will. This subordination requires discipline, work and organization. It is a process carried out over time and through collective struggle. Indeed, it is active, collective struggle that changes and reshapes desire from its individual (and, for Lukács, bourgeois and reified) form into a common, collective one.

The most renowned and compelling account of the role of revolutionary struggle in constituting communist desire – that is, in reforming individual interests into a collective one – of course comes from Lenin. Lenin constantly insists on struggling, testing, learning, developing, forging. The overthrow of the old society cannot occur without 'prolonged effort and hard-won experience'.[58] In *'Left-Wing' Communism*, Lenin presents a 'fundamental law of revolution': 'It is only when the *"lower classes" do not want* to live in the old way and the "upper classes" *cannot carry on in the old way* that the revolution can triumph.' The lower classes have to want in a communist way. If they are to overthrow capitalism and begin establishing a communist society, they have to desire as communists. Without collective, communist desire, revolutionary upheaval moves in counter-revolutionary directions. Lenin writes: 'A petty bourgeois driven to frenzy by the horrors of capitalism is a social phenomenon which, like anarchism, is characteristic of all capitalist countries. The instability of such revolutionism, its barrenness, and its tendency to turn rapidly into submission, apathy, phantasms, and even a frenzied infatuation with one bourgeois fad or another – all this is common knowledge.'[59] 'Submission', 'apathy', and 'frenzied infatuation' – here Lenin suggests failures of collective will, failures that seek the cover of a master rather than holding fast to a communist desire to steer, with courage and without certainty, the conditions we are always ourselves already making.

In this provisional sketch of a theory of communist desire, I have emphasized lack (the openness of desire) and its subjectification. I have argued that communist desire is the collective subjectification of an irreducible gap. Communist desire names the collective assumption of the division or antagonism constitutive of the political. Collectivity is the

---

58   V. I. Lenin, '"Left-Wing" Communism: An Infantile Disorder', in Robert C. Tucker, ed., *The Lenin Anthology* (New York: Norton, 1975), p. 554.
59   Ibid., pp. 602, 559.

form of desire in two senses: our desire and *our desire for us*; or, communist desire is the collective desire for collective desiring.

Statistical identity provides a contemporary figure for such a desire. As I mentioned, Badiou links the communist invariants to great popular uprisings in free rupture with counted being. As he uses it in the context of his discussion of the 'death of communism', the idea of counted being affiliates with a larger critique of the state and of law – more particularly with the work of state and law in ordering a situation and determining its facts. In a somewhat more literal criticism of counting as a mode of contemporary state power, Rancière criticizes polling as a rendering of the people as 'identical to the sum of its parts', as nothing but its demographic components.[60] Rather than agree with Badiou and Rancière, I think that it is time to consider evidence in support of a counter-thesis – namely, that in our current conjuncture a count can provide a form for expressing collectivity, even for rupturing the very setting in which it arises.

One of the slogans to emerge with particular power out of the movement to Occupy Wall Street is: 'We are the 99 per cent.' Instead of naming an identity, the number highlights a division and a gap – the gap between the wealth of the top 1 per cent and the rest of us. As it mobilizes the gap between the 1 per cent owning half the country's wealth and the other 99 per cent of the population, the slogan asserts a collectivity and a common. It does not unify this collectivity under a substantial identity – race, ethnicity, nationality. Rather, it asserts it as the 'we' of a divided people, the people divided between expropriators and expropriated. In the setting of an occupied Wall Street, this 'we' is a class, one of two opposed and hostile classes: those who have and control the common wealth, and those who do not. In other words, the announcement that 'We are the 99 per cent' names an appropriation, a wrong. It thereby also voices a collective desire for equality and justice, for a change in the conditions through which 1 per cent seize the bulk of what is common for themselves, leaving 99 per cent with the remainder.

In addition, 'We are the 99 per cent' erases the multiplicity of individuated, partial and divided interests that fragment and weaken the people. The count dis-individualizes interest and desire, reformatting both within a common. Against capital's constant attempts to pulverize and decompose the collective people, the claim of the 99 per cent responds with the

---

60 Rancière, *Disagreement*, p. 105.

force of a belonging not only that cannot be erased but that capital's own methods of accounting produce: *Oh, demographers and statisticians! What have you unleashed? As capital demolishes all previous social ties, the counting on which it depends provides a new figure of belonging!* Capital has to measure itself, count its profits, its rate of profit, its share of profit, its capacity to leverage its profit, its confidence or anxiety in its capacity for future profit. Capital counts and analyzes who has what, representing to itself the measures of its success. These very numbers can be – and in the slogan 'We are the 99 per cent' they are – put to use. They are not re-signified – they are claimed as the subjectification of the gap separating the top 1 per cent from the rest of us. With this claim, the gap becomes a vehicle for the expression of communist desire – that is, for a politics that asserts the people as a divisive force in the interest of overturning present society and making a new one anchored in collectivity and the common.

In a close engagement with Catherine Malabou's discussion of severe brain injuries, Žižek discusses the logic of dialectical transitions: 'after negation/alienation/loss, the subject "returns to itself", but this subject is not the same as the substance that underwent the alienation – it is constituted in the very movement of returning to itself'.[61] Žižek concludes, '*the subject is* as such *the survivor of its own death*, a shell which remains after it is deprived of its substance'. Proletarianization is a name for the process of this deprivation under capital. The deprivation of substance – common, social substance – leaves collectivity as its shell, as the form that remains for communist desire.

This collective form overlaps with the object-cause of communist desire – the people understood as the part-of-no-part. As I argue above, the part-of-no-part names the gap or antagonism that marks the non-identity of any ordering with its own components. It can thus be designated with Lacan's *objet petit a*, an impossible formal object produced as the excess of a process, a missingness or off-ness that calls out to us. Žižek notes that, for Lacan, the object of desire always remains at a distance from the subject; no matter how close the subject gets to the object, the object remains elusive.[62] The distinction between object and object-cause accounts for this difference; there is a gap because the object-cause is not the same as any old object to which it attaches. The object-cause is what makes an object desirable, not a property inhering in the object. One might think that the object of communist desire would be a world without

---

61   Slavoj Žižek, *Living in the End Times* (London: Verso, 2011), p. 307.
62   Ibid., p. 303.

exploitation; a world characterized by equality, justice, freedom, and the absence of oppression; a world where production is common, distribution is based on need, and decisions realize the general will. Once one starts to describe this perfect world, though, it always comes up lacking. Something is always missing: What about an end to sexism, racism, and egoism? What about an end to social hierarchies? What about religious freedom and the intolerant? What about meanness and bullying? It is no surprise that communism's critics (at least as early as Aristotle in *The Politics*) criticize communism as utopian and impossible. It seems another word for perfect. But the impossible of communist desire is not the same as its cause. The object-cause of communist desire is the people and, again, the people not as a name for the social whole but as a name for the exploited, producing majority.

For any government, system, organization or movement, the people remain elusive, incompatible with and disruptive to what attempts to reduce, constrain or represent it. Authoritarianism, oligarchy, aristocracy, representative democracy, parliamentary democracy – none of these forms worries too much about the disconnect between government and people. But the disconnect, the gap, matters for communism (and for fascism, incidentally, which deals with the gap by essentializing the people via blood, soil, and the Leader, and attempting to externalize and eliminate the remaining and unavoidable antagonism), particularly because communism is not only an association for governance, but also an organization of production.[63] The people are elusive. They exceed their symbolic instantiation as well as the images and fantasies that try to fill the gap. Communist desire – a collective desire to desire communism – occupies and mobilizes this gap, recognizing its openness (that is, the impossibility of the people) and treating it as the movement of communism itself – in the words of Marx and Engels (*The German Ideology*), 'We call communism the *real* movement which abolishes the present state of things.'[64]

I have attempted to set out an idea of communist desire in the space marked by the end of a certain left melancholy, and by an alternative to the way of the drive. Whereas some have viewed drive's sublimation as the way beyond a desire configured in terms of law and its transgression, I have sketched a different notion of desire – one that, via collectivity,

---

63   Alberto Toscano makes this point with particular power in 'The Politics of Abstraction', in Douzinas and Žižek, *Idea of Communism*, p. 202.
64   Bosteels notes the current ubiquity of this passage in *The Actuality of Communism*, p. 19.

breaks from drive's repetitive circuits. Instead of trapped in failure, getting off on and failing to reach the goal, communist desire subjectifies its own impossibility, its constitutive lack and openness. Such subjectification is inextricable from collective struggle, from the impact of changes over time that enable what James Martel calls the recognition of misrecognition – that is, the acknowledgement of false starts and errors, of fantasy constructions and myths of completeness and inevitability.[65] Precisely because such struggle is necessarily collective, it forges a common desire out of individuated ones, replacing individual weakness with collective strength.

---

65 Martel, *Textual Conspiracies*.

6 From Scientific Socialism to Socialist Science:
Naturdialektik Then and Now

Adrian Johnston

Harvard University's Marxist biologists Richards Levins and Lewontin dedicate their 1985 book *The Dialectical Biologist* 'To Frederick Engels, who got it wrong a lot of the time but who got it right where it counted.'[1] In the English-, French- and German-speaking worlds of the Western Marxisms of the mid–twentieth century up through the present, the viewpoint expressed in this dedication is an unfashionable rarity. The Engels acknowledged by Levins and Lewontin – this is the author specifically of the trilogy *Dialectics of Nature*, *Anti-Dühring*, and *Ludwig Feuerbach and the Outcome of Classical German Philosophy*, a writer who fiercely advocates a dialectical extension of historical materialism into the jurisdictions of the natural sciences – is the object of either total neglect or brusque dismissals within such still-influential movements as the Frankfurt School and Althusserianism.[2] However, in their refusal to treat this Engels as the deadest 'dead dog' of them all, these two leftist scientists implicitly urge a rescue operation in the contemporary conjuncture resembling the one Marx claims to perform on behalf of Hegel.[3] That is to say, the gesture called for here is one of saving the 'rational kernel' located at the heart of Engelsian *Naturdialektik*. (Although the exact phrase 'dialectical materialism' is not coined until 1887, by both Joseph Dietzgen[4] and Karl Kautsky,[5] I would maintain that the new materialist *Weltanschauung* of Marx and

---

1   Richard Levins and Richard Lewontin, *The Dialectical Biologist*, (Cambridge, MA: Harvard University Press, 1985), p. v.
2   Adrian Johnston, 'Repeating Engels: Renewing the Cause of the Materialist Wager for the Twenty-First Century', *Theory @ Buffalo* 15 (2011), pp. 141–82.
3   Karl Marx, *Capital: A Critique of Political Economy, Volume I*, trans. Ben Fowkes (New York: Penguin Books, 1976), p. 103.
4   Joseph Dietzgen, *Excursions of a Socialist Into the Domain of Epistemology*, trans. Max Beer and Theodor Rothstein (1887), available at marxists.org.
5   Karl Kautsky, *Frederick Engels: His Life, His Work, and His Writings*, trans. May Wood Simmons (1887/88), available at marxists.org.

Engels, as it begins to be elaborated already in Marx's 1844 *Economic and Philosophical Manuscripts*, is done no injustice by being labelled thusly.[6])

The position I seek to occupy involves a refusal to choose between three differently questionable but equally problematic options: one, the Hegelianism of the early Georg Lukács and most of post-Lukácsian Western Marxism, with its neo-Kantian dualism between nature and history and corresponding wary aversion to the natural sciences; two, the non-Hegelianism of Louis Althusser and his followers, with its neo-Spinozist formalism entailing hostility to both historicism and the empirical, experimental sciences; and, three, the anti-Hegelianism of Lucio Colletti, with its Kantian pseudo-materialism.[7] Based on my rereading of the entire sweep of Hegel's philosophy centred on issues related to *Naturphilosophie* – the upshot of this is that Hegel is seen to be far from categorically opposed to either realism or materialism[8] – I reject the alternatives put forward by Lukács, Althusser, Colletti, and those of similar minds, opting instead for an Engelsian-Leninist stance. Specifically, I am a Marxist in favour of a materialist dialectics of nature positively informed by the rich resources for this to be found in Hegel's thinking, as well as in the natural sciences themselves. However, I must append to this a crucial caveat: by contrast with the overriding emphasis on the image of an organic whole consisting of myriad interconnections between all things (this emphasis recurs throughout the works of Engels, Dietzgen, and many Soviet and British Marxists of the first half of the twentieth century interested in the links between dialectical materialism and the sciences), my pro-Engelsian transcendental materialism insists upon the importance of a counterbalancing emphasis on disconnecting gaps and splits. If Hegelian dialectics avoids one-sidedness by insisting that continuity always consists of both continuity and discontinuity (to modify a slogan shared by Schelling and Hegel), then the primary fault of Engelsian *Naturdialektik* is its having leaned into an over-the-top elevation of continuity over discontinuity. Transcendental materialism is a rectification of this lopsidedness of classical dialectical materialism.

---

6 Adrian Johnston, *Prolegomena to Any Future Materialism, Volume Two: A Weak Nature Alone* (Evanston: Northwestern University Press, 2013 [forthcoming]).

7 Ibid.

8 Adrian Johnston, 'Le Šibka narava: Substance in subjekt v Heglovi filozofiji' [trans. Erna Strnisa], *Prolbemi*, vol. 32, no. 3, 2012, pp. 117–35; Adrian Johnston, 'The Voiding of Weak Nature: The Transcendental Materialist Kernels of Hegel's *Naturphilosophie*: Part One', *Graduate Faculty Philosophy Journal*, 2012 (under review); Adrian Johnston, 'The Voiding of Weak Nature: The Transcendental Materialist Kernels of Hegel's *Naturphilosophie* – Part Two', *Graduate Faculty Philosophy Journal*, Vol. 33, no. 1, Spring 2012, pp. 103–57.

In his early gem of a book, 1975's *Théorie de la contradiction*, Alain Badiou similarly takes Engels to task for overemphasizing unity at the cost of correspondingly underemphasizing disunity (as antagonism, conflict, etc.).[9] Basing himself largely on Mao's 1937 essay 'On Contradiction'[10] – he also credits Lenin with already correcting the excessive Engelsian taste for and favouring of organicist (w)holism[11] – the young Badiou seeks not to restore balance to dialectical materialism, but to tilt the unevenness in the opposite direction by asserting the primacy of disunity over unity.[12] He proceeds to offer the following distillation of the essence of proper dialectical materialism: 'In order to be *materialist*, it is necessary to recognize that a series of terms (practice, productive forces, economic base) occupy "in general" the dominant place, that they are the principle aspect of the contradiction which unites them to the opposed term (respectively: theory, relations of production, superstructure).'[13] He tacks on to this an admission (in response to certain non-Marxist concerns) that '[i]t is therefore true that a certain type of fixity of principle is what anchors certain contents of the dialectical thesis to materialism.'[14] Then, he addresses the dialectical side of dialectical materialism:

> In order to be a *dialectician* (that is to say, not to be a mechanist), it is also necessary to recognize the negation of this fixity.
>
> If it is true that the strategic fixity ('in general') of the principle term vouches for the materialism in the dialectic, its tactical non-fixity ('in determinate conditions') vouches for the dialectic in the material-ism ... materialism is that which structures contradiction in strategically fixing the place of its terms; the dialectic is that which contradicts the structure in thinking the inversion of places, the non-fixity of the assignation of terms.[15]

Several pages later, Badiou draws from this a conclusion of immense import: it is necessary to dialecticize the dialectic itself; in other words,

9   Alain Badiou, *Théorie de la contradiction* (Paris: François Maspero, 1975), pp. 30–3, 35–6.

10   Mao Tse-Tung, 'On Contradiction', in *Mao: On Practice and Contradiction*, ed. Slavoj Žižek (London: Verso, 2007), pp. 67, 72, 74–6, 78, 86, 91, 96, 98; Johnston, *Prolegomena to Any Future Materialism, Volume One*.

11   Badiou, *Théorie de la contradiction*, pp. 42–3.

12   Ibid., pp. 21, 26, 36, 43, 48, 61–2, 65, 78, 80.

13   Ibid., p. 77.

14   Ibid., pp. 77–8.

15   Ibid., p. 78.

the dialectic must be made to become self-reflexive.[16] On several subsequent occasions he reaffirms this thesis[17] – a thesis I will rely upon later in this essay.

Not only does Badiou have Maoist reservations about Engels's version of dialectical materialism – for multiple reasons (many related to his fidelities to both Jean-Paul Sartre and Louis Althusser), he would also be allergic to the sorts of alliances with the empirical, experimental sciences of nature esteemed by Engels himself.[18] But, curiously, two proponents of an Engelsian-style rapprochement between Marxist materialism and the sciences, Sebastiano Timpanaro[19] and Lucien Sève,[20] likewise speak positively of dialecticizing the dialectic. Before segueing into an engagement with Engels's key science-related writings, a few more features of Badiou's philosophy warrant comment here.

Despite his pronounced post-Althusserian penchant for mathematical formalization and his correlatively restrictive conception of scientificity, Badiou, in a recent set of interviews, says a number of interesting things. First and foremost, he declares that, 'As regards what has to do with thought . . . I am a partisan of the doctrine of emergences. Life is a universe irreducible to matter, and thought is a universe irreducible to life. Thought is in every case a *sui generis* activity.'[21] This very much appears to be an endorsement of emergentism as a set of theoretical models in the natural sciences generally and the life sciences especially (models stressing irreducibility and complexity at different material levels). Given Badiou's repeated Koyré-inspired refusals to concede a scientific status to biology over and above molecular chemistry[22] (he reiterates this refusal in these same interviews[23]), this new reference, not to be found in his prior work, is somewhat surprising. However, recourse to emergentism is consistent not only with his youthful embrace of

---

16   Ibid., p. 81.

17   Alain Badiou, *Peut-on penser la politique?* (Paris: Éditions du Seuil, 1985), p. 84; Alain Badiou, 'Beyond Formalisation: An Interview [with Bruno Bosteels and Peter Hallward]', *Angelaki: Journal of the Theoretical Humanities* 8: 2 (August 2003), pp. 122–3; Adrian Johnston, *Badiou, Žižek, and Political Transformations: The Cadence of Change* (Evanston: Northwestern University Press, 2009), p. xxii.

18   Johnston, *Alain Badiou*.

19   Sebastiano Timpanaro, *On Materialism*, trans. Lawrence Garner (London: Verso, 1980), pp. 90–1.

20   Lucien Sève, ed., '*Nature, science, dialectique: Un chantier à rouvrir*', *Sciences et dialectiques de la nature* (Paris: La Dispute, 1998), p. 199.

21   Alain Badiou, *La philosophie et l'événement: Entretiens avec Fabien Tarby* (Paris: Éditions Germina, 2010), p. 119.

22   Johnston, *Alain Badiou*.

23   Badiou, *La philosophie et l'événement*, pp. 113–14.

the materialism of the Marxist tradition (as incarnated in Maoism in particular) – the 'materialist dialectic' of his 2006 masterpiece *Logics of Worlds* could readily be interpreted in this context as involving a non-biological version of the notion of strong emergence qua the immanent genesis of the thereafter transcendent[24] (as could numerous remarks by Alfred Sohn-Rethel on the rise of 'abstractions' out of natural, physical, empirical and/or historical grounds, remarks arguably foreshadowing Badiou's materialist dialectic[25] and being foreshadowed by the Engels of *Anti-Dühring*, who strives to formulate a materialist narrative explaining even the genesis of pure mathematical constellations and constructs[26]).

But Badiou's affirmation of emergentism betrays – to reach for a Hegelian adjective – a one-sided conception of this doctrine on his part. Theories of emergence are spontaneously speculative in Hegel's precise sense, insofar as they strive to think the dialectics of continuity and discontinuity. Badiou, with his insistence upon *sui generis* irreducibility (i.e. life as irreducible to matter and thought as irreducible to life), lopsidedly highlights only the discontinuous side of the idea of emergence. As for the flip-side of continuity, and in tension with his recent appeal to emergentism, his philosophy alternates between omitting and forbidding natural-scientific accounts of how matter generates out of itself autonomous strata of more-than-material entities and events (such as life and thought). Minus such accounts, recourse to emergentism risks being merely a fig leaf covering disavowed, non-materialist dualism(s).[27]

Whatever the limitations of Badiou's thought as regards the relations between science and materialism, I wish to touch, in passing, upon two other facets of his philosophy relevant to my present pursuits, facets with which I agree (and these in addition to his 1975 criticisms of Engels, to be redeployed in my readings of the latter below). First, in his interviews with Fabien Tarby,[28] Badiou rightly points out that materialism does not automatically entail determinism.[29] It does so only under the assumption of the validity of an underlying mechanistic, reductive and/or eliminative metaphysics. I concur with Badiou on this, although, as will become

---

24   Alain Badiou, *Logics of Worlds: Being and Event, 2*, trans. Alberto Toscano (London: Continuum, 2009), pp. 9–10, 33, 569.

25   Alfred Sohn-Rethel, *Intellectual and Manual Labour: A Critique of Epistemology*, trans. Martin Sohn-Rethel (London: Macmillan, 1978), pp. 57, 67–8, 71, 74–5, 201, 203.

26   Frederick Engels, *Anti-Dühring: Herr Eugen Dühring's Revolution in Science* (Moscow: Foreign Languages Publishing House, 1959), 2nd edn, pp. 58–9, 61.

27   Johnston, *Alain Badiou*.

28   See note 21.

29   Badiou, *La philosophie et l'événement*, pp. 144–8.

increasingly evident in what follows, he and I differ on the formulation of a non-deterministic materialism.

The second facet of Badiou's philosophy which I enthusiastically embrace in this context is his now-famous distinction between the materialist dialectic and 'democratic materialism' as articulated in the preface to *Logics of Worlds* (with democratic materialism admitting the existence of brute physical bodies and culturally relative languages, and nothing more). This distinction elegantly captures some fundamental features of the historical situation of late-capitalist societies at the end of the twentieth and the beginning of the twenty-first centuries.[30] In connection with my efforts to wed today's life sciences to a certain Marxist materialism, I see current ideological scientisms parasitizing biology and its branches – these phenomena include, among other things, developments subsumable under the heading of 'biopolitics', intellectually bankrupt sociobiology and its myriad academic offshoots, media-popularized genetic determinisms, and pharmaceutical industry disinformation – as engaged in the activity of painting a capital-complicit portrait of 'human nature' that can and should be combated mercilessly not only by philosophy and political theorizing, but by these modes of thought as armed specifically with life-scientific insights contesting such scientistic caricatures and idols.

Of course, Badiou does not ally his materialist dialectic with biology so as to delegitimize democratic materialism according to its own ostensibly-but-fraudulently scientific standards. This would be to employ a Trojan-horse tactic of immanent critique. However, although I differ tactically with Badiou, my tactics are guided in part by his perceptive diagnosis of the prevailing ideological Zeitgeist as democratically materialist. To be more precise, the scientistic renditions of human nature against which I believe a post-Engelsian materialism to be the best bet are arguably permutations of democratic materialism, a sub-variant of it I might label 'capitalist biologism', for which there are only mechanical exchanges between wholly free-standing inner essences and external existences. This ideology has a long history, clearly flowing from, among other points of origin, Hobbes, Smith and company. Contemporary capitalist biologism, as I conceive it, makes unsubstantiated appeals to the life sciences so as to depict human beings as non-dialectical juxtapositions of, on the one hand, 'nature' as a necessary bundle of innate urges (the 'bodies' of Badiouian democratic materialism, viewed as gene machines

---

30   Badiou, *Logics of Worlds*, pp. 1–9.

programmed by evolutionary pressures), and, on the other hand, 'nurture' as contingent clusters of fungible objects (the 'languages' of democratic materialism, this time as shifting bundles of commodities and commodified relationships). In an unsatisfying ideological fudge of the distinction between freedom and determinism, people are seen as propelled by an irresistible genetic destiny into proliferating networks of socially constructed choices between competing goods and services. For the capitalist biologist, the life of humanity is reduced to an ongoing negotiation between the two lone independent parties of fixed instincts and fluid providers of their satisfactions. There are only these economies, contracts and transactions (what Jacques Lacan labels 'the service of goods'[31]). The sciences are supposed to substantiate this bleak and boring picture . . . and either to medicate or to kill those who cannot or will not make peace with it.

To move from Badiou back to Engels, although I agree with Badiou's criticism of Engels's inordinate privileging of motifs of unity (as continuity, interconnectedness, holism, relatedness, totality, and so on), I consider it to be both possible and productive to rework Engels's dialectics of nature from within. That is to say, whereas Badiou's critique of Engelsian *Naturdialektik* is external, mine is immanent. Fleshing this out requires a close examination of three pivotal texts: *Dialectics of Nature*, *Anti-Dühring*, and *Ludwig Feuerbach*.

In the introduction to *Dialectics of Nature*, Engels historically situates philosophy and science with respect to each other. He maintains that the early modern sciences of the seventeenth and eighteenth centuries, although empirically ahead of ancient Greek philosophy, nonetheless lag theoretically behind this chronologically much earlier form of thought.[32] The Greeks arrive at their insights through theoretical intuition, whereas post-Baconian, post-Galilean science achieves similar discoveries through a more reliable and trustworthy method of careful empirical investigation.[33] Under the heading of 'ancient Greek philosophy', Engels evidently has in mind here an ontological vision along the lines of a Heraclitian flux doctrine, a metaphysical picture of *phusis* as a ceaseless flow of interpenetrating liquid kinetics.[34] He interprets the modern sciences as finally

31   Jacques Lacan, *The Seminar of Jacques Lacan, Book VII: The Ethics of Psychoanalysis, 1959–1960*, ed. Jacques-Alain Miller, trans. Dennis Porter (New York: W.W. Norton & Co., 1992), pp. 303, 313–15, 318.

32   Frederick Engels, 'Introduction', in *Dialectics of Nature*, ed. and trans. C. P. Dutt (New York: International Publishers, 1940), pp. 6–7.

33   Ibid., pp. 13–14.

34   Ibid., pp. 6–7.

having come around to substantiating this old process metaphysics *avant la lettre* after the many intervening centuries.[35] Already, Engels's favouring of images of seamless wholeness is on display here (as elsewhere, such as in *Anti-Dühring*, when he says, 'The real unity of the world consists in its materiality'[36]).

Apropos philosophy, both *Anti-Dühring* and *Ludwig Feuerbach* shift attention from the Greeks to Hegel as the chronologically proximate philosophical source of inspiration for historical and dialectical materialism. In *Anti-Dühring*, Engels identifies Hegel's pre-Darwinian categorical rejection of notions of evolution qua natural history as the major flaw, the Achilles' heel, of his *Naturphilosophie*.[37] For both Marx and Engels, Darwinian evolutionary theory is a scientific event shattering for good the idea of nature as ahistorical, as nothing more than an endless, eternal repetition of the same recurring cycles (an idea arguably held to by Hegel in his *Philosophy of Nature*). Darwin's historicization of nature, then so new and open to future potential paths of advance,[38] itself entices Marx and Engels to imagine the possibility of a single systematic unification of the human and natural sciences on a solidly materialist basis (as opposed to Hegel's allegedly idealist systematization).[39] Moreover, Engels points to Darwin as providing the most convincing evidence of all for the thesis that nature in itself is objectively dialectical.[40] He also observes that Marxist dialectics in general – this would include its *Naturdialektik* – is not a teleology of the necessary[41] (just as Darwinian evolution is contingent and non-teleological).

Anti-Dühring and *Ludwig Feuerbach* contain the usual Marxist objections to and polemics against Hegelian idealism, with Engels reiterating in step with Marx that, 'ultimately, the Hegelian system represents merely a materialism idealistically turned upside down in method and content'.[42] However, this negative refrain is tempered by several acknowledgments of Hegel's significant intellectual achievements. For the Engels of *Anti-Dühring*, the anti-evolutionism of the Hegelian philosophy of nature should not be construed as detracting from or eclipsing entirely its many

---

35   Ibid., pp. 6–7, 24–5.
36   Engels, *Anti-Dühring*, p. 65.
37   Ibid., pp. 17–18.
38   Ibid., p. 106.
39   Ibid., pp. 39, 41
40   Ibid., p. 36.
41   Ibid., p. 185.
42   Frederick Engels, *Ludwig Feuerbach and the Outcome of Classical German Philosophy*, ed. C. P. Dutt (New York: International Publishers, 1941), p. 24.

other invaluable features.[43] In this vein, he declares approvingly, 'The natural philosophers stand in the same relation to consciously dialectical natural science as the utopians to modern communism'[44] (Sève seconds these sentiments, speaking of the ambiguous unevenness of the Hegelian philosophy of nature[45]). For Engels, Hegel's approach to nature supposedly through a metaphysical purism of a priori concepts is the 'mystical shell' of his *Naturphilosophie*, to be cast aside as a dry, lifeless husk.[46] But the primacy granted to movement, to restless dynamics and processes, in Hegel's thinking is, in Engels's eyes, the truly momentous and progressive side of Hegelian philosophy – and this despite, on the Engelsian account, this revolutionary elevation of mobile negativity being contradictorily shackled to the stasis of a frozen framework of idealist dogmatism.[47] The post-Hegelian way forward, as Engels sees it, is to reverse Hegel's privileging of philosophy over science; he recommends granting science pride of place over philosophy, retaining from the latter the theoretical tools of formal logic and dialectics to be put at the disposal of the former.[48] Furthermore, he suggests this also entails the gesture of abandoning presumed access to absolute philosophical truth, resting content instead with the infinite pursuit of inexhaustible relative scientific truths approximating ever more closely to reality in itself.[49]

Dietzgen expresses similar views, albeit in a somewhat more confused and unsystematic fashion than Engels (this is due to his being a theoretical autodidact – a tanner by trade who, perhaps more than anyone, fits Jacques Rancière's representation of philosophy's poor cobbler[50]). Dietzgen's version of science-informed dialectical materialism, to a much greater extent than Engels's, is glaringly marked by strong Baconian and Hobbesian empiricist hues in the field of epistemology (and, like Hobbes in particular, Dietzgen seeks to combine the epistemology of empiricism with an ontology blending materialism, monism and nominalism, although he ends up closer to a Spinozistic dual-aspect, as distinct from a Hobbesian flat, ontology).[51] Neither Engels nor Dietzgen seems to take notice of just how

---

43   Engels, *Anti-Dühring*, p. 18.

44   Ibid.

45   Sève, '*Nature, science, dialectique*', pp. 49–50, 52, 54–6.

46   Engels, *Ludwig Feuerbach*, pp. 43–4.

47   Engels, *Anti-Dühring*, pp. 37–9; Engels, *Ludwig Feuerbach*, pp. 11–13.

48   Engels, *Anti-Dühring*, p. 40.

49   Ibid., pp. 56–7; Engels, *Ludwig Feuerbach*, pp. 14–15.

50   Jacques Rancière, *The Philosopher and His Poor*, ed. Andrew Parker, trans. John Drury, Corinne Oster and Andrew Parker (Durham: Duke University Press, 2004), pp. 19, 23, 35, 51.

51   Joseph Dietzgen, *The Nature of Human Brain-Work, and The Positive Outcome of Philosophy*, trans.

problematic redeployments of empiricist-style epistemologies are in the wake of Hegel and the dialectics of his to which they appeal. Anyhow, that said, Dietzgen's philosophical reflections, like those of Engels, stress both the fundamental oneness of being as rooted in its monistic material nature,[52] as the real universality of flux and change,[53] and the relativity and approximate character of all truths as extracted from empirical facts.[54]

Discounting Anton Pannekoek's gross overestimation of Dietzgen's philosophical abilities,[55] the overlaps between his and Engels's variants of dialectical materialism highlight the shortcomings of their positions. They both severely underestimate the extent to which the empirical, experimental sciences of nature necessarily depend upon the support provided by undergirding metaphysical foundations (something already brought out very clearly by the Hegel of the *Phenomenology of Spirit* and *Philosophy of Nature*). Dietzgen especially remains at a pre-Hegelian stage with his invocations of brute, raw sensory-perceptual givens as factual states of affairs disclosed to the mind directly by the extra-mental world (he sometimes flirts with lapsing into a naive realist correspondence theory of truth). When Engels claims that *Naturdialektik* is not about projecting or superimposing formal, philosophically prefabricated conceptual templates onto the objective-qua-non-subjective real of nature *an sich* – he insists that dialectical materialism discovers dialectical structures and processes already independently there in nature[56] – he forgets (or does not consider worth mentioning) that Hegel presents his manner of proceeding in every work from the *Phenomenology* onward in exactly the same way. When Sève trumpets Engels as the true secularizer of Hegelian *Naturdialektik*[57] and underscores the objective realism of Engels's dialectics of nature,[58] he too exhibits an obliviousness to the methods and contents of Hegel's absolute idealism (as including an objective realism with respect to a 'real world' said to be dialectical *an und für sich*).[59] What

W. W. Craik (Chicago: Charles H. Kerr & Co., 1928), pp. 76–79, 81, 85–6, 88–9, 94–8, 100–1, 117–19, 143.

52   Ibid., pp. 88, 96, 99, 107.

53   Ibid., p. 102.

54   Ibid., pp. 153–4.

55   Anton Pannekoek, *Lenin as Philosopher: A Critical Examination of the Philosophical Basis of Leninism*, ed. Lance Byron Richey (Milwaukee: Marquette University Press, 2003), pp. 91–100, 110–11, 121, 138, 160.

56   Frederick Engels, 'Dialectics', in *Dialectics of Nature*, pp. 26–7; Engels, *Anti-Dühring*, pp. 19, 36.

57   Sève, '*Nature, science, dialectique*', pp. 68, 71, 76.

58   Ibid., pp. 152, 161, 164, 174–6.

59   Johnston, 'A Weak Nature Alone'; Johnston, 'The Voiding of Weak Nature: Part One'; Johnston, 'The Voiding of Weak Nature: Part Two'.

is worse, Engels's tendency to speak loosely of there being dialectical 'laws' governing nature courts the danger of a regression to a pre-Hegelian formalism relying upon a non-dialectical, *Verstand*-level distinction between the forms of laws and the contents of the entities and events ruled thereby.[60]

However, I come to praise Engels and Dietzgen, not to bury them. The protracted backlash against Engelsian *Naturdialektik* has tried for long enough to perform this premature burial once and for all. Bearing in mind that Marx's historical materialism, as centred on the praxis-driven dialectics of labouring social subjects and objects both natural and artificial, requires supplementation by a dialectical-materialist account of the immanent natural genesis of this active human subjectivity,[61] I want to zero in on how Engels and, with less rigor, Dietzgen furnish precisely this. They do so primarily by bringing into play the then-available resources of biological renditions of human beings.

A few comments on the interlinked histories of the sciences and materialism, particularly as relevant to and understood by Engels, are helpful as preliminaries at this juncture. *Anti-Dühring* echoes Marx's first thesis on Feuerbach in disclosing the vulnerability of historically earlier types of materialism to idealism – both to idealist objections and to itself slipping inadvertently into insidious, disavowed modes of idealism.[62] But Engels does not wag his finger at these earlier materialisms as being the products of intellectual laziness or wilful blindness on the part of their partisans. Instead, consistent with the historical sensibilities of Marxist materialism, he explains that the nineteenth-century advent of crucial developments in the life sciences makes possible the transition from non-dialectical to dialectical materialism. To be more precise, Engels, in *Ludwig Feuerbach*, argues that philosophical materialism can, does and must change in tandem with advances in the natural sciences (this argument being of a piece with his previously mentioned inversion of the purported Hegelian prioritization of philosophy over science).[63] The anti-clerical mechanistic materialism of eighteenth-century France – this politically engaged materialism is, before Feuerbach, the historically nearest predecessor of the subsequent materialist outlook of Marx and Engels[64] – remains mechanis-

---

60 Engels, 'Dialectics', pp. 26–7; Engels, *Anti-Dühring*, pp. 193–6.
61 Johnston, *Prolegomena to Any Future Materialism, Volume Two*.
62 Engels, *Anti-Dühring*, pp. 190–1.
63 Engels, *Ludwig Feuerbach*, pp. 25–6.
64 Karl Marx and Frederick Engels, *The Holy Family*, trans. R. Dixon, in David McLellan, ed., *Karl Marx: Selected Writings* (Oxford: OUP, 1977), pp. 149–55.

tic, Engels proposes, because the natural sciences, at that stage of their development, were grounded on the mechanics of Newtonian physics as the most advanced of the sciences at the time. Hence, the French materialists could not but be mechanistic in their fight against idealist spiritualisms – and this necessarily and appropriately, in light of these thinkers' historical situation both intellectually and politically.[65] Likewise, Dietzgen's continual references to the human brain qua object of more-than-mechanistic science as the material basis of *Geist* hint at the crucial importance of the young discipline of biology for his dialectical materialism[66] (Engels, too, emphatically points at the brain[67]).

Dietzgen, despite his enthusiasm for the life sciences in connection with Marxist materialism, is well aware of the need to guide these sciences along the narrow path between mechanistic materialism and outright idealism. In 1869, he observes, 'The faculty of thought is still an unknown, mysterious, mystical being for natural science. Either it confounds the function with the organ, the mind with the brain, as do the materialists, or it believes with the idealists that the faculty of thought is an imperceptible object lying outside of its field.'[68] Later on along the same lines, Dietzgen comments:

> The spiritualist or idealist *believes* in a spiritual, [which] means a ghost-like and inexplicable nature of force. The materialist thinkers, on the other hand, are *unbelieving*. A scientific proof of belief or unbelief does not exist. The materialist has this advantage over his idealist opponent, that he looks for the transcendental, the nature, the cause, the force, not *behind* the phenomenon, not *outside* of matter. But he remains behind the idealist in that he ignores the difference between matter and force, denies the problem.[69]

Elsewhere he blames linguistic limitations for the long-entrenched (but nevertheless surpassable) deadlock between a lopsided materialism of inert, dense matter and an equally lopsided idealism of ideational energies and dematerialized spirits.[70] Consonant with the Marx of the 'Theses on Feuerbach', Dietzgen contends that the sole materialist way to jump off

---

65   Engels, *Ludwig Feuerbach*, pp. 26–7.
66   Dietzgen, *Nature of Human Brain-Work*, pp. 84–6, 88, 99–100, 132.
67   Engels, *Ludwig Feuerbach*, pp. 50, 52–3, 56.
68   Dietzgen, *Nature of Human Brain-Work*, p. 121.
69   Ibid., p. 140.
70   Dietzgen, *The Positive Outcome of Philosophy*, *The Positive Outcome of Philosophy*, p. 362.

this see-saw between one-sided sides is to build a new materialism, one that is neither contemplative nor mechanistic and that integrates within itself in a non-reductive manner the 'active side' of subjects, with their theoretical and practical activities.[71]

Dietzgen's distinctions between, on the one hand, 'matter', and, on the other hand, 'force' and/or 'mind' are proposed as Hegelian/Schellingian-style dialectical identities of identities and differences.[72] And, implicitly translating the Marxist logic of the social dialectics of infrastructure and superstructure into the terms of the mind-body problem, he speaks of the relative (rather than absolute) difference of the mental from the material (evoking the 'relative autonomy' of the superstructural in relation to the infrastructural).[73] Near the conclusion of *The Nature of Human Brain-Work* as well as in *The Positive Outcome of Philosophy*, he insightfully signals that a dialectical-materialist supersession (i.e. an *Aufhebung*) of the impasse between non-dialectical materialism and idealism brings about not only a becoming-natural of the spiritual, but simultaneously a reciprocal becoming-spiritual of the natural.[74] In other words, a materialism that is also a non-reductive naturalism – such is dialectical materialism strictly speaking for both Engels and Dietzgen – must transform conceptions of nature in parallel with altering ideas about subjectivity in its naturalization of the latter. For any dialectically sensitive position, rendering denaturalized, more-than-material subjects fully immanent to material nature changes prior images of both the subjective and the natural at one and the same time. Although Dietzgen leaves the details of this in a sketchy haze – like Engels, he also fails to discern just how much of this Hegel had already anticipated in his underappreciated *Realphilosophie*[75] – I think he is absolutely correct as regards these criteria stipulating what a robust and defensible dialectical materialism has to include.

Engels, drawing on his extensive research into the life sciences, labours to construct a much more detailed picture of a non-reductive (quasi-) naturalist theory of subjectivity consistent with dialectical materialism. However, in all three of his books dealing with *Naturdialektik*, he issues overview statements revealing him to be on the same page as Dietzgen. In

71 Johnston, *A Weak Nature Alone*.
72 Dietzgen, *Nature of Human Brain-Work*, pp. 135–8.
73 Dietzgen, *Positive Outcome of Philosophy*, pp. 359, 364.
74 Dietzgen, *Nature of Human Brain-Work*, pp. 173–4; Dietzgen, *Positive Outcome of Philosophy*, p. 330.
75 Johnston, 'A Weak Nature Alone'; Johnston, 'Voiding of Weak Nature: Part One'; Johnston, 'Voiding of Weak Nature: Part Two'.

the introduction to *Dialectics of Nature*, he provides a synopsis of what is arguably the most important chapter of the whole book, the essay entitled 'The Part Played by Labour in the Transition from Ape to Man' (I will focus sustained attention on this piece shortly). Tacitly relying upon one of his three Hegel-derived dialectical 'laws' – this would be the one positing the occurrence of leap-like transitions between quantities and qualities – Engels describes the emergence of human out of natural history as the internal production of a discontinuity (i.e. the leap into human history) out of a preceding continuity (i.e. the natural history from which human history originally springs).[76] He speaks in Hegelian fashion of 'that mammal in which nature attains consciousness of itself – man'[77] (in *Ludwig Feuerbach*, and in resonance with Marx's recognition of the sapient sentience of human beings as a distinctive feature setting them apart from other animals and the rest of the natural universe,[78] he distinguishes nature from humanity as unconsciousness from consciousness[79] – thereby also echoing the Schellingian-Hegelian idea of nature as 'petrified intelligence'). The evolutionary step from non-human primates to humans, itself embedded in the lengthy contingent sequences of continually transforming natural and animal forms, is said to make 'the gulf between man and monkey an unbridgeable one'.[80] Once again, the speculative identity of identity (as the continuity of natural evolution) and difference (as the discontinuity of an evolutionarily generated break with nature) proves to be an integral aspect of *Naturdialektik*.

In *Anti-Dühring*, Engels momentarily places stress on the immanence of humanity to evolving, historicized nature. He does so seemingly for reasons of a primarily epistemological sort. In this context, Engels clearly assumes that the preceding two-and-a-half centuries of the march of the modern sciences represents the progressive consolidation of an ever-firmer rational grip on empirical, physical reality. On the basis of this assumption, he claims, unwittingly recapitulating Hegel's absolute idealism (with its objective realism), that the ultimate condition of possibility explaining the evident isomorphisms between the concepts of minded subjects (i.e. humans) and the objects of the asubjective world (i.e. nature) is the real ontological immanence of the former to the latter. Epistemological

---

76   Engels, 'Introduction', pp. 17–18.
77   Ibid., p. 17.
78   Johnston, *A Weak Nature Alone*.
79   Engels, *Ludwig Feuerbach*, pp. 48–50.
80   Engels, 'Introduction', p. 17.

problems of the access of subjectivity to objectivity are less puzzling for a dialectical materialism systematically combining the science of human society (i.e. Marx's historical materialism) with that of historicized nature (i.e. Darwinian biology), insofar as it does not dualistically posit a matter-transcendent mind that then has to be somehow reconnected with its extra-mental Other[81] (Sève reiterates this Engelsian argument[82]). For Engels (as for Dietzgen), the distinction between human thinking and natural being is a distinction internal to natural being itself.

Attention can now be shifted onto the text of *Dialectics of Nature*, specifically 'The Part Played by Labour in the Transition from Ape to Man'. This 1876 essay, I would maintain, is the closest Engels comes to supplying Marx's historical materialism with its required dialectical-but-naturalistic account, consistent with Darwinism, of human beings as labouring social creatures. Its opening paragraph states:

> Labour is the source of all wealth, the economists assert. It is this – next to nature, which supplies it with the material that it converts into wealth. But it is also infinitely more than this. It is the primary basic condition for all human existence, and this to such an extent that, in a sense, we have to say that labour created man himself.[83]

In fact, labour, given the Marxist conception of humanity's *Gattungswesen* ('species-being'), initially is itself no more than an inner facet of the natural world. Human species-being, as one variety of animal life among many others, physically dictates that humans, like all other animals, struggle with their natural material surroundings in order to sustain themselves as living beings (hence Engels's identification of labour as 'the primary basic condition for all human existence'). This is an instance of nature as a not-Whole non-One, shot through with internal antagonisms and tensions, wrestling with itself: the human beings who wrestle with nature are themselves immanent to nature, are parts of it.

A further speculative twist to be appreciated in the preceding quotation is the reversal Engels brings about between agent and action. Intuitive notions of agency (here, the labouring subject) and activity (here, this subject's labour) usually portray agency as enjoying

---

81   Engels, *Anti-Dühring*, p. 55.
82   Sève, '*Nature, science, dialectique*', pp. 52, 73–6, 151, 154.
83   Frederick Engels, 'The Part Played by Labour in the Transition from Ape to Man', in *Dialectics of Nature*, p. 279.

ontological priority over activity. In this non-dialectical ordering of precedence, the relation of influence is a one-way street, with an already-there agent (again, the labouring subject) determining and producing a corresponding action (again, the subject's labour). From this perspective, actions do not correlatively-but-inversely determine and produce agents. By sharp contrast, for both Marx and Engels, reciprocal inter-actions between subjects and objects, mediated by practices qua actions mutually modifying both these poles in parallel, are the rule. Thus, in the perpetually ongoing activity of labouring, humans continually change themselves at the same time as they alter their others (i.e. the enveloping environs of natural entities and forces). Hence, labour creates its subject ('labour created man himself') as much as it is created by it. In other words, the human being is, by nature (as per the species-being), the simultaneous subject-object of labor.

Drawing on the fresh stores of ammunition from Darwinian biology available to him, Engels alights upon the human hand, with its opposable thumb, as a naturally evolved physical feature of human anatomy that has enormous significance. He situates this body part at the nexus of the dialectical interactions through which natural history immanently sunders itself by giving rise to human subject-objects of labour who themselves, through their nature-prompted actions, catalyze the explosive emergence of denaturalized social history. At one point, Engels asserts, 'the hand is not only the organ of labour, *it is also the product of labour*'.[84] Darwinian evolution's precise modes of historicizing nature themselves permit plug-ging into the apparatus of Marxist materialism what could be called 'bio-plasticity' (along the lines so crucial to Catherine Malabou in her own substantial efforts to invent a new dialectical materialism for the twenty-first century). This bio-plasticity is a pivotal component of a specifically materialist dialectics of human beings as self-transformative subject-objects.

Adding speech to labour, Engels proceeds to describe a complex ensem-ble of entangled, interpenetrating factors responsible for the ascent out of natural matter of the more-than-natural structures and phenomena of concern to Marx's historical materialism. With the hypothesis in the background that the human brain's evolution was driven forward by hand-directed labour, he elaborates:

---

84   Ibid., p. 281.

The reaction on labour and speech of the development of the brain and its attendant senses, of the increasing clarity of consciousness, power of abstraction and of judgement, gave an ever-renewed impulse to the further development of both labour and speech. This further development did not reach its conclusion when man finally became distinct from the monkey, but, on the whole, continued to make powerful progress, varying in degree and direction among different peoples and at different times, and here and there even interrupted by a local or temporary regression.

This further development has been strongly urged forward, on the one hand, and has been guided along more definite directions on the other hand, owing to a new element which came into play with the appearance of fully-fledged man, viz. *society*.[85]

Engels goes on to contend that these evolutionarily sparked revolutions (as nature-immanent ruptures with nature) understandably prompt the advent of idealist worldviews throughout humanity:

By the co-operation of hands, organs of speech, and brain, not only in each individual, but also in society, human beings became capable of executing more and more complicated operations, and of setting themselves, and achieving, higher and higher aims. With each generation, labour itself became different, more perfect, more diversified. Agriculture was added to hunting and cattle-breeding, then spinning, weaving, metal-working, pottery, and navigation. Along with trade and industry, there appeared finally art and science. From tribes there developed nations and states.

Law and politics arose, and with them the fantastic reflection of human things in the human mind: religion. In the face of all these creations, which appeared in the first place to be products of the mind, and which seemed to dominate human society, the more modest productions of the working hand retreated into the background, the more so since the mind that plans the labour process already at a very early stage of development of society (e.g. already in the simple family), was able to have the labour that had been planned carried out by other hands than its own. All merit for the swift advance of civilisation was ascribed to the mind, to the development and activity of the brain. Men

---

85   Ibid., p. 285.

became accustomed to explain their actions from their thoughts, instead of from their needs – (which in any case are reflected and come to consciousness in the mind) – and so there arose in the course of time that idealistic outlook on the world which, especially since the decline of the ancient world, has dominated men's minds. It still rules them to such a degree that even the most materialistic natural scientists of the Darwinian school are still unable to form any clear idea of the origin of man, because under this ideological influence they do not recognise the part that has been played therein by labour.[86]

I want to highlight a few facets of this multifaceted description of how the very material history of the factual natural genesis of denaturalized humanity ironically sets the stage for its own occlusion by preparing the triumph of anti-materialist fictions as religions, spiritualisms, and so on. In the elongated movement from natural to human history via literally manual labour, labour engaged in by social beings (i.e. humans à la Marx with their peculiar *Gattungswesen* qua self-denaturalizing nature as working gregarious animals) triggers a cascade of ever-more-intricate divisions of labour, in which a split between manual and intellectual labour eventually opens up in societies. In short, manual labour produces out of itself the divide between itself and intellectual labour. What is more, the intellectual labour thereby produced erases the memory of its material historical origins and, in so doing, propagates ideologies that come to colour the consciousness of intellectual and manual labourers alike for countless generations thereafter. Philosophers and non-philosophers both end up being vulnerable to the seductions and temptations of idealism, to misconstruing themselves and their societies as marching on their heads.

Before jumping forward from Engels to his handful of avowed contemporary heirs in the life sciences, I wish briefly to underscore another note sounded in *Dialectics of Nature*. In this text Engels, well before everything from the ecological green thinking of the past several decades to certain strains of the 'speculative realism' movement in current Continental philosophy (Dietzgen,[87] Georgi Plekhanov,[88] Lenin,[89] and Pannekoek,[90]

86   Ibid., p. 289.

87   Dietzgen, *Nature of Human Brain-Work*, pp. 87, 92, 95, 112.

88   George V. Plekhanov, *Fundamental Problems of Marxism*, ed. James S. Allen, trans. Julius Katzer (New York: International Publishers, 1969), pp. 30–1, 45, 83, 90.

89   V. I. Lenin, *Materialism and Empirio-Criticism* (Peking: Foreign Languages Press, 1972), pp. 18–19, 38, 45–6, 68–9, 95, 139, 142–5, 152–3, 177–8, 195, 203, 205, 216, 305, 310–14, 420, 426.

90   Pannekoek, *Lenin as Philosopher*, pp. 109–10.

among others and in addition to Engels, vehemently defend realist views being revived today with little to no reference to the long-established Marxist tradition), foregrounds the greater-than-human dimensions of physical being as material nature. He muses about the inevitable extinction of humanity in its entirety, the life of the human species being equally as mortal in relation to the history of the universe as the life of an individual organism[91] (Timpanaro approvingly underlines these moments when Engels reflects on the demise and disappearance of finite humanity as a whole[92]). He also presciently warns, 'Let us not . . . flatter ourselves overmuch on account of our human conquest over nature. For each such conquest takes its revenge on us.'[93]

In light of this, what is the nature of Engels's legacy, transmitted via the British Marxist and Soviet scientists and philosophers of science of the decades of the twentieth century prior to the Second World War, as it stands nowadays in the life sciences? In the book they dedicate to Engels, Levins and Lewontin endorse Engelsian *Naturdialektik* generally, and the sorts of speculations spelled out in 'The Part Played by Labour in the Transition from Ape to Man' specifically.[94] They embrace Engels's insistence that human and non-human animals alike are organisms participating in a subject–object dialectic with their environments.[95] Levins and Lewontin (and Steven Rose, too) repeatedly emphasize both that organisms and environments are not truly separable from each other, and that organisms are not just passively determined by their environments but act to determine their environments in turn.[96] These two biologists concur with Engels that 'human society arises out of animal social organization, but as it arises, it transforms the significance of adaptations and creates new needs'.[97] Consciously following in Engels's footsteps, they seek to cultivate a balanced appreciation of the mixed continuities and discontinuities between humans and the rest of (animal) nature,[98] with this

---

91 Engels, 'Introduction', p. 18.
92 Timpanaro, *On Materialism*, pp. 18, 36, 38–9.
93 Engels, 'The Part Played by Labour in the Transition from Ape to Man', pp. 291–2.
94 Levins and Lewontin, *Dialectical Biologist*, pp. 69–70.
95 Engels, 'The Part Played by Labour in the Transition from Ape to Man', pp. 289–90; Levins and Lewontin, *Dialectical Biologist*, p. 274.
96 Levins and Lewontin, *Dialectical Biologist*, pp. 89, 99, 111; Richard Lewontin, 'Genes, Environment, and Organisms', in Richard Lewontin and Richard Levins, *Biology Under the Influence: Dialectical Essays on Ecology, Agriculture, and Health* (New York: Monthly Review Press, 2007), p. 231; Steven Rose, *Lifelines: Biology Beyond Determinism* (Oxford: OUP, 1997), pp. 18, 140–3, 171, 244–5, 279, 306–8.
97 Levins and Lewontin, *Dialectical Biologist*, p. 46.
98 Ibid., p. 133.

balance, by their Engelsian lights, once again compelling recourse to a dialectical materialism steering between the Scylla and Charybdis of, on the one hand, mechanistic and reductive materialism, and, on the other, all sorts of idealisms.[99] And, whereas Engels places the human hand at the intersection between criss-crossing subjective and objective processes, Levins and Lewontin, for the same basic reasons, foreground the plastic cerebral cortex as the embodiment epitomizing humans' status as hybrid subject-objects.[100]

However, although it is Levins and Lewontin who dedicate a book to Engels, Rose is more faithful to orthodox Engelsian dialectical materialism insofar as this doctrine favours images of ultimate wholeness when all is said and done. To be more exact, Rose's book *Lifelines: Biology Beyond Determinism* appears to be philosophically inconsistent in its wavering between embracing strong emergentist models (with their anti-reductive and anti-determinist upshots) and unnuanced affirmations of the monistic oneness and self-consistency of material being as an ontologically seamless totality. He repeatedly qualifies his commitment to explanatory diversity (for instance, the irreducibility of biological to physical explanations) as strictly epistemological, coupling this epistemology of irreducible plurality with an ontology of unity: 'Our world may be – is, I would claim – an ontological unity, but to understand it we need the epistemological diversity that the different levels of explanation offer.'[101] He later reiterates that 'we require epistemological diversity in order to understand the ontological unity of our world',[102] and that 'we live in a material world which is an ontological unity, but which we approach with epistemological diversity'.[103]

And yet, given other of Rose's assertions, it seems he needs the irreducibility of emergent phenomena to be a matter of real being and not just scientific thinking, to be ontological in addition to epistemological. That is to say, his world has to be really diverse instead of unified, a de-totalized not-Whole rather than an organic One-All. Indulging in the problematic equivocation between freedom and mere indeterminacy (a slippage criticized well before Rose's book by Timpanaro[104]), he speculates that nature, especially at its organic levels, is so complex and overdetermined that, merely in its self-standing objective existence, it defies all determinist

---

99   Ibid., pp. 133, 135–6.
100   Ibid., p. 137.
101   Rose, *Lifelines*, p. 95.
102   Ibid., p. 296.
103   Ibid., p. 304.
104   Timpanaro, *On Materialism*, p. 40.

hypotheses put forward by reductionist biologists.[105] Underscoring his ontologizing of what he elsewhere inconsistently treats as strictly episte- mological, he states, 'indeterminacy is not merely a matter of ignorance, or lack of adequate technology; it is inherent in the nature of life itself'.[106]

A further source of tension with Rose's prevailing Engelsian (w)holism is generated by his astute diagnoses of images of Nature-with-a-capital-N – these images of what supposedly would be balanced and harmonious on its own were it not for humans are precious to environmentalists, and nowadays an accompanying horde of advertisers and their consumers – as ideological illusions with no basis in the life sciences[107] (Lewontin makes the same critical observations[108]). Rose does not clarify how and why his periodically proclaimed faith that the natural world is ultimately a smooth monistic unity (and this despite what he affirms as the irreducible diversity of the plurality of both natural and human sciences) is not symptomatic of a lingering, undi- agnosed attachment on his part to exactly the same rudimentary vision of nature held to by eco-ideologues. But instead of chastising Rose for a lack of theoretical rigor, I intend to trace his vacillations back to tensions already internal to Engels's materialist dialectics of nature, and to put these tensions to work in the service of laying the foundations for a new *Naturdialektik*.

The second chapter of *Dialectics of Nature*, entitled 'Dialectics', opens with the Engels of notoriety much criticized by anti-Engelsian Western Marxists for promoting an arid a priori Hegelian formalism of a pre- Marxist kind fancifully projected onto a nature beyond history. Admittedly, there is something to these criticisms in relation to charges regarding the instrumental, methodical formalization of Hegel's philos- ophy in this context. However, what these same criticisms overlook is the possibility of an immanent instead of an external critique of Engelsian dialectics.

The first sentence (actually, sentence fragment) of Engels's chapter devoted to dialectics – he opens it with a parenthesis – reads, '(The general nature of dialectics to be developed as the science of interconnections, in contrast to metaphysics.)'[109] Obviously, Engels one-sidedly subsumes his post-Hegelian conceptual toolkit under the heading of unity by defining dialectics as 'the science of interconnections'. He then infamously lists his

---

105 Rose, *Lifelines*, pp. 6–7, 245, 309.
106 Ibid., p. 15.
107 Rose, *Lifelines*, pp. 228, 246, 307.
108 Lewontin, 'Genes, Environment, and Organisms', pp. 232–3.
109 Engels, 'Dialectics', p. 26.

'three dialectical laws': one, 'The law of the transformation of quantity into quality and *vice versa*'; two, 'The law of the interpenetration of opposites'; three, 'The law of the negation of the negation.'[110]

What Engels apparently fails to realize, under the influence of his lopsided organicist monism, is that the first of his three laws of dialectics in particular is double-edged, with one of its edges directly cutting against his (w)holistic overemphasis on unity, integration, connectedness, and so on. Hegel's dialectics of quantity and quality, adopted as a principle or rule by Engels, is the original conceptualization of the structures and dynamics integral to the much more recent life-scientific paradigm of emergentism (as operative in the writings of Levins, Lewontin and Rose, among many others). In light of Hegelian speculative reason's handling of continuity and discontinuity (contra the non-speculative understanding's treatment of this pair as two mutually exclusive binary opposites), the discontinuities catalyzed by and operative within the interactions between quantitative and qualitative dimensions must be granted their place as well. I interpret some of Levins and Lewontin's ideas as moving more in this direction.

As we have seen, Badiou observed in 2006 that the traditional conflict between idealism and materialism has been superseded under late capitalism by a new intra-materialist antagonism between democratic materialism and the materialist dialectic. Already in the 1970s, Levins and Lewontin had similarly observed that, within and around the sciences, idealism-versus-materialism had been replaced by reductionism-versus-dialectics.[111] But, unlike Rose, they unambiguously and unwaveringly adhere to an ontologized strong-emergentist schema in which dialectical processes resembling those of Hegelian quantity and quality give rise to relatively autonomous levels and layers of embodied being irreducible to the other material strata from which they arose.[112]

For my purposes, certain of Levins and Lewontin's specifications of their anti-reductivist dialectics of nature are of special significance. First of all, in both *The Dialectical Biologist* and *Biology Under the Influence* (their two co-authored collections of essays), they repeatedly speak of 'weak constraints' as regards the concrete localizations of living organisms within intricate intersections of multiple regions of relations, entities and forces.[113] On one of these occasions, they explain:

---

110   Ibid.
111   Levins and Lewontin, *Dialectical Biologist*, p. 254.
112   Ibid., p. 288.
113   Ibid., p. 140; Lewontin and Levins, *Biology Under the Influence*, pp. 16, 53.

Biological objects . . . are intermediate in size and . . . internally functionally heterogeneous. As a consequence their behavior cannot be determined from a knowledge of only a small number of properties, as one can specify the orbit of a planet from the planet's distance from the sun, its mass, and its velocity, without being concerned about what it is made of.

Biological objects are at the nexus of a very large number of individually weak forces. Although there are indeed interactions among these forces (and the interactions are often of the essence), it is also the case that there are very large numbers of subsystems of causal pathways that are essentially independent of one another, so that their effects on an organism appear as random with respect to one another.[114]

The counterbalance against the Engelsian privileging of interconnectedness is obvious here. But I perceive a further step that should be taken at this point. I can introduce this additional move thusly:

[T]ake the United States federal tax code as an example of a symbolic system. This code is a body of technical legal stipulations so massive that no single person, not even the most knowledgeable tax expert, has a complete understanding of the entire network of laws and how these laws fit together with one another. Moreover, year after year, successive legislative sessions of Congress change the code, adding, subtracting, and modifying laws. Of course, this means that the creation of ever-more loopholes in the tax code is a foregone conclusion, since those altering this body of laws cannot know in advance what unforeseen possibilities will arise from the structural interactions between the already-less-than-fully-understood prior set of existing laws and the changes (as additions, subtractions, and modifications) made to these laws. Firms dealing with accounting and tax advice make their money by discovering and exploiting the loopholes in the body of laws forming the entirety of the US federal tax code.[115]

As I have suggested before,[116] this example of tax law as a symbolic system arguably holds, at least by analogy (if not by homology or isomorphism),

114   Ibid., p. 28.
115   Adrian Johnston, *Žižek's Ontology: A Transcendental Materialist Theory of Subjectivity* (Evanston: Northwestern University Press, 2008), p. 170.
116   Ibid., pp. 170–1.

for 'the nexus of a very large number of individually weak forces' within which Levins and Lewontin situate biological beings (i.e. it holds for real as well as symbolic systems, for natural as well as non-natural structures and dynamics). If, plausibly, the weakness of the multiple influences and causes which Levins and Lewontin describe functions as per my illustration of symbolic systems surpassing a certain threshold of complexity, then, however rarely, the weak shackles of these forces sometimes come undone and fall to the ground thanks to their own disharmonious, contradictory clashes with each other, their inner incompatibilities.

Weak overdetermination à la Levins and Lewontin leads (or even perhaps leaps) out of itself to under- or non-determination, however occasional and exceptional might be these loophole-like short circuits immanently transpiring within natural materialities, these zones of anomie opened by a self-sundering substance as necessary-but-not-sufficient conditions of possibility for the autonomy of denaturalized more-than-materialities (such as the subjective agents of socio-historical change not forever doomed to alienated servitude to whatever counts as the purportedly 'natural' status quo). This is a big step along the road from dialectical to transcendental materialism, a transition entailing the sublation of the former by the latter. Marx's historical materialism, with its presuppositions regarding human species-being – this *Gattungswesen* includes an effective non-epiphenomenal conscious volition belonging to minded and like-minded human beings, in addition and related to their need-driven social labouring – requires this transcendental materialist supplement. Although transcendental materialism is deeply indebted to Engels's dialectical materialism, Engels does not quite manage, in his admirable efforts towards this goal, to outfit Marxism with a systematic quasi-naturalist materialism dovetailing with and firmly buttressing Marx's historical-materialist critique of political economy.

Even more significantly, Levins and Lewontin stipulate an implicit modification to Engels's third law of dialectics (the law of the negation of the negation). Whereas Engels harnesses the Hegelian concept of determinate negation (as opposed to the abstract negation of the sub-rational understanding) in the service of a picture of the material real as a tightly woven tapestry of exhaustively entwined threads, his two biologist descendants put forward a notion of determinate negation introducing discontinuities rather than establishing and sustaining continuities. They contend, 'Nothing is more central to a dialectical understanding of nature than the realization that the conditions necessary for the coming into being of some state of the world may be destroyed by the very state of nature to which they gave rise.'[117] More so than Engels's formalization of dialectics as an instrumental method, Levins and Lewontin's characterization of *Naturdialektik* clearly involves generalizing specifically from Marx's Hegel-inspired dialectical analyses of socio-historical development hitherto, as propelled forward by the negative energy of class struggles (culminating, of course, in communism's destruction of capitalism after capitalism has made possible and given rise to communism). For Marx, 'Human anatomy contains a key to the anatomy of the ape'[118]; likewise, for Levins and Lewontin, historical dialectics contains a key to the logics of natural dialectics. What Engels articulates gropingly in his discussion of the transition from apes to humans, his scientist offspring crystallize with greater lucidity.

This newer, post-Engelsian dialectics of nature tacitly relies upon a meta-dialectical dialecticization of dialectics along the lines of what Badiou, Timpanaro and Sève all demand, as we have seen. More precisely, in addition to the indeterminate negations of *Verstand* and the determinate negations of *Vernunft* (with the second as interpreted by Engels), Levins and Lewontin hint at a third type of negation, itself a permutation of Hegelian determinate negation qua dialectical. This third variety I might depict as the non-dialectical side of determinate negation, with this depiction entailing a meta-dialectics of the dialectical and the non-dialectical internal to determinate negation.

Apart from whatever inherent philosophical interest it might possess, what, if any, payoff does my transcendental materialist *Aufhebung* of dialectical materialism yield relative to the guiding, overriding concerns of the Marxist tradition as a distinct political and theoretical orientation? Broadly and summarily speaking, I see four primary ways in which this approach is constructive and useful for Marxism. One, my repetition of a gesture first boldly performed by Engels and Lenin (i.e. recruiting the natural sciences to the side of Marxist materialism) turns the life sciences, themselves in a pre-eminent cultural and institutional position in the Western world today, from supporting to contesting the Hobbesian-Smithian portrait of 'human nature' – and along with this lending further support to Marx and Engels's load-bearing materialist hypotheses regarding the species-being of humanity. Two, transcendental materialism's meta-dialectics of nature helps to

117   Lewontin and Levins, *Biology Under the Influence*, p. 31.
118   Karl Marx, *Grundrisse: Foundations of the Critique of Political Economy*, trans. Martin Nicolaus (New York: Penguin Books, 1993), p. 105.

debunk, both philosophically and scientifically, contemporary scientistic ideologies (such as those related to what Rose labels 'neurogenetic determinism'[119]) that falsely naturalize status-quo social relations and forms of subjection, as ideology in various socio-historical guises typically tries to do; on the active front of a live intellectual war of position, this updated materialism strives to unmask bio-scientism's specious rationalizations for a mind-boggling array of infrastructural and superstructural features of late capitalism. Three, it pursues what I see as the valuable goal of thoroughly immunizing Marxist materialism from the threats of three intellectual and ideological dangers: covert idealisms (à la post-Lukácsian antipathy to the natural sciences in Western Marxism), overt idealisms (if only by association with the dubious company of conscious or unconscious neo-Kantians or the theologically inclined), and non-dialectical materialisms (to take a handful of examples, what Badiou dubs democratic materialism, what I describe as capitalist biologism, Rose's neurogenetic determinism, and similar manifestations that are now ubiquitous). Four, despite carrying out this immunization, my position allows for the outlining of a contemporary materialism that is both fully compatible with the core of Marx and Engels's shared *Weltanschauung*, as well as for striking a delicate balance between affirming freedom and admitting determinism, in such a way that optimism about revolutionary subjective agency and realism about objective material conditions and constraints can be varyingly combined in ways appropriate and sensitive to shifting concrete conjunctures (thereby allowing for a tactically and strategically wise, sober conviction that avoids deviating in the direction of either wild-eyed Panglossianism or dull-eyed resignation).

A main line of attack resorted to by Marxists hostile to Engels and his dialectics of nature is one sadly mirroring an all-too-familiar non-Marxist canard. This commonplace refrain mindlessly writes off Marxism in its multifaceted entirety by equating it wholesale with Stalinism. According to this popular and oft-repeated mantra, Stalin's USSR is the inevitable and logically consequent outcome of Marx's ideas, with the reality of bureaucratic state terror purportedly revealing, with the benefit of twentieth-century historical hindsight, the unrealistic and disaster-prone nineteenth-century utopianism of communism's champions. Opponents of a dialectical materialism affiliated with the natural sciences (this includes a number of Western Marxists) sometimes might be tempted to conjure up the ghost of Stalin's favoured 'barefoot scientist', the Ukrainian

---

119   Rose, *Lifelines*, pp. 272–99.

agronomist Trofim Lysenko.[120] Lysenko represents for Soviet science what Stalin represents for Really Existing Socialism as a whole – namely, a terrifying nosedive into rigid dogmatism, superficial polemics, cynical institutional manoeuvring, and paranoia-driven purges.

Just as the figure of Stalin serves anti-communists as ostensibly a reduction-to-the-absurdly-horrific of Marxism in its entirety, so too does Lysenko serve anti-Engelsians in rationalizing their rejection of every conceivable dialectical-materialist philosophy of nature and science. Timpanaro points out the lack of strong connections between Stalin's philosophical writings (expounding his doctrine that came to be dubbed 'diamat') and Marxism's science-linked materialisms, from Engels through the non-Lysenkoist scientists and philosophers of science in the East.[121] Levins and Lewontin, in a chapter of *The Dialectical Biologist* entitled 'The Problem of Lysenkoism', seek to thwart the cheap-and-easy manoeuvre of exploiting the figure of Lysenko so as to forbid as politically dangerous and intellectually pointless any mixing of Marxism and science.[122] For a plethora of good reasons, no self-respecting Marxist accepts as valid and compelling the stale anti-Marxist argument that uses Stalinism to condemn Marxism *überhaupt*. Any Marxist who turns around and exploits Lysenkoism, as the corresponding scientistic sub-variant of Stalinism, to deploy the exact same type of argument against dialectical-materialist appropriations of the natural sciences should be ashamed. Similarly, not only must today's radical leftists cease feeling pressured into interminable self-flagellation by all those to their right who demand they paralyze themselves into inaction by ceaselessly apologizing for the miseries of Really Existing Socialism; Marxist thinkers at the dawn of the twenty-first century ought to stop saying they are sorry for the tragedy of Lysenkoism. Before doing this, some contemporary Marxists will first have to learn and appreciate the historical truth, that they have been standing in the shadows of this, their unconscious guilt, for quite a while already.

At this moment, I cannot resist a passing invocation of Walter Benjamin's deservedly famous and celebrated essay, 'Theses on the Philosophy of History'. I invoke Benjamin at this juncture in connection

---

120 Helena Sheehan, *Marxism and the Philosophy of Science: A Critical History – The First Hundred Years* (Amherst: Humanity Books, 1993), 2nd edn, pp. 220–8.

121 Timpanaro, *On Materialism*, p. 33; Joseph Stalin, *Dialectical and Historical Materialism* (New York: International Publishers, 1940), pp. 7–11, 15–17, 20–21.

122 Levins and Lewontin, *Dialectical Biologist*, pp. 163–96.

with two observations resembling each other. The first of these is made by Marxist Alfred Sohn-Rethel. In his book *Intellectual and Manual Labour*, he underscores the weightiness of the stakes of his historical-materialist genealogy of mathematical and natural-scientific modes of thought by contending that socialism, in the absence of a self-critical Marxist assessment of science and technology, threatens to degenerate into inegalitarian technocracy[123] (by 1951, when Sohn-Rethel had completed his manuscript,[124] this degeneration seemed to be a fait accompli in the USSR and its satellites). The second, and similar, observation I have in mind here is made by non-Marxist Michel Foucault near the end of the concluding lecture of his Collège de France course of 1975–76. This seminar session (17 March 1976) is the occasion on which Foucault introduces the notions of 'biopower' and 'biopolitics',[125] which, as is common knowledge, have become incredibly influential in contemporary socio-political theorizing. Near the very end of this academic year, he charges that 'One thing at least is certain: Socialism has made no critique of the theme of biopower.'[126] It thereby allegedly dooms itself to remain imprisoned in the same essential sort of power structures holding sway over the Western capitalist world too.[127] In Foucault's view, an adequate ideological critique of biopower and its politics, let alone a revolution against it, had yet to materialize.[128]

In the Collège de France seminars of the late 1970s (especially the consecutive annual courses 'Security, Territory, Population' [1977–78] and 'The Birth of Biopolitics' [1978–79]), Foucault, manifestly under the influence of Aleksandr Solzhenitsyn's 1973 *Gulag Archipelago* and paving the way for France's repentant ex-Maoist *nouveaux philosophes*,[129] displays what comes across as a deliberate, wilful ignorance of the history and theories of the multifaceted Marxist tradition. Mimicking a stale, standard liberal gesture, he insinuates, with perhaps calculated crudeness, that

123   Sohn-Rethel, *Intellectual and Manual Labour*, p. 3.

124   Ibid., p. xiv.

125   Michel Foucault, *'Society must be defended': Lectures at the Collège de France, 1975–1976*, ed. Mauro Bertani and Alessandro Fontana, trans. David Macey (New York: Picador, 2003), pp. 239–63.

126   Ibid., p. 261.

127   Ibid., pp. 261–3.

128   Michel Foucault, *Security, Territory, Population: Lectures at the Collège de France, 1977–1978*, ed. Michel Senellart, trans. Graham Burchell (New York: Picador, 2007), pp. 150, 215–16; Michel Foucault, *The Birth of Biopolitics: Lectures at the Collège de France, 1978–1979*, ed. Michel Senellart, trans. Graham Burchell (Basingstoke: Palgrave Macmillan, 2008), pp. 131, 162–4.

129   Richard Wolin, *The Wind from the East: French Intellectuals, the Cultural Revolution, and the Legacy of the 1960s* (Princeton: Princeton University Press, 2010), pp. 342–8.

Marxism *tout court* deserves to be lumped together with the most abhorrent aspects of Really Existing Socialism *à la* Stalin.[130] Moreover, he misrepresents Marxists as obsessively preoccupied in historically unoriginal and unimaginative ways with 'the state' qua the centralized ensemble of the organs of government administration.[131]

Foucault's anti-Marxist polemics and provocations aside, neither he nor Sohn-Rethel show any awareness of the fact that, starting with Engels and continuing through Dietzgen, Plekhanov, Lenin, Nikolai Bukharin, Boris Zavadovsky, Mao Tse-Tung and many others, Marxism (particularly its non-Western strains) indeed faces up to the challenge of engaging critically with science generally and the life sciences in particular. For instance, biology, the science of the living, was submitted to intense philosophical scrutiny and heated political debate by both scientists and non-scientists in the Soviet Union from the 1920s through the 1940s, for better and (with Lysenko) worse. Engels's writings on the sciences gave rise to a now largely forgotten tradition in the philosophy of science. The Marxian-Engelsian philosophical orientation with respect to the sciences has been obliterated from the memories not only of those who consider this sub-discipline within philosophy to be the exclusive province of analytic philosophers going back to the early twentieth century of the Vienna Circle and Oxbridge, but also of the vast majority of Western Marxists and, more broadly still, Continental philosophers as a loose, large group.[132] When, as per Sohn-Rethel, Really Existing Socialism atrophied into an oppressive bureaucracy of party technocrats; and if, as per Foucault, a revolutionary Marxism-in-power did not manage to evade the clutches of biopower, this certainly was not due, as their erroneous diagnoses suggest, to a lack of concerted efforts (informed by the philosophical sophistication of dialectical materialism) to rethink from top to bottom the social and economic ramifications for living beings of the complex overlappings of politics and science, of (to resort to Giorgio Agamben's post-Foucauldian biopolitical parlance) a *zoe* caught up in *bios* and a *bios* caught up in *zoe* in ways scientifically, politically and philosophically problematizing this very distinction itself. Nevertheless, the inaccuracy of Sohn-Rethel's and Foucault's observations as regards the past does not mean they cannot

130 Foucault, *Security, Territory, Population*, pp. 200–1; Foucault, *Birth of Biopolitics*, pp. 190–2.

131 Foucault, *Security, Territory, Population*, pp. 355–6; Foucault, *Birth of Biopolitics*, pp. 76–7, 92, 187.

132 Sheehan, *Marxism and the Philosophy of Science*, pp. 2–3, 6.

act as signposts for present and future Marxism(s): those Marxists who neglect to grasp the sciences will be grasped by them; the breadth and depth of the economic and political significance of scientific theories and practices cannot be safely repressed or effectively escaped.

With reference to Benjamin, I would suggest that Engels's dialectical-materialist engagement with the sciences, and the carrying forward of this project primarily by Soviet Marxists in the early twentieth century, is, for the past fifty or more years of radical leftist political thinking in the West, an 'image of the past that is not recognized by the present as one of its own concerns', which, as Benjamin goes on to warn, 'threatens to disappear irretrievably'.[133] In his sixth and following thesis on the philosophy of history, he cautions, '*even the dead* will not be safe from the enemy if he wins. And this enemy has not ceased to be victorious.'[134] Historical materialism *à la* Benjamin combats these dangers by 'brushing history against the grain'.[135] Moreover, a Marxist historical materialist is also obligated to brush the history of Marxism itself against the grain – at least from time to time, and especially in situations of crisis.

With these pertinent Benjaminian worries in mind, my rallying cry to return to Engels is motivated partly by the hunch, and the hope, that uncovering the obscured grains of the past he and his sympathizers left for the future might equip fighting leftists in the here-and-now with powerful new arms in the war against a globalized late capitalism fundamentally reliant upon the natural sciences both economically and ideologically. I strongly suspect that turning science into a Trojan horse, one already conveniently situated at the beating heart of biopolitical, techno-scientific capitalism, is a much more promising strategy for the left than sticking exclusively to cultural ideology critique and/or hurling objections against the high walls of scientific fortresses from positions outside them. As every Hegelian knows, the only critiques really worth making are immanent ones. In resurrecting the scientifically minded Engels, I seek, as Benjamin varyingly puts it, 'to seize hold of a memory as it flashes up at a moment of danger',[136] to take 'a tiger's leap into the past',[137] to 'blast out'[138] and bring back to light an overshadowed historical

---

133   Walter Benjamin, 'Theses on the Philosophy of History', in *Illuminations: Essays and Reflections*, ed. Hannah Arendt, trans. Harry Zohn (New York: Schocken Books, 1969), p. 255.
134   Ibid., p. 255.
135   Ibid., pp. 256–7.
136   Ibid., p. 255.
137   Ibid., p. 261.
138   Ibid., pp. 261, 263.

sequence previously entombed as a virtual spectre in the historical past, but more pregnant than ever with possibilities *à venir*.

In the early twenty-first century, immanently converting the sciences to dialectical materialism, internally raising them to the dignity of these their notions, is an urgent imperative under the shadows of the simultaneously threatening and promising risks situated in such socially central spheres as ecology, genetics, health and agriculture. The anticlerical fighting spirit of eighteenth-century French materialism must be revived, this time in the fight against a new church – that of capitalism's flashy, gadget-bejewelled techno-scientism (or, in familiar French theoretical terms, a fight against Althusser's hegemonic educational 'Ideological State Apparatuses'[139] and/or Lacan's now-dominant 'university discourse'[140]). I believe this option not only to be advisable on the tactical and strategic grounds of hard-nosed political and propagandistic practice as indispensable to a Gramscian 'war of position' (if not a 'war of manoeuvre').[141] For me, this is a matter of recognizing that much of what is revealed by today's sciences, in an actuality whose obscurity renders it no less actual, ultimately testifies in favour of Marxian-Engelsian dialectical materialism (in line with Sève's characterization of the critical function of *Naturdialektik* with respect to the sciences,[142] drawing out this testimony requires philosophical-theoretical interventions). With the Marxist insight into the partisanship of truths in view (for the sciences as for all other disciplines, objectivity and neutrality are not synonymous), the radical left can and should have confidence that, beneath both intra- and non-scientific encrustations of ideologically distorted and distorting scientisms, the empirical and experimental sciences are not incorrigibly complicit with prevailing status-quo ideologies (Althusser), the irrational rationalizing of fully administered worlds (Adorno, Horkheimer, et al.), and/or the machinations of biopower (Foucault/Agamben). Instead, the sciences are ripe for joining in movements of history straining against the barriers and currents of the capitalist era – an era in which they have nonetheless

---

139   Louis Althusser, 'Ideology and Ideological State Apparatuses: Notes towards an Investigation', *Lenin and Philosophy and Other Essays*, trans. Ben Brewster (New York: Monthly Review Press, 2001), pp. 88–9, 98–9, 102–6.

140   Jacques Lacan, *The Seminar of Jacques Lacan, Book XVII: The Other Side of Psychoanalysis, 1969–1970*, ed. Jacques-Alain Miller, trans. Russell Grigg (New York: W. W. Norton & Co., 2007), pp. 168, 206.

141   Antonio Gramsci, *Prison Notebooks, Volume III*, ed. and trans. Joseph A. Buttigieg (New York: Columbia University Press, 2007), Sixth Notebook, §138, p. 109; §155, p. 117; Seventh Notebook, §16, pp. 168–9.

142   Sève, *'Nature, science, dialectique'*, p. 140.

rapidly matured over the past two centuries.[143] In reviving the Engelsian project of theorizing the sciences through the lenses of dialectical materialism, capitalism can be shown to be irrational not only in terms of its demand for alienating submission to the anarchy of markets, but also in the strictest philosophical and scientific senses.

In his 2010 book *Living in the End Times*, Slavoj Žižek proclaims, 'A resuscitation of the "critique of political economy" is the *sine qua non* of contemporary communist politics'.[144] As he rightly maintains, most Marxists in the West during the past several decades have left the core of the mature Marx's thought by the wayside (he accuses Badiou of this too).[145] Many of these theorists limit Marxism to functioning as a matrix solely for ideology critique at the level of the study of cultures. In traditional Marxist terms, infrastructure falls away and superstructures become the only objects of theoretical interest.

I would supplement Žižek's proclamation concerning the necessary condition for the current renewal of communism (i.e. repeating anew Marx's historical-materialist critique of political economy) with a declaration of my own, already signalled above: the sine qua non of contemporary Marxist materialism is a revival of a dialectics of nature nurtured by cutting-edge science and capable of combating the practical and ideological complicity of scientists and scientisms with a globalized late capitalism ever more reliant on them (i.e. repeating anew Engels's dialectical-materialist philosophy of the natural sciences). The criticisms of science used by Marxists in the West to rationalize leaving *Naturdialektik* by the historical wayside are simultaneously too critical and not critical enough: on the side of being too critical, such Marxists, with an all-or-nothing purist absolutism, construe the embeddedness in capitalism of the empirical and experimental sciences of modernity as wholly and completely compromising these fields to the very core; on the side of not being critical enough, such Western Marxists fail to take up the struggle against ideological scientisms on the battlefield of the sciences themselves, conceding too much ground to their opponents in advance. In this vein, Timpanaro justifiably warns, 'Unless it confirms and deepens materialism (in the way that Engels sought to achieve in the Marxist field), Marxism

---

143   Sohn-Rethel, *Intellectual and Manual Labour*, p. 135.
144   Slavoj Žižek, *Living in the End Times* (London: Verso, 2010), p. 185.
145   *Badiou, Žižek, and Political Transformations: The Cadence of Change* (Evanston: Northwestern University Press, 2009), pp. 182–5, 129–34.

becomes a philosophy confined to arts graduates or pure philosophers.'[146] In *The Origin of the Family, Private Property and the State*, Engels, who considers the modern sciences to be crowning achievements of human civilization, declares as a dialectician that 'everything civilization brings forth is double-edged, double-tongued, divided against itself, contradictory'.[147] The radical left of the twenty-first century must seize and ruthlessly deploy the contradictions of contemporary science and its extra-scientific entanglements, remembering with confidence that these scientific swords can slice in multiple directions.

Lenin's marvellous 1922 article 'On the Significance of Militant Materialism', with its expression of his trust in the spontaneous materialist leanings of science, argues for the importance of recruiting natural scientists as radicalized public representatives of atheistic dialectical materialism (Timpanaro later reiterates the points made in this piece by Lenin[148]). As regards this forcefully proposed programme, he maintains that failing to recruit these types of intellectuals would be not merely to miss an opportunity; it would be, for communist militants, a self-defeating abandonment of these knowledge-workers to the fate of becoming agents of capitalism formidably endowed with potent intellectual firepower and socio-cultural prestige. Left to their own devices without proper politico-philosophical education, guidance and orientation – I see this as being true of scientists today as well as in Lenin's time – they are prone to lapsing into and lending their support to ideologies and scientisms uncritically caught up in the spiritual cobwebs and chains enveloping stagnant conjunctures.[149] I wish to reissue Lenin's 1922 call for 'a kind of "Society of Materialist Friends of Hegelian Dialectics"' – one including, as Lenin insists, converted scientists and the fruits of their endeavours as digested by Marxian–Engelsian materialism.[150] Capitalism's scientific labourers must be allowed and encouraged to enlist in the ranks of its other intellectual and manual grave-diggers. The left stands to lose a great deal by ignoring or shunning such cross-disciplinary cooperation and solidarity. Timpanaro insightfully remarks that the 'daily experience of the degradation of science from an instrument of liberation to one of oppression . . .

146 Timpanaro, *On Materialism*, p. 63.
147 Friedrich Engels, *The Origin of the Family, Private Property and the State*, trans. Alick West (New York: Penguin Books, 1985), p. 97.
148 Timpanaro, *On Materialism*, pp. 12, 15.
149 V. I. Lenin, 'On the Significance of Militant Materialism', in *Selected Works: One-Volume Edition* (New York: International Publishers, 1971), pp. 660–7.
150 Ibid., p. 665.

gives rise to the (one-sided and mistaken) reduction of science to ideology'.[151] Leftists desperately need to learn to resist this understandable, but nonetheless misleading, anti-scientific impulse. The hour is overdue for awakening some of the mighty dead, and for beginning again with Engels, that dear, invaluable comrade of Marx.

---

151   Timpanaro, *On Materialism*, p. 258.

7   Remembering the Impossible: For a Meta-Critical Anamnesis of Communism

Frank Ruda

Unthinkable Communism, Impossible Philosophers

The problem is to have an idea . . .

Alain Badiou

Today, communism seems impossible.[1] And it also seems as if all that the word 'communism' stood for throughout its history will never again experience something like a new beginning. What the word 'communism' has stood for in history thus far is as follows: overcoming the dreadful *division* and specialization *of labour* that grounds the division of society into antagonistic classes; a different, non-statist form of organization; and finally the equality of anyone with anyone.[2] But all these characteristics seem to be radically invalidated by all previous attempts to put 'communism' into practice and give it a concrete and practical existence.[3]

At least this is what the sirens of the dominant ideology – which one might call, with Badiou, 'democratic materialism' – emblazon everywhere: non-statist organization works only in relation to market dynamics and individual profits; the reduction of specialized skills (without constant re-specialization) among labour forces is considered simply a sign of underdevelopment, and reference to any form of equality other than the abstract equality of those who are able to buy the same commodities – that is to say, talk of an equality of everyone with everyone else – is viewed as a mildewed relic of earlier ways of thinking. It is as if, in 1923, Georg

---

1   For their critical and helpful comments on previous versions of this article I owe gratitude to Eva Marlene Heubach, Mike Lewis, Mark Potocnik and Aaron Schuster.
2   For these characteristics of communism, see Alain Badiou, *Le courage du présent*, in *Le Monde*, 13 February 2010.
3   For how to conceive of this invalidation, see Alain Badiou, *Peut-on penser la politique?* (Paris: Seuil, 1985), and Alain Badiou, *The Communist Hypothesis* (London/New York: Verso, 2010), pp. 1–40.

Lukács was thinking of our own times rather than his when he wrote in his *History and Class Consciousness*:

> In this way the very thing that should be understood . . . becomes the accepted principle by which to explain all phenomena . . . namely the unexplained . . . facticity of bourgeois[4] existence as it is here and now and acquires the patina of an eternal law of nature . . . enduring for all time.[5]

What we have, even if it is experiencing one crisis after the other, is presented everywhere as if it were all that is thinkable. The word 'communism' thus names something which here and now seems to refer to something unthinkable. Communism is impossible – this is what history has shown, so it cannot be (or, more precisely, should not be) thought.

What happened and was experienced within history under this name should not be thought, and one should not imagine another communist beginning.[6] 'Communism' stands for nothing but endless crimes, and names nothing but terrorist regimes.[7] What is is all there is, and although what is is not perfect, it is still the least worst imaginable option. One consequence of this naturalization of the given 'there is' might be rendered, following a thought experiment of Fredric Jameson, in the following way. Today it seems far more plausible to the majority of the inhabitants of this planet that a comet might hit the earth than that there will be the slightest possible change within the predominant, i.e. capitalist, system. Today it seems that the only comet that might come not from outer but from inner space, originates in the greed of morally degenerate investment bankers who are pushed to their degeneracy by the very system they are working for. To

---

4   Today, one might say 'of democratic materialist' existence. For this notion see Alain Badiou, *Logics of Worlds: Being and Event, 2* (London/New York: Continuum, 2009), pp. 1–9; and Badiou's seminars in recent years, available at entretemps.asso.fr.

5   Georg Lukács, *History and Class Consciousness: Studies in Marxist Dialectics* (Cambridge, MA: MIT Press, 1999), p. 157. This is what Mark Fisher recently referred to as 'capitalist realism'. See Mark Fisher, *Capitalist Realism: Is there no Alternative?* (Hants: Zero Books, 2009).

6   The New York conference on the 'Idea of Communism' (after London and Berlin), organized by Alain Badiou and Slavoj Žižek, was entitled Communism: A New Beginning?

7   From this starting point, reactionaries love to draw the following conclusion: if within history any form of collective will of any universal good only brought out the worst, the only proper ethical position is to avoid willing the collective and universal good. This position is dear to many so-called 'philosophers' or those who hold 'left-wing positions' today: from the French 'New Philosophers' to 'informed' and 'enlightened' system theoreticians (like Norbert Bolz), from German Green Party philosophers (Micha Brumlik, for example) to leftist newspapers (like the German *TAZ*).

avoid the catastrophic effects of their wrongdoing,[8] all we need is a good dose of ethical responsibility in the upper echelons of society, which can easily be backed up by the objective evaluation of financial rating agencies. In this way we would get rid of the predators, and could live a happy life in what would finally be 'global capitalism with a human face'.[9]

But today it is not just communism that seems impossible. One can easily find strands within philosophy that also seem to be radically outdated and invalidated by history. Who would today still defend a full-blown Cartesian, Hegelian or Platonist position, after all the famous 'turns' within theory: the linguistic turn, the performative turn, and so on? After the implementation of the pragmatist and praxeological hegemony within philosophical discourse, and the predominance of ordinary language or analytical philosophy of mind *tout court*? Interestingly enough, even capitalists today seem to admit that there is a certain something to the thought of Marx. Everyone seems to enjoy the (moral) advantages that come with being critical of the system, with being at least to some degree anti-capitalist.[10] Marx comes in handy even for the broker or conservative politician next-door, even for most philosophers defending the present state of things. But the same cannot be said about Plato, Descartes or Hegel. We seem to be in a situation that comes *after* the validity of the idea of communism, and in a 'global state of philosophy'[11] which is also the state of an *after*. The philosophical situation is structured in such a way that we are situated *after* a phase in which we were able to believe in eternal ideas, irrefutable truths, absolute knowledge, or the dualism of being and appearance. Today, by contrast, we believe that nothing eternal could take place in our world; we believe that non-relative truths are unthinkable, and stick to the essential relativity of all knowledge and to the absolute naturalization of appearances. When we were still able to believe otherwise, we were also still able to believe in

---

8   A far-reaching analysis of this mechanism can be found in Alain Badiou, 'This Crisis is the Spectacle: Where is the Real?' in Badiou, *Communist Hypothesis*, pp. 91–100.

9   Slavoj Žižek, *In Defense of Lost Causes* (London/New York: Verso, 2008), p. 459. One can also claim that we today experience a perverse version of this capitalism with a human face in the guise of a socialism for the rich. If you are rich enough you will be saved no matter what you do; if you are not, you will not be.

10   As I shall argue, this is why anti-capitalism is never enough – one needs an additional political supplement. I want to suggest, following the recent works of Badiou and Žižek, that such a supplement might lie in a critique of the present assimilation of the signifier 'democracy' in the frame of liberal-parliamentarianism. To render this suggestion in a Kantian formula, one can say that *anticapitalism without a critique of democracy is impotent*; but also it holds that *any critique of democracy without anti-capitalism is blind*.

11   Alain Badiou, *Being and Event* (London/New York, Continuum, 2005) p. 1.

communism as something irrefutable, eternal and thinkable. But the situation has changed: we seem to have no choice.

Who – with the exception of a handful of militant thinkers mainly from Slovenia,[12] for example – would today dare to defend a full-blown Hegelian position without any hesitation? Being an Hegelian is acceptable as long as one gets rid of the traumatic kernel of Hegel called 'absolute knowledge'. For we know that we are all finite and have no access to anything absolute. Within the philosophical field, the only possible Hegelian position today is based on a liberal reading – centring, for example, on his so-called theory of mutual recognition.[13] What becomes of Hegel today, in these (liberal) interpretations, culminates in the end in a position that sacrifices his most fundamental claims, and sinks into historicism or relativism, or leads to a hypostatization of the social domain in which the most crucial imperative becomes to respect the opinions of the other. These are then understood as being normative commitments, and one draws the conclusion that the social bond of inter-subjectivity lies at the basis of every (political) practice.[14] But this simply means that all there is are relative and historically varying practices; nothing trans-historical can or will ever see the light of day – although, as one must immediately add, Hegel himself mistakenly believed so. Only in this castrated way is Hegelianism still defensible today, and the same can be said of most of the claims of Descartes (with regard to the subject of the *cogito*[15] or to the creation and existence of truths) or Plato (with regard to the disciplined organization of a society ruled by guardians and the philosopher king – who is considered to be a clear symptom of Plato's explicit totalitarianism; or concerning the existence of something which does not immediately coincide with the sensible sphere).

The distinction between eternity and appearance, between the soul and the body – everything reminiscent of dualism – is judged to be as radically

---

12   I am here thinking of Slavoj Žižek, but also of Mladen Dolar and Alenka Zupančič.

13   Paradigmatically this can be seen in Axel Honneth, *The Struggle for Recognition: The Moral Grammar of Social Conflicts* (Cambridge, MA: MIT Press, 1995). But it is also present in the works of the 'Pittsburgh Hegelians'.

14   Usually the story is told as a development within the history of philosophy. Whereas one gets certain normative commitments (explicit or implicit) with Kant, what Hegel adds is precisely the social dimension – normative commitments are embedded in the dynamic role-play of the individuals striving for the realization of their good. The problem with this reading is that it relates the struggle for life between master and slave from Hegel's *Phenomenology* to objective spirit, where, as Hegel explores, this very struggle is already overcome.

15   Along these lines, Descartes is usually not only attacked for being a dualist but also for ignoring the social dimension of the constitution of subjectivity.

outdated, as impossible, as the idea of communism seems to be.[16] We are in a situation that lies *after* communism and *after* what has been thought by Plato, Descartes and Hegel under such names as the Idea, *cogito*, absolute knowledge, the cunning of reason, and so on. It is just not possible, as a philosopher, to develop a moral theory of tolerant mutual recognition and at the same time propagate communism – as communism clearly never stood for something that was just relative, tolerant or mutual. It has always been scandalous in some sense. And it always implied an organization that in many ways was 'beyond good and evil', to use Nietzsche's terminology; an organization for and maybe even of eternity; an organization which at least in principle aimed at putting the impossibility of inegalitarian statements and actions into practice. So, to link the diagnosis of the political domain to that of the philosophical situation, one can claim the following: one essential category that today appears in politics with the signifier 'communism' and in philosophy with the names of Plato, Descartes and Hegel is the category of the impossible. This does not imply that Plato, Descartes and Hegel are communist thinkers. But it implies that what is suppressed in their position is something that is also attacked under the name 'communism' – i.e. something that presented itself as non-relativist and non-historicist, which is to say: eternally true. The question I want to address here is quite a fundamental one: What is the task of philosophy in times when the impossible within politics and philosophy – although in different guises – prevails? Where to begin when one takes the question of a new beginning of communism to be a philosophical question?[17]

Today, after the disappearance of idealism and what might be called the death of God, all of us have become materialists. And the contemporary form of materialism that is offered to us has two fundamental axioms: there are only bodies and languages; or, there are only

---

16 One of the worst attacks within the philosophical field is to be accused of dualism. This might indicate that, today, dualism is worth defending. The question then is: Which dualism? I have traced certain implications of this in Frank Ruda, 'Exiting the Woods: Cartesianism for the 21st Century (to come)', forthcoming in *Monokl*, Istanbul, 2013.

17 The question of communism today, as I see it, has to be treated first and foremost as a philosophical question and not a political one. Treating it as a directly political question would lead either into leftist nostalgia or melancholia for what has been experienced under this name within history – and thus the precise historical situation we are in is neglected; or it would be seen as a direct call for action – which again leads to a blindness to the singular coordinates of the historical situation or to actions that at the same time do not really change anything. I have attempted to develop a distinction between pseudo-actions and real action following Badiou and Žižek in Frank Ruda, 'Remembering, Repeating, Working Through Marx: Badiou and Žižek and the Re-Actualizations of Marxism', in *Revue Internationale de Philosophie*, Brussels 2012.

individuals and communities.[18] Idealism is passé, over, and if one calls
someone an idealist one usually means that this someone has not yet
been properly educated in the laws of the contemporary world. Mostly
they seem to be fools within the ivory tower of philosophy. There is no
choice but to be a materialist. As Badiou noted, one of the most basic
imperatives which democratic materialism relies upon is the following:
live without an idea.[19] Living without an idea is the predominant ground-
work common to all slogans along the lines of 'Enjoy without limits', 'Be
flexible', and so on. But a life without an idea implies the reduction of
this very life to mere survival.

At this point, one might ask: Why is there a problem with the materialist conviction that man is unable to live for anything but his own
interests?[20] Already the early Marx criticized one effect of this sort of
ideology by insisting that capitalism reduces all human animals to the
substratum of their animality.[21] Although a lot of things seem to have
changed, today, democratic materialism leads to precisely the same
result.[22] But how is this possible, as we seem to act in a quite human
manner while purchasing Apple products, consuming Starbucks
coffee or enjoying internet porn? Firstly, by way of diagnosis, I want
to argue here that there can be, and is, a regression from humanity to
animality: there can be a (reductive) privation. But I also want to
defend the following thesis, which is one crucial claim of what I call
meta-critical anamnesis: there is no relation between the human and the
animal. In a more dialectical manner, I want to argue that there is no
relation between the human and the animal, but there is something
like a human animal which therefore is the embodiment of this very
non-relation between the human and the animal.[23] Human animals are
embodiments of this non-relation, so there is no pure non-relation,
which is important to bear in mind.[24] This thesis will become clearer in

18   See footnote 4.
19   See, for example, Badiou, Communist Hypothesis, p. 67.
20   As this is precisely what living without an idea means: live only with regard to the satisfaction
of your self-interest and be a self-seeking egotist, for anything else is by definition not possible.
21   I am here obviously thinking of Marx's 1844 manuscripts. See Karl Marx The Economic and
Philosophical Manuscripts of 1844 and the Communist Manifesto (New York: Prometheus, 1988).
22   One can find an interesting comparison between the capitalist situation of the nineteenth
century and ours in Alain Badiou, Le Réveil de l'histoire. Circonstances, 6 (Paris: Lignes, 2011), pp. 17–27.
23   I have also developed this in my Can Animals be Political? A Question of Philosophy and Indifference
(forthcoming).
24   This is important to keep in mind if one is not to fall into certain – idealist – traps. There can
never be something simply human without the animal substratum. To claim that we could be fully
human means to defend the idea of abolishing our very embodiment, which seems to me to be a very

the development of my argument, and will lead me to the elaboration of my central proposition: philosophy today needs to take the form of a *meta-critical anamnesis*.

Animal Humanism and the Bio-Materialism of the Possible

But that the existence of a human being who lives merely for enjoyment (however busy he might be in this respect) should have a value in itself even if as a means to this he was as helpful as possible to others who were likewise concerned only with enjoyment, because he participated in all gratification through sympathy: of this reason could never be persuaded.

Immanuel Kant[25]

Why, today, are human animals reduced to their animality? As is well known, Badiou's thesis is that capitalism is the regime that takes seriously the fact that man is also an animal.[26] It offers a pathological (in the Kantian sense of the term) model of everyday life, and leads to an understanding of the subject that centres on its animal constitution, its body, since bodies can be defined and are thereby naturalized. We all, in a very anti-Spinozist manner, seem to know very well what a body can do and what it requires to feel well. The contemporary capitalist idea of the subject is thus a bio-subjective model of embodied subjectivity, and ultimately man is considered to be 'a biped without feathers whose charms are not obvious'.[27] Capitalism reduces every-*body* to its commercial capacities, its particular interests, to its small desires and fetishisms, and thereby produces a generalized commercial animality. As Marx already claimed when he spoke of the worker who is reduced to the mere functioning of his stomach, capitalism presents an all-encompassing system that reduces everyone down to his bodily, animal, and thus purely organic constitution.

Hence, the contemporary imperative is to live one's life in a purely bodily, this is to say animal manner, without attachments, without an idea. The image of humanity that capitalism presents is a historically specific

---

problematic conception. Somewhere along these lines the interesting – but no less problematic – position of Jambet and Lardreau can be situated. See Guy Lardreau and Christian Jambet, *L'ange. Ontologie de la révolution* (Paris: Grasset, 1975).

25   Immanuel Kant, *Critique of the Power of Judgment* (Cambridge: CUP, 2000), p. 93.

26   See Alain Badiou, Frank Ruda and Jan Völker, 'Wir müssen das affirmative Begehren hüten', in Alain Badiou, *Dritter Entwurf eines Manifest für den Affirmationismus* (Berlin: Merve, 2008), pp. 45–6.

27   Alain Badiou, *Ethics: An Essay on the Understanding of Evil* (London/New York: Verso, 2001), p. 12.

construction and an ideological interpretation of what a body is (which is based upon the conviction that there is something like the 'one body'[28] with which one lives). The simple continuation of life, i.e. survival, entails that we be put in the position of passive 'subjects' – and one can easily see why significant numbers of passive voters, for example, are thereby considered to be more important in politics than real militants.[29] What the capitalist-materialist ideology produces is the abstract equality of individually circulating, objectified animal bodies that share the same form of (biological) constitution, and can circulate in the same way that objects do. And they circulate in what, for Badiou, is the contemporary name for the non-world that we live in: *the market*.[30] This is why democracy became 'the emblem and custodian for a conservative oligarchy whose main (and often bellicose) business is to guard its own territory as animals do under the usurped name *world*'.[31] It is this reduction that suspends the world, diminishes it, and leaves behind a mere environment which at the same time should give all of us cause for concern. In the last instance, this yields the humdrum claptrap of environmental or human rights concerns that present themselves as asserting rights of the species. And this is because the reduction of human beings to their animal species is closely linked to one threat any species faces: domestication. For the simplest negative definition of a species is: that which can be domesticated. And the mode of democratic-materialist domestication, as part of its ideological project, is precisely such a naturalist reduction to animality, which I want to call *animal humanism*. Animal humanist life is a subjectively impoverished life, even when one has the contingent luck of being objectively quite well off. It is a life without an idea – or, in other words, a life without thought.[32]

---

28   I here refer to the brilliant formulation of a 'oneness of the body', as described in Lorenzo Chiesa, 'The Partisan's Morale Provisoire' (unpublished typescript).

29   For a reconstruction of the Sartrean distinction between active and passive numbers, see, for example, Alain Badiou, *Pocket Pantheon: Figures of Postwar Philosophy* (London/New York: Verso, 2009), pp. 14–35.

30   Badiou: '[M]arket is the name of a world which is not a world'. Alain Badiou, 'Philosophy and the "War against Terrorism"', in Badiou, *Infinite Thought* (London/New York: Continuum, 2003), p. 162. There is even some weird form of neo-pagan animism involved here, as idioms like 'the markets are not satisfied' and similar omnipresent sayings indicate.

31   Alain Badiou, 'The Democratic Emblem', in Giorgio Agamben, Alain Badiou, Daniel Bensaïd and Wendy Brown, Jean-Luc Nancy, Jacques Rancière, Kristin Ross and Slavoj Žižek, *Democracy in What State?* (New York: Columbia University Press, 2011), p. 8.

32   Animal humanism, as can be seen in a lot of different domains, does not attempt to produce any form of thought, for thought is what stands in contradiction to its very concept. It also should be clear here why capitalist-animal-humanism is fundamentally a doctrine of the state, as, to modify Heidegger's formula, the state does not think.

Capitalism thus produces indifference: the abstract and objective bodily equality of all human animals embedded in the environment of the market in which they have to compete with one another. And this material production of indifference – everyone becoming a self-seeking animal-body that tries to be the better predator[33] – works even better because, to use Stephen Jay Gould's term,[34] it exapted the perfect state-form to realize it, namely democracy. Today the very form of democracy is conditioned by the capitalist content, and the very form of capitalism is conditioned by the democratic content. Capitalist content in democratic form presents itself in the hegemony of interests and pathological desires, and finally in the beastly constitution of man, that dominate all contemporary 'political' discussions, human rights debates, and so on. This is an effect of what I call *animal humanism*. Democratic content in capitalist form is present in most of the practical interpretations of democratic principles – for example, of freedom as a freedom of the worker to sell his own labour-power. This is what democratic materialism comes down to. Badiou is right to emphasize that any state is indifferent towards equality. And the contemporary capitalist democratic state form organizes the produced abstract conformity (of individual or communal bodies) through the processes of so-called free elections that are indifferent towards all singularities. *Elections* are statist means to *organize indifference*, and this organized indifference is indifferent precisely with regard to any point of the real.[35] But free elections are today themselves sold as a means of the very realization of freedom: one can vote for all that is politically possible. From this one can infer why today the category of the *possible* has become an instrument of oppression. Why should that be?

In politics, the reliance on the possible has three eventual consequences:[36]

1. The privileging of the possible implies that one has always already opted for one particular model of change: change as an extension of the possible.

---

33 This seems to be the precise starting point for the utterly reactionary project of John Gray. See his *Straw Dogs: Thoughts on Humans and Other Animals* (New York: Farrar, Straus & Giroux, 2007).

34 Stephen Jay Gould, 'A Crucial Tool for Evolutionary Biology', in *Journal of Social Issues* 47:3 (1991), pp. 43–65.

35 As Badiou once claimed, 'The vote is in essence contradictory to principles, just as it is to every idea of emancipation and protest.' Alain Badiou, *Polemics* (London/New York: Verso, 2006), p. 91.

36 I am here referring to arguments Badiou developed in his seminars. See entretemps.asso.fr.

2. This process of extension implies that equality can only be conceived of in a gradual manner, as a gradually realized state of the extended regime of the possible – here one should remember the French battle cry: *Tout ce qui bouge n'est pas rouge*. Not everything that moves is red.

3. Siding with the possible thus inevitably implies siding with the primacy of inequality over equality, for there is always something that seems impossible in a given realm of the possible.

This is because siding with the possible implies that a change of the framework of what seems possible itself becomes impossible. It systematically becomes impossible to transform the situation in any other way than by extending the possible. But one thereby ends up with a historically specific and circumscribed realm of possibilities that can be actualizable. To extend, in a seemingly infinite manner, what is possible is already to accept a final limit-point of this very extension. This is why 'communism' – an organization of the impossibility of inegalitarian statements here and now – seems impossible, since this is precisely what communism in its history stood for. But such an organization simply cannot be reached by a gradual extension of the possible.

Today the possible is a stable, statist regime that, although it constantly seems to change, never truly changes. In other words, to side with the regime of the possible is to support a return to the actual state of things, and to stick forever with the actual and existing state. This is why it implies a circumscribed realm of thinkability.[37] Consequently, the allegedly infinite extension of the possible is necessarily limited and finitized by something which appears to be impossible within a given historical situation. And such an impossibility becomes naturalized just as much as the regime of the possible attempts to naturalize itself.

To abide by what seems possible is thus to redouble the impossibility: there is a general impossibility of changing the laws of change – i.e. the extension of the possible – and this always implies the impossibility, which takes different concrete forms, of organizing impossible inegalitarian statements. This is why communism is today presented as impossible – starting with the possible means of naturalizing it, and of naturalizing the impossibilities it encounters. In other words, the impossible is simply (i.e. forever and ontologically) impossible. All this is linked to the fact that today the most fundamental paradigm of the possible is the natural. For

37   Sylvain Lazarus, *Anthropologie du nom* (Paris: Seuil, 1996).

naturalization signifies that the only orientation offered by the possible is inscribed in the axiomatic equation:

possible = 'existence = individual = body'.[38]

What is possible is what is bodily and individually natural. What is possible is what is there – in the bodies that exist as naturally determined by their needs, and so forth. This capitalist materialism of the possible is in the last instance a materialism of the biological and animal body that stands under the paradigm of the natural, the naturalized possible. It is a *bio-materialism of the possible*.[39]

So, to resume: *animal humanism* is the direct outcome of the ideological framework of democratic materialism, which implies a materialism without an idea. This leads to the most radical – which is to say, material – reduction of humans to their animal substructure, and presents an immense production and organization, moreover an administration of indifference.[40] The abstract uniformity of individual and collective circulating bodies produces an abstract equivalence and indifference between these very bodies. But what to do with this situation, philosophically speaking? The answer I want to offer is that philosophy should not wish to remain confined to academia and avoid becoming a purely administrative discourse of knowledge – the university discourse, so to speak.[41] It must therefore be engaged philosophy.[42] It has to intervene to clarify the situation, and it can do so – against the dominant current – if it assumes the task of a *meta-critical anamnesis*. If the question of a new beginning of communism can be treated as a philosophical question, it thus has to be treated as a question of a meta-critical anamnesis. So my main task in the following is to elaborate what *meta-critical anamnesis* is, and then to specify

---

38   Badiou, *Logics of Worlds*, p. 2.
39   This is also why, as Zupančič remarked, starting from the regime of the possible, one contemporaneous concrete form of naturalization that eventually occurs is a racism of success: a racism that presents success as a natural category inscribed into our individual bodily capacities and lifestyles. See Alenka Zupančič: *The Odd One In: On Comedy* (Massachusetts/London, MIT Press, 2007), pp. 5–7.
40   An interesting analysis of the production of indifference in capitalism, although from a rather non-radical background, can be found in Georg Lohmann, *Indifferenz und Gesellschaft. Eine kritische Auseinandersetzung mit Marx* (Frankfurt: Suhrkamp, 1991).
41   As I attempted to indicate in the beginning, the philosophy of university discourse today is, without any doubt, what is called analytical philosophy (in all its pragmatist versions). Even though analytical philosophy considers itself to be dialectical, as shall become clear in the following, it is not, as it remains within a limited scheme of dialectical thinking (it avoids thinking what I call a *dialectic of dialectics and non-dialectics*).
42   Thereby, and maybe only thereby, it cannot but be heir to Sartre.

its relation to communism. Hence, the following will first present certain preliminary remarks on a *meta-critical anamnesis of communism*.[43]

Hence, the meta-critical anamnesis of communism, as that which answers the question of communism's new beginning, is itself just beginning. But I want to start from one very simple but fundamental insight: if, today, communism seems impossible, any meta-critical and anamnetic approach to communism has to deal with what seems impossible. I want to claim that a meta-critical anamnesis consists of three different features, which will also structure this chapter:

1. an idealism without idealism[44]
2. a dialectic of dialectics and non-dialectics[45]
3. a Cartesian stance for the twenty-first century (to come).[46]

Philosophy as meta-critical anamnesis is something that cannot but be considered as in a strict party-line relationship with the philosophical stance of Badiou.

Idealism without Idealism; or, Philosophy as Anamnesis

One can claim that, given the predominance of democratic materialism today, the old ideological battle, to put it in Althusser's terms, between idealism and materialism[47] that always determined philosophy throughout its history is entering a new phase. With the complete withering away of idealism, one can claim that the split that separated idealism from materialism is now reappearing within materialism. This is one possible rendering of how one might conceive of the distinction that Badiou has introduced between *democratic materialism* and *materialist dialectics*. If idealism is impossible, then the only thinkable option is materialism; but as

---

43   All this needs much more elaboration. I will attempt to present a more detailed account of this in a book in preparation with the working title 'Indifference and Repetition' (which I owe to Aaron Schuster), mainly focusing on Descartes, Kant, Hegel, Marx, and ultimately Plato (especially his way of challenging the sophist).

44   I develop this much more extensively in my 'Idealism without Idealism: Badiou's Materialist Renaissance', in *Angelaki* (forthcoming).

45   For a longer version of this, see my 'Thinking Politics Concretely: Negation, Affirmation and the Dialectics of Dialectics and Non-Dialectics', in *Thinking – Resisting – Reading The Political* (forthcoming), also available at blip.tv.

46   See my 'Exiting the Woods'.

47   See Louis Althusser, 'Philosophy as Revolutionary Weapon', at marxists.org; and Alain Badiou, 'Philosophy as Creative Repetition', at lacan.com.

materialism is still an 'ideological atmosphere',[48] as Badiou puts it, one might assume that the repetition of the distinction between idealism and materialism within materialism itself brings forth an idealistic material-ism, a bad one, and a proper materialist materialism. I want to argue, on the contrary, that the contemporary inscription of the distinction between idealism and materialism in the domain of materialism itself should be framed in a more dialectical way. To cut a long story short: I will claim that this repetition contains a moment of reversal – a moment which materialistically reverses the distinction between good and bad material-ism within materialism itself; or, better: it introduces a moment of torsion within materialism. Following Badiou, I will argue that democratic mate-rialism can be understood as materialism without an idea, as *materialism without idealism*, and that any materialist dialectical approach should be conceived of as an *idealism without idealism*.

A good place to begin can be found in Descartes. One finds a remark-able passage in his *Meditations on First Philosophy* where he asks why it is that we can be deceived at all. And one part of the answer he gives is that there can be error and mistake due to the attribute in which we are the most God-like, the freedom of our will. I can be mistaken because I am free without limits: 'When the will is considered not relationally, but strictly in itself, God's will does not seem any greater than mine . . .'[49] But this means that the freedom of my will is so infinite that it can even will two radically incompatible things at the same time. In addition to this, Descartes states in a famous letter from 1644: 'And further, if God willed to make some truths necessary, that is not to say that he willed this of necessity. For it is one thing to will that they are necessary, and another to will this of necessity, or to be necessitated to will it.'[50] Sartre insisted that, for Descartes, God is so free that his freedom should be identified with radical contingency;[51] freedom is the contingency of creating a world in one way or another. Descartes's point is that my will (which makes me God-like) is so free that it can will A and Not-A at the same time. The

---

48   Badiou, *Logics of Worlds*, p. 3.
49   René Descartes, *Philosophical Essays and Correspondence* (Indianapolis/Cambridge: Hackett Publishing, 2000), pp. 124–5. This contingency of God's free will is fundamentally necessary. Otherwise he would be obliged to create truths, and one would thus suppress the contingency of freedom involved. Here one might again trace a Cartesian heritage in the works of speculative realists like Meillassoux. Descartes was the first philosopher to insist radically on the necessity of contingency.
50   Ibid., p. 220.
51   Jean-Paul Sartre, 'Cartesian Freedom', in Sartre, *Literary Philosophical Essays* (Vancouver: Collier Books, 1967).

Cartesian philosophy of the Subject thereby begins by confronting what he articulates as follows: 'I can be free without being inclined both ways. Indeed, the more strongly I incline in one direction the more free my choice is. When no reason inclines me in one direction rather than another, I have a feeling of indifference – that is, of its not mattering which way I go – and that is the poorest kind of freedom.'[52] His point is that one is only radically free when one takes sides; freedom is side-taking, and not the opportunity to select between possible choices.[53] It is only real, realized, in a decision – not in the abstract existence of two sides of a choice, in which one might dwell forever.[54] Freedom consists, as one might say with Badiou, in 'treating a point',[55] in a decision which condenses all the alleged differences into one single choice. And freedom consists in choosing and pursuing the consequences of such a decision.

For Descartes, this means that I can only err when I have already misperceived the nature of my freedom. This is the case when I mistake my own nature as possibility to will A and Not-A at the same time. So, when I only remain in the domain of this *yes and no* at the same time, I am not free. This is the reason for me to become indifferent – and this is one way to understand the fundamental effect of the contemporary demo-cratic-materialist ideology. Democratic materialism is a *bio-materialism of the possible*, of indifference abolishing true choice. It is a regime of the A and Non-A at the same time.

One can thus learn from Descartes that philosophy has to intervene against this (or better: against any sort of) indifference. *Philosophy is engaged philosophy against indifference* and, although I cannot develop this argument in detail here, when Badiou claims that politically we are in the same situation as Marx in the 1840s,[56] what one can infer is that in a certain sense philosophically we are in the same situation as Descartes in the 1640s. For philosophy has to creatively repeat the Cartesian gesture against indifference. I will return to this point.

To resume: as soon as I feel I am doing A, but nevertheless do Non-A – as soon, to take up Žižek's example, as I think I partake in a collective

---

52   Descartes, *Philosophical Essays*, p. 125.

53   As he has it: '[T]he more I am inclined toward one direction . . . the more freely do I choose that direction.' Ibid.

54   The insistence on the possibility of having a choice of two thinkable options is therefore also what leads directly to indecisiveness. See Descartes' analysis of this in René Descartes, *The Passions of the Soul: Les passions de l'âme* (Indianapolis: Hackett, 1989).

55   For this see Badiou, *Logics of Worlds*, pp. 397–448.

56   Badiou, *Communist Hypothesis*, pp. 259–60.

project while buying a mochaccino at Starbucks, and conceive of this as the very incarnation of my freedom – I become indifferent. Or, to put this into more dialectical terms: if my own freedom is that which makes me God-like, it is precisely not something natural (or naturalizable) as today's democratic materialism claims; rather, it is something which in myself, although I am *also* a natural being, is anti- or even a-natural[57] – it is the other, the inhuman within the subject. Freedom is my nature, and it is that which makes me God-like; but God is the creator of nature, and thus His and also necessarily my freedom cannot be simply natural. So, Descartes's point is that *human beings are free beings whose very nature is something a-natural*. But this enables them at the same time to misperceive their own a-natural nature in a way that suspends this very (a-natural) nature by naturalizing it.

There is no relation between the human and the animal – they are two different substances, as Descartes would say; but there is such a thing as a human animal, which is an embodiment of this non-relation. And embodiment means: there is a material incarnation of this without-relation, of a non-relation. And this embodiment of non-relation is an embodiment of freedom, a natural incorporation of something a-natural. Freedom is not and never will be a natural given, which amounts to saying that it is the a-natural.[58] Against the naturalization of freedom, which is the reduction of human animals to animal embodiment under democratic materialism, one should insist on the necessary a-naturality of freedom, which makes the human animal into a *human* animal. Freedom therefore demands a true choice, hard work, discipline and strict organization in pursuing its consequences. This is what, maybe unsurprisingly, communism was always about.

One might also say that, today, democratic capitalist materialism somehow works like the *genius malignum*, the evil genius of Descartes – deceiving us about pretty much everything. Maybe it is the most evil genius imaginable, as capitalism takes the body-soul distinction and extrapolates the body. To put it again into more Cartesian terms: in a beautiful passage from his *Meditations*, he reflects on the 'cogito, ergo sum' proof: 'I am, I exist – that is certain. But for how long? For as long as I am thinking. But

---

57   This is one possible way of understanding why human animals are embodiments of the non-relation. Following Descartes, one can claim that they are natural incorporations of something a-natural.

58   This is why one is never simply free from the beginning, from the moment one is born; freedom always implies hard work and discipline. Žižek has demonstrated this nicely in his reading of Zack Snyder's movie *300*. See Slavoj Žižek, 'The True Hollywood Left', at lacan.com.

perhaps no longer than that; for it might be that if I stopped thinking I would stop existing; and I have to treat that possibility as though it were actual . . .'[59] The reduction within capitalism might be said to function in perfect alignment with this argument: capitalism deceives us in such a way that we, as embodiments of the non-relation between the human and the animal, think we do not exist in any way other than the bodily. Or, to put it another way: we very well know that we exist as *human* animals, but we nevertheless act as if we were not; we act in a purely animal-like fashion – taking the position of animals that no longer dare to think, of animals that have been tricked by the evil genius of capitalism and its democratic-materialist ideology.

Here one can also turn to Plato. And one can clarify what philosophy in such times as ours can learn from an utter idealist. It is this: philosophy has to assume an anamnetical task. The lesson that can already be learned from Descartes can be rendered in the following way: to avoid becoming indifferent, the human animal has to be reminded that its very nature – its freedom – is a-natural. Human animals are an embodiment of the non-relation between the human and the animal, *natural incarnations of a-naturality*. And this a-natural nature is only real when it takes sides, when it decides upon something. This insight even made it to Hollywood recently. As one of the characters of Zack Snyder's 2011 movie *Sucker Punch*[60] states: 'If you do not stand for something, you fall for anything.' But when does one really stand for something? It is here that the idealist Plato can help. As Badiou has underlined, Plato's fundamental question has always been, 'What is a good life?' or: 'What is a life worthy of an idea?' This was (and maybe still is) *the* question of philosophy, *the* question of Plato.[61] And Plato – the first ever to defend the idea of the idea – gives the following answer to this question: one does not fall for anything, but stands for something, when one upholds and clings to an idea. And, as Badiou has shown on several occasions, an idea is always an exception to the simple existence of what there is – of individual bodies, collective

---

59   Descartes, *Philosophical Essays*, p. 120.
60   I here subscribe to Žižek's claim that Snyder is one of the paradigmatic figures of the Hollywood Left. *Sucker Punch* can be said to be an impressive combination of Hegelian themes (there are precisely four steps to liberation and to the formation of a subject which overcomes – imaginary – impossibilities) and Brechtian moments (as the movie directly addresses the viewer claiming: 'You have all the weapons you need, now fight!'). I will present an analysis along these lines in Frank Ruda, 'We are all Hot Girls in a Mental Asylum: The 'Hollywood Left' and Contemporary Democracy', in Frank Ruda and Jan Völker, ed., *Art and Contemporaneity* (Zürich: diaphanes, 2013 [forthcoming]).
61   See his seminars on 'Pour aujourd'hui, Platon!', at entretemps.asso.fr. See also Alexandre Koyré, *Discovering Plato* (New York: Columbia University Press, 1968).

languages and opinions. An idea is always the somehow scandalous, inhuman, a-natural exception to the given natural realm of opinions.

Turning to Plato, one might claim that the first task of philosophy in our times is to do the 'difficult work of resurrecting the idea'[62] against the omnipresent reduction of human animals to animality. And as we are living in a time when there seems to be no idea available, philosophy has to work for its very resurrection – this is to say, for a new beginning of the idea which has been and is addressed under different names, one of these names being 'communism'.

Thus it is precisely the *idea of an idea* that one needs to resurrect from idealism under present materialist conditions.[63] This is how to inscribe the distinction between materialism and idealism into materialism itself. It is not a simple return to idealism, as we are in a situation where we can only be materialists. Rather, it means to invert materialism to will that they are necessary and to necessarily will it or to be necessitated to will it – i.e. to oppose the materialism without an idea that leads to animal humanism with a *materialism of the idea, a materialism of the a-natural, inhuman freedom of the human animal*. This can be done by inscribing a true Two:[64] the Two comprising (1) what there is, and (2) an exception. One can also render this as follows: yes, there is only individual and collective animal-humanist life, except that there is an idea of communist life. Such a renaissance of idealism under materialist conditions can be characterized by a formula Badiou once used to describe his own enterprise. In a text called *Metaphysics and the Critique of Metaphysics*, he referred to his own philosophy as 'metaphysics without metaphysics',[65] and I think that one can conceive of the necessary philosophical act that re-inscribes the

---

62   Ibid.

63   This is what a materialist reversal of materialism might look like: one turns to idealism to resurrect the (form or idea of the) idea and reinsert it into the materialist grounding of any contemporary position. It can give an answer to the question Badiou articulates in his seminars on Plato: 'Do we have an idea of the idea?' The answer for any dialectical and materialist position today needs to be: yes. The problem is what the consequence of such a 'yes' will have been.

64   This is also consistent with Badiou's position, although he is often rendered as a thinker of something like a primordial ontological multiplicity. That this is a problematic reading of his meta-ontological conception is easy to demonstrate – as he insists on the primacy of the Two (the one and the pure multiple on one side and the void on the other). His thinking thus remains coherent with what he claimed early on: 'Dialectics states that there is the Two, and intends to infer the One from it as a moving division. Metaphysics posits the One, and forever gets tangled up in deriving the Two. There are others, like Deleuze, who posit the Multiple, which is never more than a semblance since positing the multiple amounts to presupposing the One as substance and excluding the Two from it.' Alain Badiou, *Theory of the Subject* (London/New York: Continuum, 2009), p. 22. See also my 'Exiting the Woods', where I retrace this in greater detail.

65   Alain Badiou, 'Metaphysics and the Critique of Metaphysics', *Pli* 10 (2000), p. 190.

distinction between idealism and materialism into materialism along these very lines. This means: philosophy as a dialectical-materialist enterprise must imply an *idealism without idealism*. This is precisely why philosophy today has to be anamnetical. For any idea (this is what one can learn from Plato) is essentially good, and this leads to the following task: philosophy has to remind us of this very fact.

That any non-relative idea seems to be impossible right now does not matter. It has already seemed impossible several times before (and in multiple situations). No one, for example, really believed in radical transformation in the 1840s. So, philosophy can and should recall the impossible and remind us that it has already taken place, and more than once, before became possible. But, for such an anamnetical task, historical specificity is of the utmost importance. One needs to take into account all the experiences – the failures – that already exist, and learn from them without drawing the Thermidorian conclusion[66] of predominant materialism, namely that any attempt to realize a universal collective good ultimately leads to the instantiation of the worst imaginable. So, although it is true that we are thinking *after* Plato, Descartes and Hegel, we have to avoid the obscurantism of a naturalized possible/impossible distinction that reduces everybody to the animal substratum and to a life without any collective project – or without any relation to something absolute (i.e. to an idea). In our historically specific conditions, philosophy has to be an anamnesis to remind us that the impossible – under the name of communism – has already become possible in the past. One can see why Descartes, Hegel and Plato become important for this very task.

Already, Descartes' philosophical method was directed against any form of deception or failure in judgment; he famously started to doubt everything that had ever deceived him, which thus could not be trusted any longer. One can deduce from this that, in a similar way, philosophy can remind us that the evil genius of capitalism, also in its democratic-materialist guise, cannot and should not be trusted. Capitalist democratic materialism attempts to animalize the human animal, or to humanize the animal aspect of it. Descartes's method can make us into sceptics. And one can link this doubt to an insight Hegel formulated in his *Aesthetics* where he claimed that the human is the only animal that knows it is only an animal, and due to this very knowledge is more than an animal.[67]

---

66   For the logic of the Thermidorian, see Alain Badiou, *Metapolitics* (London/New York: Verso, 2012), pp. 124–40.

67   See G. W. F. Hegel, *Aesthetics: Lectures on Fine Art*, vol. 1 (Oxford: Clarendon, 1975), p. 80.

Philosophy's task is to keep this very knowledge alive. One can therefore combine the Cartesian method and the Hegelian insight with what I claim needs to be recovered from Plato.

Philosophy's task is anamnetical. It has to remind us of the fact, as one might put it, that we are embodiments of the non-relation, and that it is in our nature to be able to do the a-natural, the impossible; that we are able to live under an idea. Philosophy takes up the method of doubt to restore the knowledge of the *human* animal and remind us of the idea of an idea. It is in this way that it can emancipate us from any reductive naturalization.

Dialectics of Dialectics and Non-Dialectics: Meta-Critical Philosophy

But, to counter the animal humanist reduction of human beings to animals, something more than this is needed. It is important to ask the following question: How are we to assure the historical concreteness of this anamnetical task? Hence, taking up the idea of an idea and developing an *idealism without idealism* is only one part of philosophy's job today. One needs to relate it to the precise historical situation that we are in. As Badiou suggested, it is comparable to the situation Marx faced in the 1840s. What was his situation? No one knew what 'communism' or 'revolution' could signify (as today), and this is precisely why he formulated it as a hypothesis. This is what needs to be repeated. We need a repetition of what Marx did in the 1840s: we need new theses on Feuerbach (i.e. democratic materialism), a new economic-philosophical manuscript (i.e. a theory of alienation and a theory of human species-being) and a new communist manifesto.[68]

The early Marx dealt first and foremost with Hegel. More precisely, he reworked Hegelian dialectics, and especially the concept of negation. Think for example of his famous definition of the proletariat as a negation of everything that the bourgeoisie includes in its definition of a human being.[69] If we are truly in a comparable situation, philosophy today has to

---

68   This is a necessary implication of the comparison between Marx's situation and ours. The early Marx, before co-authoring the *Manifesto*, started working on Feuerbach (as one might claim: the democratic materialism of his time), on Hegel and on bourgeois economics (although this can all be seen as a part of his reworking of dialectics). The results of this are, among other things, essentially the theses on Feuerbach, the 1844 Manuscripts, and the *Manifesto*. If our situation is comparable, our task is to redo these works.

69   This can be found in Karl Marx, 'A Contribution to the Critique of Hegel's Philosophy of Right: Introduction (1843–44)', in Marx, *Early Writings* (London: Penguin, 1992), pp. 243–58. I have presented a reading of this definition in relation to Marx's (in-)humanism in Frank Ruda, 'Humanism

repeat Marx. It has to work through dialectics – which is to say, it has to work through the motor of dialectical thought: negation. This can bring out a new, or renewed, materialist dialectics able to conceive anew of the impossible in our singular historical conditions. But how are we to repeat the Marxian gesture today?

In an important article, Badiou offers what is in my view the first outlines of how to do so.[70] He distinguishes three forms of negation that provide essential coordinates for a renewed materialist dialectics, relating all of them back to the Aristotelian *Metaphysics*. Therein Aristotle shows that thinking in general is determined by three principles: 1. The principle of identity: any proposition is equivalent to itself, i.e. to its truth content; 2. The principle of contradiction: it is impossible that in the same context the proposition A and the proposition not-A can be true at the same time; and 3. The principle of the excluded middle: for a proposition A it holds that it is either true or false – either A is true or not-A is true. Negation, in this model, is structured in a twofold manner. First it has the power of exclusion: the proposition A excludes the validity of the proposition not-A. Secondly, it presents a forced decision: either A or not-A is valid; there is no third option. For classical negation never holds that 'yes' and 'no' are valid at the same time, but always holds that either 'yes' or 'no' is valid. But one can easily see that there are not only classical forms of negation. Within the framework of these three principles, other logical forms of negation may be inferred.

Negation is only classical when it follows the principle of contradiction and the principle of the excluded middle. One can also think a negation that follows only the principle of contradiction but not the principle of the excluded middle; a negation that follows the principle of the excluded middle but not the principle of contradiction; and, finally, a negation that follows neither of the two principles. This last form of negation loses all power of negation because it neither prescribes a decision nor does it exclude anything – it knows negation only as itself negated. The second form of negation, only following the principle of contradiction but not of the excluded middle, is what Badiou calls the *intuitionist logic of negation*; the third, only following the principle of the excluded middle but not of contradiction, he calls *paraconsistent*.

It is important to note that, for Badiou, the classical logic of negation corresponds to the discourse of ontology. For his definition of being qua being, the principle of extensionality is fundamental: an element of a set belongs to the set or does not belong to it. A (the element belongs to the set) is true or false, there is no third option. The difference between two multiplicities may thus follow only from the fact that an element of one set is not an element of another. If one accepts this framework, this means that any form of negation that complies with the principle of contradiction and of the excluded middle is not only classical but also ontological. What is then the status of the intuitionist logic of negation? Badiou's answer is: it is the logic of appearance. The ontological determination of what a multiple is can be distinguished from how it appears – with what intensity, whether it appears in the shadows or the brightest light. Although one can show that the intuitionist logic of negation is consistent with the classical one – something cannot appear absolutely and with maximal intensity and at the same time not appear in a world – it is not true that, in the realm of appearances, one has to decide between A and not-A.

A multiplicity cannot appear and not appear at the same time, but it can appear in multiple ways or with multiple intensities. There is a multiplicity of third options. The principle of contradiction is therefore valid, but the principle of the excluded middle is not: A can appear as B between the absolute appearance, A, and the absolute non-appearance, not-A. This form of negation is therefore not only intuitionist but linked to the discourse of appearance: phenomenology.

To comprehend the third form of negation – the paraconsistent one, following the principle of the excluded middle but not of contradiction – one has to introduce, besides ontology and phenomenology, what Badiou calls an event. An event is related as much to being as to appearance. One can thus ask: 1. What sort of multiplicity does an event name (ontologically)? and 2. How does an event appear (phenomenally)?

1. An event is a contradictory multiplicity whose definition is that it belongs to itself – it has the property that is axiomatically prohibited for any other multiple. This means that, on the level of ontology, an event is neither classical (it does not comply with the principle of contradiction) nor intuitionist. From this perspective it can be called paraconsistent. An event might be in itself nothing but paraconsistent, and yet its definition would also comprise that it is nothing but the ensemble of the consequences it will have yielded. It is measured only by the consequences it will have been able to generate, and can thus only be thought within the

linkage of being and appearances. Because, if the event is not a transcendent intervention, one has to claim that there is nothing substantial that might count as an event. One has to claim that the only things that appear are the consequences that it has (an event is an event due to its consequences). So, how does an event appear? Phenomenally, it is the identity of appearance and disappearance. That is to say: what it is disappears whenever one attempts to substantialize it; and this very disappearing is its 'substance', its appearance.

An event is the vanishing mediator that appears to be paraconsistent – a yes and no at the same time; but this does not change the fact that one can only decide what it will have been if one considers whether it had concrete consequences or not. Therefore, its (ontologically) paraconsistent form necessitates a (logical) decision. When it is not clear if something has happened or not, a decision – a 'yes' or a 'no' – is needed. An event therefore conjures the classical form of negation; it demands the power of exclusion and the power of decision. If an event is nothing but the ensemble of the consequences that it yields, one can claim that these are measured by the fact that one either said 'yes' or 'no' to the forced choice that it necessitates; and also by what follows from the acceptance of the choice or the indifference towards it. An event constructs a diagonal towards the classical, intuitionist and paraconsistent form of negation. But what does that mean?

One can state that an event is a sudden change in the laws that regulate the realm of appearance. Something that seemed impossible now appears in the form of a formerly unthinkable possibility. Therefore it is not directly the creation of 'something' new, but rather the creation of a new, formerly nonexistent possibility. If an event were the creation of something new, it would mainly be destructive. But it also makes it possible to integrate something old into the construction of something new – or, to put it differently: the dialectical relation is not simply between the old and the new, but between the new of the previous sequence (the old new) and the new (the new new). This is why it is imperative for any new beginning of communism to take already-existing experiences into account – in such a way that it is able to integrate 'something' old into the composition of 'something' new.

The greatest change that an event can inaugurate is the transformation of something that does not appear in a world (for example, not-A does not appear in it) into something that does appears in that world (i.e. into A). This transformation is eventual, and follows the classical logic of negation. At the same time the consequences of the event have to be thought through from the perspective of the two other logics of negation – the intuitionist and the paraconsistent logics. The consequences of the event are either classical (not-A appears instead of A) or intuitionist (not-A appears as B, which does not replace the appearance of A by the appearance of not-A). Or, finally, the consequences of the event are paraconsistent. In this case, the fundamental framework of appearance is respected, and the distinction between A and not-A is not touched at all. From the perspective of the world, everything remains the same; the event and the non-event are identical, and their consequences are null – i.e. there is no event.

If any world of appearance is organized intuitionistically, then any radical form of action – i.e. any revolution – has to follow the classical logic of negation. Pseudo-actions, i.e. alleged revolutions, follow the paraconsistent logic. True action has to be organized classically, and mobilizes the double power of negation – of exclusion and forced decision; but the development of consequences of the exclusive decision takes place in a world governed by intuitionistic logic, in which multiple ways of its manifestation are possible. This is a necessary prerequisite to prevent grounding the consequences in one single 'yes' or one single 'no'. And it has to be remarked that an event – due to the fact that it conjures within the phenomenal world the form of a classical negation – is not shared by everyone. Not everyone answers the forced choice with a 'yes'; some remain untouched.

Hence, one needs to think a relation between the three logics, because the ontologically paraconsistent event appears as classical negation (something has happened or has not happened, and there is no third option) within an intuitionist framework in which a multiplicity of consequences are possible, and at the same time there is a paraconsistent opposition to it, because not everyone shares the initial 'yes' as an answer to the forced choice. Within the procedure of unfolding the consequences – which Badiou calls fidelity[71] – there is always a temptation to transform the 'yes or no' into a 'yes and no'. 'Yes' something has happened, but 'no' I do not have to draw consequences from it. This is the paradigmatic form of the paraconsistent temptation, or of fetishistic disavowal. Such a position implies precisely not to assume the consequences that are implied in

71   On Badiou's conception of fidelity, see Alain Badiou, *Being and Event*, pp. 201–64, and my 'Von der Treue als subtraktiver Institution', in Gernot Kamecke and Henning Teschke, eds, *Ereignis und Institution: Anknüpfungen an Alain Badiou* (Tübingen: Narr, 2008), pp. 69–96.

what I decided upon. This is why there are today two materialisms: a *paraconsistent reactionary materialism of fake freedom and a fake Two*, in the guise of a 'yes and no' at the same time; and a *true materialist dialectics*. A *materialism of organized indifference* on one side, and a *materialism of equality and a-natural freedom* on the other.

This is why there has to be a continually perpetuated series of 'yeses' – and also why the only imperative of an ethics of truth is 'Continue!'[72] Freedom has to be sustained and because it takes place within a concrete world, to sustain it one has to continually subtract from all the empirical differences – national, local, etc. – that appear to be natural in and for the world. The 'yes' has to be repeated in the situation that has already changed due to a former 'yes'. The subjective *determinate affirmation* (the 'yes', as I call it) has to be capable of repeatedly sustaining itself, to sustain classicism in the face of a world that changes through the consequences that unfold within it; but how that is to be done cannot be foreseen. But one needs to uphold the prescription that it will have been possible to do so. This is what philosophy reminds us of: even in times when there seems to be no possibility of affirming anything, we can affirm this prescription.

So the 'yes' has to be sustained although it is unforeseeable how to do so, and it might even seem impossible. Only in this way can the contingent emergence of a new possibility retroactively gain consistency; or, to put it differently: only via the consequences that unfold step by step, or point by point – i.e. through the continuity of 'yeses' – can an event be retroactively considered as what it will have been, or in this sense gain objectivity. Objective is only what will have been objective by the retroactive effect of the consequences that are nothing but the sustained classicism of subjective determinate affirmation in a changing world that changes precisely due to the effects of these determinate affirmations. One can also say that *the constant upholding of the subjective determinate affirmation of the emergence of the retroactively objective classical negation, inside the intuitionist framework and against any paraconsistent temptation, is a dialectical development that always (which is precisely what retroactivity means) relies upon something that is not itself dialectically deducible: namely, an event.*

If the consequences that change the world are engendered by an event, which itself is nothing but what it will have generated, in order not to fall back into extrapolating only one form of negation (the intuitionist one,

---

72   Badiou, *Ethics*, p. 52.

for example), one has to insist upon the following claim: for materialist dialectics to remain materialist it has to introduce something that cannot be deduced dialectically – otherwise the event would be substantialized.

It is this relation between the three logics of negation that presents the matrix of a new dialectical conception. It is dialectical in that it is a relation of different types of negation, and it is materialist because it considers the concrete consequences produced by the relations between the negations. Why is this new dialectical skeleton necessary today? Because of the historical specificity that conditions us. We are thinking *after* Plato – so one cannot uphold a conception of truth or the idea which considers it to be given; *after* Descartes – God cannot be the guarantor of anything; and *after* Hegel – there is no self-unfolding of the idea, or, to put it more simply: there is no reason in history. For a materialist, it is clear: there are no given ideas, no already-existing truths, no one truth of history. Thus, we have to think in a way that is adapted to historical specificity and that is also materialist. We are the ones to produce truths. We are the ones responsible for our own destiny. It might happen in New York, occupying Wall Street; it might happen in the Arab world. But philosophy, (re-)turning to Plato, Descartes and Hegel, has to remind us that we are able to produce truths, eternal ones, because we have already demonstrated that we are. Thus one still has to remain faithful to what has been bequeathed to us by the three of them: the ideas of the subject, of truth, and of the absolute. What follows from this is that materialist dialectics, in order not to fall back into the specific shortcomings of previous attempts to realize the communist hypothesis,[73] must constantly remind itself that this unfolding is grounded in something that, following the logic of retroactivity, is prior to it – although it is only accessible, only objective, after this very unfolding. Materialist dialectics, in order not to totalize dialectics – and thereby hypostasize only one form of negation[74] – has to be a dialectics of dialectics (the drawing of consequences) and non-dialectics (the contingent emergence of a new possibility).

---

73   One cannot but insist that every attempt hitherto has been a radical failure. Otherwise one remains blind to the very historical condition that necessitates our reworking of dialectical and materialist thought – this is to say: essentially blind in reworking the concept of negation.

74   This is precisely what previous modes of dialectical thinking have attempted in those very moments when they were put into practice. One famous hypostasis, for example, was the Leninist mode of dialectics. For this, see also Alain Badiou, 'Politics: An Expressive Dialectics', in Mark Potocnik, Frank Ruda and Jan Völker, eds, *Beyond Potentialities? Politics between the Possible and the Impossible* (Berlin: Diaphanes, 2011), pp. 13–22. See also Frank Ruda and Jan Völker, 'Was heißt es, ein Marxist in der Philosophie zu sein?' in Alain Badiou, *Ist Politik denkbar?* (Berlin: Merve, 2010), pp. 135–65.

This can also instruct us with regard to what *meta-critical anamnesis* is. For Badiou, as we know, philosophy stands in the position of meta-ontology with regard to its scientific condition and of meta-politics with regard to its political condition.[75] I want to claim that, from this, it follows that a philosophy which tries to intervene in a concrete situation cannot simply be critical. Philosophy will never be critical theory. It has to be meta-critical (theory). If philosophy were to be critical, it would still be linked to the situation, insisting on unmentioned possibilities that have not yet been realized; or it would start by distinguishing what is from what ought to be. Philosophy as critical theory would draw a distinction in the sense of the Greek *krinein*,[76] analyze tendencies, as Ernst Bloch did,[77] and in one way or another stick to only one form of negation as the motor of transformation. It would thus bind itself, in one way or another, to the given realm of the possible. Subtracting it from this bond means insisting that no form of true change is dialectically deducible. There is change that, from the immanence of a given situation, seems impossible. To affirm paraconsistency in a very specific sense against the materialist-democratic position is essential: but it needs to be thought and affirmed as an ontological paraconsistency (of the event) not as intuitionistic paraconsistency (of ideological seduction or disavowal). It has to be affirmed as that which forces a choice, forces us to be free. This is why philosophy has to affirm the contingent, unforeseeable and scandalous emergence of a new impossible possibility – that of an event which is not dialectically deducible.

This is why philosophy as meta-critical anamnesis has to comprise an element of a dialectic of dialectics and non-dialectics.[78] A meta-critical stance – a term resurrected and advocated by my comrade Lorenzo

---

75   See Alain Badiou, *Conditions* (London/New York: Continuum, 2009).

76   Here one should note that *krinein* also means 'to choose, to decide' – thus I imply that it is not that philosophy decides, but that it insists on the necessity of taking a choice. For this, see also Badiou's remark on the task of philosophy in Alain Badiou, 'Thinking the Event', in Alain Badiou and Slavoj Žižek, *Philosophy in the Present* (Cambridge/Malden: Polity, 2009), pp. 1–48.

77   See for example Ernst Bloch, 'Tendenz – Latenz – Utopie', in *Werke* (Frankfurt: Suhrkamp, 1985).

78   Here one would also need to develop why the relationship between the dialectical development of consequences and their non-dialectical 'origin' has to be conceived of in a dialectical manner. One can render this in a much too short and abstract way by saying that one thinks the relation between the two either as a relation of a 'without' or of an 'and'. Either there is the 'dialectical *and* the non-dialectical' side, which implies that there is a dialectical and a non-dialectical stratum of thought; thinking the relation of the terms then would come down to thinking the 'and' between them. This is precisely the path of vitalism. Against this one should claim that there is no relationship between them, although there are dialectical consequences of a non-dialectical event – this is what it means to think the 'without' (relation) between them. Any dialectics thinks the 'without' and not the 'and'. Dialectics is always thinking non-relation.

Chiesa[79] – is necessary because it enables philosophy to turn itself against itself, and to draw a line of demarcation against reactionary tendencies within itself. Critical philosophy draws an idealist line of demarcation; meta-critical philosophy draws a line of demarcation of an idealism without idealism, or simply: a truly materialist party-line of demarcation.

'Meta-critical' implies being self-critical – implies a *philosophical torsion*, against any fake (liberal, pragmatist, etc.) dialectics. But also it has to take into account that, under changed historical conditions, the very means that remind the human animal of the possibility of the impossible need to be renewed. Thus it is not a critique of the present, but a critique of the means of remembering the impossible: it is a meta-critique. And it thus has to work for the renewal of those means; it implies a working-through of dialectics and negation. Philosophy has to be *meta-critical anamnesis*.

Countering Indifference or Cartesianism for the Twenty-First Century

By remembering Descartes, a meta-critical anamnesis understands the human animal as a natural embodiment of a-natural freedom and methodically doubts the ideology of the evil capitalist genius. By remembering Plato, a meta-critical anamnesis defends the conception of a life under an idea and the idea of truth. By repeating Marx and working through Hegel, it obtains the conception of a renewed dialectical model which also renews the means to recall the impossible possibility of an event. What does all this come down to? How can a meta-critical anamnesis concretely counter democratic materialism today? Three points:

1. *Meta-critical anamnesis* means pitting a *politics of human discipline, equality and freedom* against the reactionary *animal humanist politics* of domestication. Remembering the impossible means starting with a determinate affirmation which affirms communism as a (possible) truth within politics. Philosophy can affirm that the communist hypothesis presents the only thinkable idea of politics. And, if it can, it must affirm it. It must affirm that the individual has not necessarily surrendered to the state and its contemporary animal humanist ideology. It must affirm that a new singular-collective creation of possibilities is itself possible. And it must affirm that the name

---

79 See the impressive Lorenzo Chiesa, 'Notes Towards a Manifesto for Metacritical Realism', in Ruda and Völker, *Beyond Potentialities?*

'communism' is not forever doomed. It must affirm that there are experiences – and it has to insist on the fact that 'we' have them. It must affirm the impossible possibility of a 'communist we'. And, if we have such experiences, we have to do everything in our power to continue to produce and to create them. This anamnetical affirmation is an affirmation addressed to everyone: as a concrete, singular affirmation of the existence of communist experiences, it is at the same time a universal, collective affirmation, because it is an affirmation of their internal trans-temporality, their truth. Against the fetishism of failure so dear to liberals, libertarians or 'social chauvinists', as Lenin liked to say, a *meta-critical anamnesis* has to uphold this form of affirmation of a singular-collective 'we' that is of a communist nature. This is why, at least in and for philosophy, one should determinately affirm that we can and therefore must be communists. There can be a new beginning, and everything, as always, will begin with a concrete, determinate 'yes'. A philosophical 'yes'.

2. If we are politically in the same situation as Marx was in the 1840s, philosophy today, as I outline it above, seems to be in a comparable situation to that of Descartes in the 1640s. Thus, a *meta-critical anamnesis* has to repeat the Cartesian gesture against indifference under changed conditions. What can this mean? Badiou has articulated a radical diagnosis of the present in the following form: the twenty-first century has not yet begun. The reason, it can be argued, is that we are still thinking – for example within politics – in the terms of the twentieth century; we still, for example, refer to 'revolution' in the manner that Lenin or Mao did.[80] This is one reason why he called our times 'a time of disorientation'.[81] Disorientation here can be understood as one direct effect of the (ideological) predominance of the fake Two of democratic materialism over any materialist dialectical stance. We are all lost in the ossified realm of bodies and their pathological constitution; in the commerce of languages (the expression of arbitrary opinions); the alleged complexity of our individualities and their relationship to the communities we think that we belong to even if we are arbitrarily born into them (family, nation, state, and so on). How can we oppose this stance?

---

80 For an analysis of the last century, see Alain Badiou, *The Century* (Cambridge/Malden: Polity, 2007).
81 Badiou, *Le courage du présent*.

I want to suggest that it is Descartes who offers some means of coming up with a *different indifference against the indifference* produced by democratic materialism. Against the *disorienting indifference* of the fake Two, one needs to put up a *subtractive indifference* of a true Two which is constitutive for any true or 'generic orientation of thought'.[82] This subtractive indifference subtracts – as Descartes did – all the seemingly unavoidable particular differences and naturalizations of the 'there is'. Badiou has in a recent seminar outlined what this act of subtractive indifferentiation today can mean.[83] These are first moments of a concrete subjective stance against democratic materialism: one needs first an indifference with regard to numbers, secondly with regard to the established regime of the possible, thirdly with regard to particularities, fourthly concerning the alleged antinomy between the authoritarian and the tolerant, and finally concerning the separation of repetition and projection. The first mode of indifference implies that a numerical majority is not a criterion of truth – a point already articulated by Descartes: ten militant people count more than a million passive ones; the second mode implies the diagnosis that today the possible is a repressive category; the third that a truth can only begin from something which is valid for anyone and disregards the particularities of different life-worlds; the fourth that one cannot know in advance which form of discipline, which form of authority, will have been adequate. Any idea generates its own norms and one can never know in advance if someone will get hurt in the course of its development.[84] The fifth mode of indifference, finally, implies the insight that an exception is neither a simple repetition – it is not synonymous with tradition – nor a pure projection, since any new projected idea is, as is well known, always threatened to become a nicely marketable product. An exception is rather the synthesis of repetition (as something unthinkable or impossible within a given historical situation has already taken place a couple of times before) and projection: a synthesis of singularity and universality.

All these indifferences are needed for a contemporary

---

82 Badiou, *Being and Event*, p. 510.

83 I here reconstruct what can be found in: Alain Badiou, *Images du temps présent. Séminaires 2003-04*, at www.entretemps.asso.fr.

84 This is an insight that is particularly valid when one relates politics to love. After a love encounter, none of those involved knows in advance if someone will get hurt at some point in the history of the love's unfolding.

re-actualization of Descartes's gesture in the frame of a *meta-critical anamnesis* that insists on the possibility of the impossible, the contingent occurrence of an absolute contingency which allows for the thinkability of the unthinkable (equality), for the emergence of the a-natural human freedom which makes all of us into embodiments of the non-relation between the human and the animal. Thus philosophy in times of disorientation does not have a critical duty in any traditional sense. It not only distances itself from the world of the 'there is'; it has to come up with a renewed notion of the contingent emergence of the absolute (the event and a truth which unfolds post-eventally) – i.e. of our a-natural freedom – and it can only do so by remembering that it has already taken place several times under different historical conditions, and taking this into account. *Meta-critical anamnesis* can do so by remembering communism.

3. Thus philosophy has to be Cartesian in a re-actualized way: it has to be a Cartesianism for the twenty-first century (still to come).[85] It can take this meta-critical stance – propagating the thinkability of unthinkable and impossible communism – in reminding the human animal that it can act in a human, or better inhuman because a-natural way. We thus not only have to change the world of bodies, languages, individuals and communities, but also, by becoming indifferent towards it and its alleged evidences, we also (and maybe first and foremost) have to change ourselves. Because we can. And we can because we already did so. Philosophy recalls actions of the impossible, thoughts of the unthinkable under changed conditions. This is philosophy as *meta-critical anamnesis*. Then (with meta-critical anamnesis as one of its preconditions) a twenty-first century will begin some day. For, *meta-critical anamnesis* is a preparation for this very beginning.

What *meta-critical anamnesis* takes up from idealism under materialist conditions is the idea of truths, the *idea of the idea*. This is what philosophy as philosophy always was, and, in order to remain philosophy, will always be conditioned by. It is still *materialist*, as it agrees that there is nothing

---

85   The twenty-first century will begin some say: it is absolutely necessary although it is impossible. This is why this claim marks a point of the real, as the real in the Lacanian version is precisely what is impossible and necessary at the same time. The only thing to recall is that, although one can be absolutely sure that the twenty-first century will begin some day, it might take a couple of thousand years to happen.

but bodies and languages; but it is at the same time dialectical, as it introduces an exception into what there is. It relies on a dialectics of the exception. It is *formalist*, as it is conditioned by the form of the idea of truth – as truths stand in exception to the realm of the simply given. But the dialectics of the exception has also to be thought *dialectically*: it is a *dialectics of dialectics and non-dialectics*, not totalizing dialectics. Because in reminding us, human animals, *philosophy reminds itself* – or, in other words: it asserts and defends the seemingly impossible possibility of truth, which is the only task philosophy has ever had throughout its history. Because by asserting itself and reminding itself of its role, philosophy can counter one threat: the disappearance of one condition, of one field of practice – this is to say, for our contemporary non-world, the disappearance of emancipatory politics. For, if there is only universalized indifference and survivalist animal humanism, politics disappears; it becomes a mixture of administration and corruption.[86] Philosophy as *meta-critical anamnesis* is thus first and foremost a self-affirmation of philosophy. Affirmation that affirms philosophy as philosophy. But by affirming itself it affirms something else. Because philosophy is only philosophy and can remain philosophy when it is conditioned by something that is not philosophy. This is what it learned from idealism. Thus, in affirming itself it also affirms the (historically specific) truths (or, at least, their impossible possibility) that it is conditioned by. And truths are never philosophical – they always emerge in extra-philosophical domains of practice, in politics for example.

Philosophy as *self-affirmative meta-critical anamnesis*, seeking new means to remind us of our unthinkable capacities, our a-natural freedom, of the possibility to live a life under an idea, thus also affirms the impossible possibility of the existence of politics, i.e. communism. In affirming itself, philosophy finds within itself something which conditions its own constitution but at the same time is radically autonomous from philosophy. The affirmation of philosophy leads to the affirmation of true practices outside philosophy:

A meta-critical and anamnetical self-affirmation of philosophy therefore leads to the recollection of the extimate truth-kernel of philosophy. Communism is one of the (multiple) hearts that are able to keep philosophy alive. This

---

86 One way of reading the contemporary situation would be to present it as different combinations of these two terms: there is corruption and then there is the administration of its effects; there is administration as the very precondition for corruption, and there is corruption as the only thing that keeps administration running.

is why one answer to the question this volume has addressed (communism: a new beginning?), taken as a philosophical question, is: one condition for a new beginning of communism is the self-assertion, *die Selbstbehauptung* of philosophy. *Selbstbehauptung* of philosophy as recalling the impossible possibility of the existence of emancipatory politics. The name of it, right now, could be, perhaps always will be: communism. So: communism, a new beginning? Yes. And for this we need philosophy. Let us always remember that there is always the impossible possibility of a new beginning; in always new situations. This is *meta-critical anamnesis*. This is philosophy.

8   Communism Today

Emmanuel Terray

The debate on the communist hypothesis, it seems to me, essentially boils down to the following question: Should the communist project, such as it has been elaborated since the nineteenth century, be set down among the great utopias that have marked the history of Western political thought – from Campanella to Thomas More and Fourier – or, rather, is it still able to provide meanings and perspectives to our struggles today?

I would like to note, firstly, that for me this question is not a new one. In 1992, in the wake of the fall of the Berlin Wall and the Velvet Revolution in Prague, at a time when all the Western intelligentsia were either bemoaning or celebrating the death of communism, I published a little book with Actes Sud, entitled *Le Troisième jour du Communisme* ('The Third Day of Communism'); as an epigraph for this text, I used a verse from the Gospel of Matthew (17:23): 'They will kill him, and on the third day he will be raised to life.' This book advanced two ideas. Firstly, it tried to explain the disastrous end of actually existing socialism – this was, I argued, *the consequence of the transformation of the communist movement into a 'secular religion'*. Starting from the thesis of a Marxist science of history and society, from the formation of a vanguard party, entrusted with this science, and invested with the mission of guiding the proletariat to the revolution, and from the rather messianic conception of the working class as the universal class responsible for putting an end to class society, a veritable Church was created, with its own dogmas, rituals, hierarchy and inquisition. In this Church, History with a capital H took the place of God; but that did not fundamentally change the nature of the institution – namely, one founded upon the hypothesis of an enlightened elite charged with the fate of the people, and upon the values of order, obedience and discipline. It is hard to see how an organization conceived of in this manner could have become an instrument of collective emancipation.

But secondly, I recalled – to use Mao's formulations – *that where there is exploitation, there is struggle, and where there is oppression, there is resistance.*

Since the end of actually existing socialism did not at all mean the end of capitalist exploitation and the manifold oppressions that go with it, but on the contrary had every chance of aggravating it – given the disappearance of a threat that had, in the past, often jolted the bourgeoisie towards prudence and compromise – *it was easy to foresee that the communist phoenix would soon rise from the ashes*, just as, after the abortion of the French Revolution and Napoleon's dictatorship, the republican and democratic ideal, declared dead in 1815, was little-by-little resuscitated and reinvigorated, so that it had triumphed across all of Europe a century later. The same causes produce the same effects, and you did not have to be a rocket scientist or some divinely inspired prophet to predict that the communist hope would soon be resurrected – a resurrection whose first omens we can all observe today.

In a second text, written in 2007, with the slightly provocative title 'De Lénine à Proudhon' ('From Lenin to Proudhon'),[1] I turned back to the same questions, but from a rather different angle: the strategy of the Communist Parties, as we know, consisted of trying to *seize state power in order to then put it to use* as a lever for carrying out social transformation and securing the victory of the emancipation project. This strategy thus relies on the all-decisive hypothesis that *the state is an instrument adequate to this project* – and it is on precisely this point that we might question it. There can be no doubt that the state is an effective instrument for carrying out *certain* social transformations: in particular we might recall the role that it played in the period of primitive accumulation laying the ground for the advent of capitalist society. But when the transformation we have in mind is that of collective emancipation, the generalization of freedom and equality across all domains of social life, is the state still the appropriate tool? This is doubtful: by definition, the state is an authority separate from, exterior to and above society; its very existence relies on the opposition between those who govern and those who are governed, between those who rule and those who are ruled. Since communism must necessarily advance by way of the abolition of this opposition, we can say that there exists a *manifest contradiction between the goal pursued – communism – and the means employed – the state and the party that mirrors it.*

This is the reason why Lenin evoked the *withering-away of the state* as a process that would have to begin immediately after the conquest of power, and as one of the urgent tasks of the new government. However, in the

---

1   Republished in my *Combats avec Méduse* (Paris: Galilée, 2011).

USSR this task was, in fact, postponed in favour of others deemed more pressing: namely, the defence of the Revolution against its domestic and foreign enemies, the collectivization of agriculture, and industrialization. In the Stalin era, this postponement was theorized, it being specified that the dictatorship of the proletariat, far from withering away, would have to go through a period of intensive reinforcement before it could give way to communism. It would be mistaken to see in this development the simple reflection of the circumstances particular to the Soviet Union of the 1920s: in fact, *there has never been an institution that worked towards its own disappearance*. On the contrary, like Spinoza's *unaquaeque res*, institutions have a tendency to persevere in their own being and to work for their own reproduction; the thesis of the withering-away of the state is thus shown to be utopian, a last concession to utopia by the incorrigible realist Lenin.

Hence, the *recourse to Proudhon*: for him, the conquest of state power must mean its immediately being dismantled, and any survival, even in part, of this authority would be a lever for the old oppressions and inequalities to take root again. The state must be eradicated at once, and its functions handed over to the community of associated producers. Given the catastrophic fate of actually existing socialism, such theses suddenly acquire a striking contemporary relevance. In any case, it seems clear to me that *the late-nineteenth-century debate between anarchists and communists has to be reposited on new bases*, in the light of the experience acquired since then.

When I refer to the two texts that I have just cited, it is not to assert some sort of lineage, but rather to make quite clear that *we have a history and an experience* that we cannot just sweep away. This history and this experience are the history and experience of a *failure*: the failure of the project of social transformation such as it developed through the course of the twentieth century according to the perspectives set out by Marxism. But each failure also offers *lessons to be drawn*, and we must take these lessons on board if we are not to start off again along the same route and commit the same mistakes. In the second part of this text, I would like to sketch a brief list of the questions posed to us by a past that is, whether we like it or not, *our* past.

A first series of questions revolve around the notion of *property*. Marx defined communism as the *abolition of private property* in the means of production, in favour of their collective appropriation.

First question: *Should this abolition concern all means of production, no matter what they are?* Including the land and the equipment used in agricultural labour? Including the artisans, and small and medium enterprises? To put it another way: *What are we prepared to leave to the domain of private property*, in terms of capital goods, durable consumer goods, housing, and so on?

Second question: *What do we mean by 'collective appropriation'?* In the experience of actually existing socialism, collective appropriation was very widely taken to mean nationalization or state control, along with all that implies in terms of centralized and bureaucratic management. Only in the domain of agriculture was any place left for other forms of property – in this case cooperatives. But do we have to box ourselves into this dilemma between private property and state control? Should we not, rather, experiment with *other forms of property: municipal property, for example in building plots and urban services; or cooperative property in artisanal businesses and SMEs* – the objective being to leave to the state only those major public services whose technological demands require a centralized management (energy, transport, and so on).

Linked to this question of property is the *question of the relationship between the market and the plan*. Private property in the means of production means independent and sovereign producers, between whom there can be no relationship other than market competition. But with the collective appropriation of the means of production, the producers become *part of a whole, and it is a plan elaborated by this whole that carries out the function of guaranteeing coordination among the producers*. The blind game of competition, whose results can only be known after the event, is therefore replaced with a *conscious direction*, which entails the determination in advance of the objectives to be attained as well as the organization of the means necessary to this end. The question thus posed is: In the economy of the new society, *what should be reserved to the plan, and what should be left to competition and the market?* This question should not be confused with that of private versus collective property, since cooperative enterprises could also be linked to each other by means of relations of competition and offering goods on the market.

We are then posed the question of *the democratic elaboration of the plan*. In societies as complex as our own, a Soviet-style, centralized elaboration of the plan is clearly impracticable. *Democratic planning* must be founded on cells at the base, and principally consist of harmonizing the projects elaborated by these cells. Also posed, moreover, is the question of the means by which the plan is implemented: What role is there for *binding decisions*, and what role for *incentives*? Ultimately, any effort at planning entails certain initial decisions that can and must be submitted to the community:

What share is reserved for consumption, and what share should be saved or invested? We can very well imagine that society could compromise between many different perspectives on this point.

Finally, whatever the answers to the questions of property and the plan, also posed is the question of *workplace democracy*. At the present moment, the workplace is the example par excellence of authoritarian order and hierarchical organization – and democracy, such as it does exist, only begins at the factory gate. So how do we break down this door? Here, we must resume the whole *discussion on self-management and workers' councils*, such that the abolition of private property in the means of production also leads to the abolition of wage-labour.

As concerns society, the first question posed is that regarding *equality*. The societies that existed under actually existing socialism wilfully distanced themselves from the egalitarian ideal that had characterized the early communist movement, tolerating variations of income and living standards equal to or sometimes even greater than those existing in capitalist societies. We must all ask ourselves whether *such variations should continue to exist, according to what criteria, and to what extent*. Again, many alternatives are possible, and it is for the community to settle this matter.

But the central question is, clearly, that of *democracy*. It is a commonplace, a banality, to claim that the societies of actually existing socialism died due to a lack of democracy. But what should we understand by that? Today, the word 'democracy' designates *the conjunction of individual freedoms and the parliamentary system*. Every day we feel the limits and the farce of democracy conceived in such a fashion, and no one could possibly believe that the faults of the system of actually existing socialism would have been remedied had only such a democracy been introduced. Thus we are faced with having to accomplish a great work of the imagination, in order to *devise forms of democracy applicable to all domains of social life*: housing, schools, healthcare, public services, and so on. What role should be accorded to the workers in the sectors under consideration, and what role for the service-users? Given the peril of technocratic, bureaucratic management, it is clear enough that we must carry out the *maximum of decentralization*, and strictly implement the *principle of subsidiarity*: nothing is decided at a higher level that cannot be decided at lower levels.

We should, moreover, reflect on *the means by which to ensure the independence of the major means of information and communication* with respect to the state. Undoubtedly, the solution would come by means of the creation of independent authorities disposing of their own resources, subcontracted by the state. Equally, we would have to guarantee *freedom of association and the freedom of the trade union movement*. Finally, to the extent that collective rule extends across all levels of society, we would have to see to *the reinforcement of individual freedoms* – including, in particular, *the independence of judicial authority*, the guardian par excellence of civil liberties. Only thus can representative democracy and its corollary, universal suffrage, become a truly democratic structure, and not the ersatz democracy to which it is today reduced.

Lastly, we should address the matter of our *relationship with the outside world*. In a society as deeply integrated into the international economy as our own, what possibility of engaging in a project of radical transformation would be left to us? What measures should we take to protect our sovereignty and freedom to choose the social system that suits us best? Clearly, at the same time, this poses *questions of currency, the control of the circulation of capital and of goods, and so on*. You do not have to be a prophet to predict that any attempt at radical transformation will come up against a *hostile environment*: consequently, the debates concerning world revolution and socialism in one country will again be of contemporary relevance . . .

The experience that has been gathered brings us one last lesson: whatever form it takes, the society that we want to build *will not be a society of reconciliation, calm compromise and harmony*. It will be a *conflictual society*, and we should not only accept this, but welcome it. And this conflict will not only oppose partisans of the new order to those who want to go back to the old one. It will be established in the very heart of the new society: between *the partisans of order and the partisans of movement*; between the advocates of consolidation and prudence and those who uphold experimentation, innovation and risk-taking. Recently I read the memoirs of Zhao Ziyang, the Chinese CP secretary forced from office in 1989 for having opposed the Tiananmen Square massacre. Zhao Ziyang explains how, before 1989, he had clashed with Chinese CP hierarchs on account of his desire to implement economic reforms. For their part, the hierarchs upheld the authority of the party, centralized planning, the supremacy of the state sector . . . In brief, they were men of the old values of realism, order, hierarchy and authority who have always been at the heart of right-wing thought. In a *communist society, too, there will be a right and a left*, insofar as, under no matter what regime, the dialogue between left and right essentially boils down to the dialogue between Don Quixote and Sancho Panza.

To put it another way, what we can expect from communism is *a society capable of freely and consciously deciding its own fate*. This is not the case today: capitalism is like a broken engine, and we are the impotent prey of blind forces that, in truth, no one is able to control. This is what we will change. We will regain mastery over our own destiny: we will continue to clash with each other over this destiny, but with the simple – and considerable – difference that we will be fighting over real stakes, not with impossible-to-grasp phantoms.

9   Answers Without Questions

Slavoj Žižek

In China, so they say, if you really hate someone, the curse to fling at them is: 'May you live in interesting times!' Historically, the 'interesting times' have been periods of unrest, war and struggles for power in which millions of innocents suffered the consequences. The four events that shook the world in the Summer of 2011 – the continuation of the Arab uprisings, Anders Breivik's killing spree in Oslo, the renewed financial turmoil announcing another recession, and the violent protests in UK cities with hundreds of houses and cars looted and burned – are clear signs that we are entering a new epoch of interesting times.

According to Hegel, repetition plays a precise role in history: when something happens just once, it may be dismissed as a mere accident, as something that might have been avoided through better handling of the situation; but when the same event repeats itself, this is a sign that we are dealing with a deeper historical necessity. When Napoleon lost the first time, in 1813, it looked like bad luck; when he lost the second time, at Waterloo, it was clear that his time was over . . . And does not the same hold for the ongoing financial crisis? When it first hit the markets in September 2008, it looked like an accident to be corrected through better regulations, and so forth; now that signs of a repeated financial meltdown are gathering, it is clear that we are dealing with a structural necessity.

What makes the ongoing crisis weird is the axiom followed by the large majority of 'specialists' and politicians: we are told again and again that we live in a critical time of deficit and debts where we all have to share a burden and accept a lower standard of living – *all with the exception of the (very) rich*. The idea of taxing them more is an absolute taboo: if we do this, so we are told, the rich will lose the incentive to invest and create new jobs, and we will all suffer the consequences. The only way to escape the hard times is for the poor to get poorer and for the rich to get richer.

And if the rich are in danger of losing some of their wealth, society has to help them out: the dominant notion of the ongoing financial crisis (namely that it was caused by excessive state borrowing and spending) is blatantly in conflict with the fact that, from Iceland to the US, its ultimate cause was the big private banks – in order to prevent the banks' failure, the state had to intervene with enormous amounts of taxpayers' money. How can we find our way through such a confusing situation?

Back in the 1930s, Hitler offered anti-Semitism as a narrative explanation of the troubles experienced by ordinary Germans: unemployment, moral decay, social unrest . . . behind all this stood the Jew, for evoking the 'Jewish plot' made everything clear by providing a simple 'cognitive map'. Does not today's hatred of multiculturalism and of the immigrant threat function in a homologous way? Strange things are happening, financial meltdowns occur which affect our daily lives but are experienced as totally opaque – and the rejection of multiculturalism introduces a false clarity into the situation: it is the foreign intruders who are disturbing our way of life . . . There is thus an interconnection between the rising anti-immigrant tide in Western countries (which reached a peak in Breivik's killing spree) and the ongoing financial crisis: clinging to ethnic identity serves as a protective shield against the traumatic fact of being caught up in the whirlpool of non-transparent financial abstraction – the true 'foreign body' which cannot be assimilated is ultimately the infernal self-propelling machine of Capital itself.

There are things which give us pause to think in Breivik's ideological self-justification, as well as in reactions to his murderous act. The manifesto of this Christian 'Marxist hunter' who killed more than seventy people in Oslo is precisely *not* a case of a madman's rambling; it is simply a consistent exposition of 'Europe's crisis' which serves as the (more or less) implicit foundation of rising anti-immigrant populism – its very inconsistencies are symptomatic of the inner contradictions of this view. The first thing that cannot but strike us is how Breivik constructs his enemy: the combination of three elements (Marxism, multiculturalism, Islamism), each of which belongs to a different political space: the Marxist radical left, multiculturalist liberalism, Islamic religious fundamentalism. The old fascist habit of attributing to the enemy mutually exclusive features ('Bolshevik-plutocratic Jewish plot' – the Bolshevik radical left, plutocratic capitalism, ethnic-religious identity) returns here in a new guise. Even more indicative is the way Breivik's self-designation shuffles the cards of radical rightist ideology. Breivik advocates Christianity, but remains a secular agnostic: Christianity is for him merely a cultural construct to oppose Islam. He is anti-feminist and thinks women should be discouraged from pursuing higher education; but he favours a 'secular' society, supports abortion, and declares himself pro-gay. Furthermore, Breivik combines Nazi features (in the details too – for example, his sympathy for Saga, the Swedish pro-Nazi folk singer) with hatred for Hitler: one of his heroes is Max Manus, the leader of the Norwegian anti-Nazi resistance. Breivik is not so much racist as anti-Muslim: all his hatred is focused on the Muslim threat. And, last but not least, Breivik is anti-Semitic but pro-Israel, since the state of Israel is the first defence line against Muslim expansion – he even wants to see the Jerusalem Temple rebuilt. His view is that Jews are OK as long as there are not too many of them – or, as he wrote in his 'Manifesto': 'There is no Jewish problem in Western Europe (with the exception of the UK and France) as we only have 1 million in Western Europe, whereas 800,000 out of these 1 million live in France and the UK. The US on the other hand, with more than 6 million Jews (600% more than Europe) actually has a considerable Jewish problem.' His figure thus realizes the ultimate paradox of a Zionist Nazi. How is this possible?

A key is provided by the reactions of the European right to Breivik's attack: its mantra was that, in condemning his murderous act, we should not forget that he addressed 'legitimate concerns about genuine problems' – mainstream politics is failing to address the corrosion of Europe by Islamicization and multiculturalism, or, to quote the *Jerusalem Post*, we should use the Oslo tragedy 'as an opportunity to seriously reevaluate policies for immigrant integration in Norway and elsewhere'.[1] (Incidentally, it would be nice to hear a similar appreciation of the Palestinian acts of terror, something like 'these acts of terror should serve as an opportunity to reevaluate Israeli policies'.) A reference to Israel is, of course, implicit in this evaluation: a 'multicultural' Israel has no chance of surviving, apartheid is the only realistic option. The price for this properly perverse Zionist-rightist pact is that, in order to justify the claim to Palestine, one has to acknowledge retroactively the line of argumentation which was previously, in earlier European history, used against the Jews: the implicit deal is 'We are ready to acknowledge your intolerance towards other cultures in your midst if you acknowledge our right not to tolerate Palestinians in our midst.' The tragic irony of this implicit deal is that

---

1   Editorial on 'Norway's Challenge', *Jerusalem Post* 24 July 2011.

previously the Jews themselves were the first 'multiculturalists': their problem was how to survive maintaining their culture intact in places where another culture was predominant.[2] At the end of this road lies the extreme possibility, which should in no way be discarded, of a 'historic pact' between Zionists and Muslim fundamentalists.

But what if we *are* entering a new era where this new reasoning will impose itself? What if Europe was to accept the paradox that its democratic openness is based on exclusion: there is 'no freedom for the enemies of freedom', as Robespierre put it long ago? In principle, this is, of course, true, but it is here that one has to be very specific. In a way, Breivik was right in his choice of target: he did not attack foreigners, but those within his own community who were seen as too tolerant towards the intruding foreigners. The problem is not the foreigner, it is our own (European) identity. Although the ongoing crisis of the European Union appears as a crisis of the economy and debt, it is in its fundamental dimension an *ideologico-political* crisis: the failure of referendums about the EU constitution a few years ago gave a clear signal that voters perceived the EU as a 'technocratic' economic union, lacking any vision which could mobilize people – until the recent protests, the only ideology able to mobilize people was the anti-immigrant 'defence' of Europe.

Recent outbursts of homophobia in East European post-Communist states should give us pause to reflect. In early 2011, there was a gay parade in Istanbul where thousands marched in peace, with no violence or other disturbances; in gay parades which took place at the same time in Serbia and Croatia (in Belgrade and Split), the police were not able to protect participants who were ferociously attacked by thousands of violent Christian fundamentalists. *These* fundamentalists, rather than Turkey's, are the true threat to the European legacy, so when the EU basically blocked Turkey's entry, we should raise the obvious question: What about applying the same rules to Eastern Europe?[3]

It is crucial to locate anti-Semitism in this series, as one of the elements alongside other forms of racism, sexism, homophobia, and so on. In order to ground its Zionist politics, the state of Israel is here making a catastrophic mistake: it has decided to downplay, if not outright ignore,

---

2   Incidentally, one should note here that, in the 1930s, in direct response to Nazi anti-Semitism, Ernest Jones, the main agent of the conformist gentrification of psychoanalysis, engaged in weird reflections on the percentage of foreign population a national body can tolerate in its midst without endangering its own identity, thereby accepting the Nazi problematic.

3   Not to mention the weird fact that the main force behind the anti-gay movement in Croatia is the Catholic Church, well-known for its numerous paedophile scandals.

the so-called 'old' (traditional European) anti-Semitism, focusing instead on the 'new' and allegedly 'progressive' anti-Semitism masked as the critique of the Zionist politics of the state of Israel. Along these lines, Bernard-Henri Lévy (in his *The Left in Dark Times*) recently claimed that the anti-Semitism of the twenty-first century will be 'progressive' or not at all. Pushed to its logical conclusion, this thesis compels us to invert the old Marxist interpretation of anti-Semitism as mystified/displaced anti-capitalism (instead of blaming the capitalist system, the rage is focused on a specific ethnic group accused of corrupting the system): for Lévy and his partisans, contemporary anti-capitalism is a disguised form of anti-Semitism.

This unspoken but no less effective prohibition of attacking 'old' anti-Semitism is taking place at the very moment when 'old-school' anti-Semitism is returning all across Europe, especially in post-Communist East European countries. We can observe a similar weird alliance in the US: How can the US Christian fundamentalists, who are, as it were, by definition anti-Semitic, now passionately support the Zionist policy of the state of Israel? There is only one solution to this enigma: it is not that the US fundamentalists have changed, it is that Zionism itself, in its hatred of the Jews who do not fully identify with the politics of the state of Israel, paradoxically became anti-Semitic itself – that is, constructed the figure of the Jew who doubts the Zionist project along anti-Semitic lines. Israel is playing here a dangerous game: Fox News, the main US voice of the radical right and a staunch supporter of Israeli expansionism, recently had to demote Glen Beck, its most popular host, whose comments were becoming openly anti-Semitic.

The standard Zionist argument against the critics of the policies of the state of Israel is that, of course, like every other state, Israel can and should be judged and eventually criticized, but that the critics misuse the justified critique of Israeli policy for anti-Semitic purposes. When the unconditional Christian fundamentalist supporters of the Israeli politics reject leftist critiques of Israeli policies, is not their implicit line of argumentation best rendered by a wonderful cartoon published in July 2008 in the Viennese daily *Die Presse*? It shows two stocky Nazi-looking Austrians, one of them holding in his hands a newspaper and commenting to his friend: 'Here you can see again how a totally justified anti-Semitism is being misused for a cheap critique of Israel!' Such are today's allies of the state of Israel. Jewish critics of the State of Israel are regularly dismissed as self-hating Jews – however, are not the true self-hating Jews those who secretly hate the true greatness of the Jewish people, precisely the Zionists making a pact with anti-Semites? How did we end up in such a weird situation?

The underlying problem is here the one of loving one's neighbour – as usual, G. K. Chesterton hit the nail on its head: 'The Bible tells us to love our neighbours, and also to love our enemies; probably because they are generally the same people'. So what happens when these problematic neighbours strike back? Although the UK riots of August 2011 were triggered by the suspicious death of Mark Duggan, it is commonly accepted that they express a deeper unease – but what kind of unease? Like the car burnings in the Paris suburbs in 2005, the UK protesters had no message to deliver. The contrast is here clear with the massive student demonstrations in November 2010 which also turned violent: they had a message – rejection of the higher education reforms. This is why it is difficult to conceive of the UK riots in the Marxist terms of the emerging revolutionary subject; they fit much better the Hegelian notion of a 'rabble', of those outside the organized social space, prevented from participating in social production, who can express their discontent only in the guise of 'irrational' outbursts of destructive violence, of what Hegel called 'abstract negativity'. Maybe, this is the hidden truth of Hegel, of his political thought: the more a society forms a well-organized rational state, the more the abstract negativity of 'irrational' violence returns.

The theological implications of this hidden truth are unexpectedly far-reaching: What if the ultimate addressee of the biblical commandment 'Thou shalt not kill' is God (Jehovah) Himself, and we, the fragile humans, are His neighbours exposed to divine rage? How often, in the Old Testament, do we encounter God as a dark stranger who brutally intrudes into human lives and sows destruction? When Levinas wrote that the first reaction when we see a neighbour is to kill him, was he not implying that this originally refers to God's relationship to humans, so that the commandment is actually an appeal to God to control His rage? Insofar as the Jewish solution is a dead god, a god who survives only as a 'dead letter' of the sacred book, of the Law to be interpreted, what dies with the death of God is precisely the god of the real, of destructive fury and revenge. The title of a well-known book on the Holocaust – *God Died in Auschwitz* – has thus to be inverted: God was born in Auschwitz, through its violence. Recall the story from the Talmud about two rabbis debating a theological point; the one who is losing the debate calls upon God Himself to come and decide, and when God does actually come, the other rabbi tells Him that his work of creation is already accomplished, so He now has nothing left to say and should depart, which God then does – it is as if, at Auschwitz, God came back, with catastrophic consequences. The true horror does not occur when we are abandoned by God, but when God comes too close to us.

This is why both conservative and liberal reactions to the urban unrest clearly failed. The conservative reaction was predictable: there is no justi-fication for such vandalism; one should use all necessary means to restore order; and what is needed to prevent further explosions of this kind is not more tolerance and social assistance, but rather more discipline, hard work and a sense of responsibility. What is false in this account is not only that it neglects the desperate social situation pushing young people to such violent outbursts, but, perhaps more important, the way such outbursts echo the subterranean premises of conservative ideology itself. When, back in the 1990s, the Conservatives launched their infamous 'back to basics' campaign, its obscene supplement was clearly indicated by Norman Tebbit, 'never shy about exposing the dirty secrets of the Conservative unconscious':[4] 'man is not just a social but also a territorial animal; it must be part of our agenda to satisfy those basic instincts of tribalism and territoriality'. This, then, is what 'back to basics' was really about: the reassertion of the barbarian 'basic instincts' lurking beneath the semblance of civilized bourgeois society. And do we not encounter in the violent outbursts these same 'basic instincts' – not of the lower under-privileged strata, but of the hegemonic capitalist ideology itself? Back in the 1960s, in order to explain how the 'sexual revolution' brought about the lifting of traditional obstacles to free sexuality, Herbert Marcuse introduced the concept of 'repressive desublimation': human drives can be desublimated, deprived of their civilized coating, and still retain their 'repressive' character – is not this kind of 'repressive desublimation' what we see on the streets of the UK today? That is to say, what we see there is not men reduced to 'natural beasts', but the historically specific 'natural beast' produced by hegemonic capitalist ideology itself, the zero-level of the capitalist subject.

Meanwhile leftist liberals, no less predictably, stuck to their mantra about neglected social programmes and integration efforts, which have deprived the younger generation of immigrants of any clear economic and social prospects: violent outbursts are their only means of articulating

---

4   Jacqueline Rose, *States of Fantasy* (Oxford: OUP, 1996), p.165.

their dissatisfaction. Instead of indulging ourselves in vengeful fantasies, we should make an effort to understand the deeper causes of the violent outbursts: Can we even imagine what it means to be a young man in a poor and racially mixed area, a priori suspected and harassed by the police, living in a context of misery and broken families, not only unemployed but often unemployable, with no hope for the future? The moment we take all this into account, the reasons why people take to the streets become clear . . . The problem with this account is that it simply lists the objective conditions for the riots, ignoring the subjective dimension: to riot is to make a subjective statement, to implicitly declare how one relates to one's objective conditions, how one subjectivizes them. We live in an era of cynicism where we can easily imagine a protester who, when caught looting and burning a store and pressed for the reasons for his violence, would suddenly start talking like a social worker, sociologist and social psychologist, quoting diminished social mobility, rising job insecurity, the disintegration of paternal authority, a lack of maternal love in his early childhood – he knows what he is doing, and he is nonetheless doing it, as in the famous 'Gee, Officer Krupke' from Leonard Bernstein's *West Side Story* (lyrics by Stephen Sondheim), which contains a statement 'Juvenile delinquency is purely a social disease':

> We never had the love
> That every child oughta get
> We ain't no delinquents
> We're misunderstood
> Deep down inside us there is good
>
> My daddy beats my mommy
> My mommy clobbers me
> My grandpa is a commie
> My grandma pushes tea
> My sister wears a moustache
> My brother wears a dress
> Goodness gracious, that's why I'm a mess
>
> Yes!
> Office Krupke, he shouldn't be here.
> This boy don't need a couch
> He needs a useful career

> Society's played him a terrible trick
> And sociologically he's sick
>
> Dear kindly social worker
> They tell me get a job
> Like be a soda jerker
> Which means I'd be a slob
> It's not I'm antisocial
> I'm only anti-work
> Gloryosky, that's why I'm a jerk!

They are not simply a social disease, they declare themselves as such, iron-ically staging different accounts of their predicament (or how a social worker, a psychologist, a judge would describe it). Consequently, it is meaningless to ponder which of the two reactions to the riots, conservative or liberal, is worse: as Comrade Stalin would have put it, they are *both* worse, and this includes the warning formulated by both sides about the real danger of these outbursts residing in the easily predictable racist *reaction* of the 'silent majority'. This reaction (which should absolutely not be dismissed as simply reactionary) was already taking place in the guise of a 'tribal' activity of its own: the sudden emergence of the self-organized defence of local communities (Turkish, Afro-Caribbean, Sikh . . .) quickly forming their own vigilante units to protect their hard-earned property. Here, too, one should reject the choice about which side to take in this conflict: Are the small shopkeepers defending the petty bourgeoisie against a genuine if violent protest against the system, or are the defenders repre-sentatives of genuine working people against forces of social disintegration? The protesters' violence was almost exclusively directed against their own. The cars burned and the stores looted were not those of richer neighbour-hoods: they were part of the hard-won acquisitions of the very strata from which the protesters originated. The sad truth of the situation resides in this very conflict between the two poles of the underprivileged: those who still succeed in functioning within the system versus those who are too frustrated to go on doing so, and are only able to strike at the other pole of their own community. The conflict that sustains the riots is thus not simply a conflict between parts of society; it is, at its most radical, *the conflict between non-society and society*, between those who have nothing to lose and those who have everything to lose, between those with no stake in their commu-nity and those whose stakes are the highest.

But why were the protesters pushed towards this kind of violence? Zygmunt Bauman was on the right track here when he characterized the riots as acts of 'defective and disqualified consumers': more than anything else, the riots were a consumerist carnival of destruction, a consumerist desire violently enacted when unable to realize itself in the 'proper' way (through shopping). As such, they also, of course, contained a moment of genuine protest, a kind of ironic reply to the consumerist ideology with which we are bombarded in our daily lives: 'You call on us to consume while simultaneously depriving us of the possibility of doing so properly – so here we are doing it the only way open to us!' The riots thus, in a way, stage the truth of the 'post-ideological society', displaying in a painfully palpable manner the material force of ideology. The problem with the riots was not their violence as such, but the fact that this violence was not truly self-assertive – in Nietzsche's terms, it was reactive, not active; it was impotent rage and despair masked as a display of force; it was envy masked as triumphant carnival.

The danger is that religion will fill this void and restore meaning. In other words, the riots need to be situated in a series they form with another type of violence that the liberal majority today perceives as a threat to our very way of life: namely, direct terrorist attacks and suicide bombings. In both instances, violence and counter-violence are caught up in a deadly vicious cycle, each generating the very forces it tries to combat. In both cases, we are dealing with blind *passages à l'acte*, where violence is an implicit admission of impotence. The difference is that, in contrast to the Parisian or UK outbursts, which were a 'zero-level' protest, violent outbursts which wanted nothing, terrorist attacks act on behalf of that *absolute* Meaning provided by religion.

But did not the Arab uprisings offer a collective act of resistance which avoided this false alternative of self-destructive violence and religious fundamentalism? Unfortunately, the Egyptian Summer of 2011 may be remembered as the time of the end of revolution, as the suffocating of its emancipatory potential; its gravediggers are the army and the Islamists. That is to say, the contours of the pact between the army (which is the same old Mubarak army, the big receiver of the US financial aid) and the Islamists (who were totally marginalized in the early months of the upheaval, but are now gaining ground) are more and more perceptible: the Islamists will tolerate the material privileges of the army and will gain ideological hegemony in exchange. The losers will be the pro-Western liberals, too weak in spite of all the CIA funding they are getting to 'promote democracy'; and, especially, the true agents of the revolutionary events, the emerging secular left, which was desperately trying to organize a network of civil society organizations, from trade unions to feminist groups. What further complicates the situation is the rapidly worsening economic situation, which will sooner or later bring into the streets millions of the poor, largely hitherto absent during the events dominated by the educated middle class youth. This new explosion will *repeat* the Spring explosion, bringing it to its truth, imposing upon political subjects a harsh choice: Who will succeed in becoming the force which directs the rage of the poor, translating it into a political programme: the new secular left or the Islamists?

The predominant reaction of Western public opinion to the pact between Islamists and the army will be without doubt a triumphant display of cynical wisdom: we will be told again and again that, as was clear already in (the non-Arab) Iran, popular upheavals in Arab countries always end in militant Islamism, so that Mubarak will retroactively appear as a much lesser evil – it is better to stick with the devil we know and not to play around too much with emancipation. Against this cynical temptation, one should remain unconditionally faithful to the radical-emancipatory core of the Egypt uprising.

However, one should also avoid the temptation of the narcissism of the lost cause, which admires the sublime beauty of uprisings doomed to fail. The poetry of failure, the old Beckettian motif of 'fail better' (whose clearest expression is Brecht's note on Mr Keuner: "'What are you working on?' Mr K. was asked. Mr K. replied: "I'm having a hard time; I'm preparing my next mistake"') is thus inadequate; what one should focus on are the results left behind by a failure. On the contemporary left, the problem of 'determinate negation' returns with a vengeance: What new positive order should replace the old one the day after, when the sublime enthusiasm of the uprising is over? It is at this crucial point that we encounter the fatal weakness of the protests: they express an authentic rage which is not able to transform itself into a minimal positive programme of socio-political change. They express a spirit of revolt without revolution.

The situation in Greece looks more promising, probably due to the recent tradition of progressive self-organization (which disappeared in Spain after the fall of the Franco regime).[5] But even in Greece, the

---

5 Although, even in Greece, right-wing nationalism is on the rise, directing its fury at the EU as well as at African immigrants; the left echoes this nationalist turn, attacking the EU instead of turning a critical gaze on its own past – such as analyzing how the government of Andreas Papandreou was a crucial step in the establishment of the Greek 'clientelist' state.

protest movement seems to reach its peak in popular self-organization: protesters sustain a space of egalitarian freedom with no central authority to regulate it, a public space where all are allotted the same amount of time to speak, and so on. When the protesters started to debate what to do, how to move beyond the form of a mere protest (should they organize a new political party, and so on), the majority consensus was that what was needed was not a new party or a direct attempt to take state power, but rather a civil society movement whose aim was to exert pressure on political parties. This, however, is clearly inadequate to impose a new reorganization of the whole of social life – to do this, one needs a strong body able to reach quick decisions and realize them with all necessary harshness. Who can accomplish the next step? A new tetrad emerges here, the tetrad of *people – movement – party – leader*.

The people is still there, but no longer as the mythical sovereign Subject whose will is to be enacted. Hegel was right in his critique of the democratic power of the people: 'the people' should be reconceived as the passive background of the political process – the majority is always and by definition passive; there is no guarantee that it is right; the most it can do is to acknowledge and recognize itself in a project imposed by political agents. Thus, the role of the people is ultimately a negative one: 'free elections' (or a referendum) serve as a check on party movements, as an impediment destined to prevent what Badiou called the brutal and destructive *forçage* ('enforcing') of the Truth on the positive order of Being regulated by opinions. This is all that electoral democracy can do; the positive step into a new order is beyond its scope.

In contrast to any elevation of 'authentic ordinary people', one should insist how irreducibly *violent* is the process of their transformation into political agents. John Carpenter's *They Live* (1988), one of the neglected masterpieces of the Hollywood Left, is the story of John Nada – Spanish for 'nothing'! – a homeless laborer who finds work on a Los Angeles construction site, but has no place to stay. One of the workers, Frank Armitage, takes him to spend the night at a local shantytown. While being shown around that night, he notices some odd behavior at a small church across the street. Investigating it the next day, he accidentally stumbles on several more boxes hidden in a secret compartment in a wall, full of sunglasses. When he later puts on a pair of the glasses for the first time, he notices that a publicity billboard now simply displays the word 'OBEY', while another billboard urges the viewer to 'MARRY AND REPRODUCE'. He also sees that paper money bears the words

'THIS IS YOUR GOD'. What we get here is a beautifully naive *mise-en-scène* of the critique of ideology: through the critico-ideological glasses, we directly see the Master Signifier beneath the chain of knowledge – we learn to see dictatorship *in* democracy, and seeing it hurts. When Nada tries to convince Armitage to put the glasses on, the friend resists, and a long, violent fight follows, worthy of *Fight Club* (another masterpiece of the Hollywood Left). The violence staged here is a positive violence, a condition of liberation – the lesson is that our liberation from ideology is not a spontaneous act, an act of discovering our true Self. We learn in the film that, when one looks for too long at reality through critico-ideological glasses, one gets a strong headache: it is very painful to be deprived of ideological surplus-enjoyment. To see the true nature of things, we need the glasses. It is not that we should take ideological glasses off to see reality directly as it is; we are 'naturally' in ideology, our natural sight is ideological.

This is why the long fight between Nada and Armitage is crucial for the film; it starts with Nada saying to Armitage: 'I'm giving you a choice. Either put on these glasses or start to eat that trash can.' (The fight is taking place among overturned trash bins.) The fight, which goes on for an unbearable eight minutes, with momentary exchanges of friendly smiles, is in itself totally 'irrational' – why does not Armitage agree to put the glasses on, just to satisfy his friend? The only explanation is that he *knows* that his friend wants him to see something dangerous, to attain prohibited knowledge which would totally spoil the relative peace of his daily life. The violence staged here is positive violence, a condition of liberation. How does a woman become a feminist subject? Only through renouncing the crumbs of privilege offered to her by the patriarchal discourse – from the reliance on the male protective shield to pleasures provided by male 'gallantry' (paying the bills in restaurants, opening the door for her, and so on and so forth).

When people directly try to 'organize themselves' in movements, the most they can arrive at is the egalitarian space for debate where speakers are chosen by lot and everyone is given the same (short) time to speak. But such protest movements are inadequate the moment one has to act, to impose a new order – at this point, something like a *party* is needed. Even in a radical protest movement, people *do not* know what they want, they demand a new Master to tell them this. But if the people does not know, does the party know? Are we back with the standard topic of the party possessing historical insight and leading the people? It is Brecht that gives us a clue here. In what is for some the most problematic song of *The Measure Taken*, the celebration of the party, Brecht proposes something much more unique and precise than may appear. That is to say, what appears is that Brecht is simply elevating the party into the incarnation of Absolute Knowledge – a historical agent that has complete and perfect insight into the historical situation, a subject-supposed-to-know if there ever was one: 'You have two eyes, but the Party has a thousand eyes!' However, a close reading of this poem makes it clear that something different is the case: in his reprimand to the young Communist, the chorus says that the party does *not* know everything, that the young Communist may be *correct* in his disagreement with the predominant party line:

> Show us the way which we should take, and we
> shall follow it like you, but
> do not take the right way without us.
> Without us, this way is
> the falsest one.
> Do not separate yourself from us.

What this means is that the authority of the party is *not* that of determinate positive knowledge, but that of the *form* of knowledge, of a new type of knowledge linked to a collective political subject. The crucial point on which the Chorus insists is only that, if the young comrade thinks that he is right, he should fight for his position *within* the collective form of the party, not outside it – to put it in a somewhat pathetic way, if the young comrade is right, then the party needs him even more than its other members. What the party demands is that one agree to ground one's 'I' in the '*We*' of the party's collective identity: fight with us, fight for us, fight for your truth against the party line, *just do not do it alone*, outside the party.

Movements as the agents of politicization are phenomena of 'qualitative democracy' – even in mass events like the protests on Tahrir Square in Cairo, the people who gathered there were always a minority; the reason they 'stood for the people' hinges on their mobilizing role in political dynamics. In a homologous way, the organizing role of a party has nothing to do with its access to some privileged knowledge: a party is not a figure of the Lacanian subject-supposed-to-know, but an open field of knowledge in which 'all possible mistakes' (Lenin) occur. However, even this mobilizing role of movements and parties is insufficient: the gap that separates the people themselves from the organized forms of their political agency has to be somehow overcome – but how? Not by the proximity of the people and these organized forms; something more is needed, and the paradox is that this 'more' is a *Leader*, the unity of the party and people. We should not be afraid to draw all the consequences from this insight, endorsing the lesson of Hegel's justification of the monarchy and ruthlessly slaughtering many liberal sacred cows on the way. The problem with the Stalinist leader was not an excessive 'cult of personality', but quite the opposite: he was not sufficiently a Master, but remained part of the bureaucratic-party Knowledge, the exemplary subject-supposed-to-know.

To take this step 'beyond the possible' in *today's* constellation, one should shift the accent of our reading of Marx's *Capital* to 'the fundamental structural centrality of unemployment in the text of *Capital* itself': 'unemployment is structurally inseparable from the dynamic of accumulation and expansion which constitutes the very nature of capitalism as such'.[6] In what is arguably the extreme point of the 'unity of opposites' in the sphere of the economy, it is the very success of capitalism (higher productivity, and so on) that produces unemployment (renders more and more workers useless) – what should be a blessing (less hard labour needed) becomes a curse. The world market is thus, with regard to its immanent dynamic, 'a space in which everyone has once been a productive laborer, and in which labor has everywhere begun to price itself out of the system'.[7] That is to say, in the ongoing process of capitalist globalization, the category of the unemployed acquired a new quality beyond the classic notion of the 'reserve army of labour': one should consider in terms of the category of unemployment 'those massive populations around the world who have, as it were, 'dropped out of history', who have been deliberately excluded from the modernizing projects of First World capitalism and written off as hopeless or terminal cases'[8] – so-called 'failed states' (Congo, Somalia), victims of famine or ecological disasters, caught in pseudo-archaic 'ethnic hatreds', objects of philanthropy and NGOs or (often the same people) of the 'war on terror'. The category of the unemployed should thus be expanded to encompass the wide span of the population, from the temporary unemployed, through the no-longer employable and permanently unemployed, up to people living in slums and other types of ghettos (all those often dismissed by Marx himself as

6   Fredric Jameson, *Representing Capital* (London: Verso, 2011), p. 149.
7   Fredric Jameson, *Valences of the Dialectic* (London: Verso, 2009), pp. 580–1.
8   Jameson, *Representing Capital*, p. 149.

'lumpen-proletarians') – and, finally, whole areas, populations or states excluded from the global capitalist process, like the blank spaces in ancient maps. Does not this extension of the circle of the 'unemployed' bring us back from Marx to Hegel: the 'rabble' is back, emerging in the very core of emancipatory struggles? In other words, such a re-categorization changes the entire 'cognitive map' of the situation: the inert background of History becomes a potential agent of emancipatory struggle. Recall Marx's dismissive characterization of the French peasants in his *Eighteenth Brumaire*:

> the great mass of the French nation is formed by the simple addition of homologous magnitudes, much as potatoes in a sack form a sack of potatoes . . . Insofar as there is merely a local interconnection among these small-holding peasants, and the identity of their interests forms no community, no national bond, and no political organization among them, they do not constitute a class. They are therefore incapable of asserting their class interest in their own name, whether through a parliament or a convention. They cannot represent themselves, they must be represented.[9]

In the great twentieth-century revolutionary mobilizations of peasants (from China to Bolivia), these 'sacks of potatoes' excluded from the historical process proper started to represent themselves actively. We should nonetheless add three qualifications to Jameson's deployment of this idea. First, one should correct the semiotic square proposed by Jameson, whose terms are (1) workers, (2) the reserve army of the (temporarily) unemployed, (3) the (permanently) unemployable, and (4) the 'formerly employed'[10] but now unemployable: would not a more appropriate fourth term be the *illegally employed*, from those working in black markets and slums up to various forms of slavery? Second, Jameson fails to emphasize how those 'excluded' are often nonetheless *included* in the world market. Take the case of contemporary Congo: beneath the façade of 'primitive ethnic passions' exploding yet again in the African 'heart of darkness', it is easy to discern the contours of global capitalism. Since the fall of Mobutu, Congo no longer exists as a united operating state; especially its eastern part is a multiplicity of territories ruled by local warlords controlling their patch of land with

---

9   Quoted from the text available at marxists.org.
10 Jameson, *Valences of the Dialectic*, p. 580.

an army which as a rule includes drugged children, each of the warlords having business links to a foreign company or corporation exploiting the (mostly) mining wealth in the region. This arrangement fits both partners: the corporation gets the mining rights without taxes etc.; the warlord gets money. The irony is that many of these minerals are used in high-tech products like laptops and cell phones – in short: forget about the 'savage customs' of the local population; just take the foreign high-tech companies out of the equation and the whole edifice of ethnic warfare fuelled by old passions will fall apart. Thirdly, the category of 'formerly employed' should be supplemented by its opposite, those educated with no chance of finding employment: a whole generation of students has almost no chance of finding corresponding employment, which leads to massive protest; and the worst way to resolve this gap is to subordinate education directly to the demands of the market – if for no other reason than because the market dynamic itself renders the education provided by universities 'obsolete'.

Jameson adds here another (paradoxical, but deeply justified) key step: he characterizes this new structural unemployment as a form of *exploitation* – the exploited are not only workers producing surplus-value appropriated by capital, the exploited are also those who are structurally prevented from getting caught in the capitalist vortex of exploited wage labour, up to whole zones and nations. How, then, are we to rethink the concept of exploitation? A radical change is needed here: in a properly dialectical twist, exploitation includes its own negation – the exploited are not only those who produce or 'create', but also (and even more) those who are condemned *not* to 'create'. Are we here not back at the structure of the famous Rabinovitch joke? 'Why do you think you are exploited?' 'For two reasons. First, when I work, the capitalist appropriates my surplus-value.' 'But you are now unemployed, no one is appropriating your surplus-value because you create none!' 'This is the second reason . . .' Everything hinges here on the fact that the capitalist totality of production not only needs workers, but also generates the 'reserve army' of those who cannot find work: the latter are not simply outside the circuit of capital, they are actively produced as not-working by this circuit. Or, to refer again to the *Ninotchka*-joke, they are not simply not-working, their not-working is their positive feature in the same way as 'coffee without milk' is its positive feature.

The importance of this accent on exploitation becomes clear when we oppose it to *domination*, the favoured motif of the different versions of postmodern 'micro-politics of power'. In short, Foucault and Agamben are inadequate: all the detailed elaborations of the regulating power mechanisms of domination, all the wealth of notions such as the excluded, bare life, *homo sacer*, and so on, must be grounded in (or mediated by) the centrality of exploitation; without this reference to the economic, the fight against domination remains 'an essentially moral or ethical one, which leads to punctual revolts and acts of resistance rather than to the transformation of the mode of production as such' – the positive programme of the ideologies of 'power' is generally the one of some type of 'direct' democracy. The outcome of the emphasis on domination is a democratic programme, while the outcome of the emphasis on exploitation is a communist programme. Therein resides the limit of describing horrors of the global South in terms of the effects of domination: the goal becomes democracy and freedom. Even the reference to 'imperialism' (instead of capitalism) functions as a case of how 'an economic category can so easily modulate into a concept of power or domination'[11] – and the implication of this shift of accent towards domination is, of course, the belief in another ('alternative') modernity in which capitalism will function in a 'fairer' way, without domination. What this notion of domination fails to see is that only in capitalism is exploitation 'naturalized', inscribed into the functioning of the economy – it is not the result of extra-economic pressure and violence, and this is why, in capitalism, we get personal freedom and equality: there is no need for direct social domination, domination is already in the structure of the production process. This is also why the category of surplus-value is crucial here: Marx always emphasized that the exchange between worker and capitalist is 'just' in the sense that workers (as a rule) get paid the full value of their labor-power as a commodity – there is no direct 'exploitation' here; that is, it is not that workers 'are not paid the full value of the commodity they are selling to the capitalists'. So while, in a market economy, I remain de facto dependent, this dependency is nonetheless 'civilized', enacted in the form of a 'free' market exchange between me and other persons instead of the form of direct servitude or even physical coercion. It is easy to ridicule Ayn Rand, but there is a grain of truth in the famous 'hymn to money' from her *Atlas Shrugged*: 'Until and unless you discover that money is the root of all good, you ask for your own destruction. When money ceases to become the means by which men deal with one another, then men become the

---

11   Ibid., p. 151.

tools of other men. Blood, whips and guns or dollars. Take your choice – there is no other.'[12] Did not Marx say something similar in his well-known formula of how, in the universe of commodities, 'relations between people assume the guise of relations among things'? In the market economy, relations between people can appear as relations of mutually recognized freedom and equality: domination is no longer directly enacted and visible as such.

The liberal answer to domination is recognition (the favoured topic of 'liberal Hegelians'): recognition 'becomes a stake in a multicultural settlement by which the various groups peaceably and electorally divide up the spoils'.[13] The subjects of recognition are not classes (it is meaningless to demand the recognition of the proletariat as a collective subject – if anything, fascism does this, demanding the mutual recognition of classes). Subjects of recognition are race, gender, and so on – the politics of recognition remains within a bourgeois civil-society framework; it is not yet class politics.[14]

The recurrent story of the contemporary left is that of a leader or party elected with universal enthusiasm, promising a 'new world' (Mandela, Lula) – but, then, sooner or later, usually after a couple of years, they stumble upon the key dilemma: does one dare touch the capitalist mechanisms, or does one decide to 'play the game'? If one disturbs the mechanisms, one is very swiftly 'punished' by market perturbations, economic chaos and the rest.[15] So although it is true that anti-capitalism cannot be directly the goal of political action – in politics, one opposes concrete political agents and their actions, not an anonymous 'system' – one should apply here the Lacanian distinction between goal and aim: if not the immediate goal of emancipatory politics, anti-capitalism should be its ultimate aim, the horizon of all its activity. Is this not the lesson of Marx's notion of the 'critique of *political economy*' (totally absent in Badiou)? Although the sphere of the economy appears 'apolitical', it is the secret point of reference and structuring principle of political struggles.

This is also how one should approach the Egyptian uprising of 2011: although (almost) everyone enthusiastically supported these democratic

---

12   Ayn Rand, *Atlas Shrugged* (London: Penguin, 2007), p. 871.
13   Jameson, *Valences of the Dialectic*, p. 568.
14   Ibid.
15   This is why it is all too simple to criticize Mandela for abandoning the socialist perspective after the end of apartheid: Did he really have a choice? Was the move towards socialism a real option?

explosions, there is actually a hidden struggle for their appropriation going on. The official circles and most of the media in the West celebrate them as the same thing as the 'pro-democracy' velvet revolutions in Eastern Europe: a desire for Western liberal democracy, a desire to become like the West. This is why uneasiness arises when one sees that there is another dimension at work in protests there – the dimension usually referred to as the demand for social justice. This struggle for reappropriation is not only a question of interpretation, but has crucial practical consequences. We should not be too fascinated by the sublime moments of all-national unity – the key question is: What happens the day after? How will this emancipatory explosion be translated into new social order? As I have noted, over the last few decades, we witnessed a whole series of popular explosions which were re-appropriated by the global capitalist order, either in its liberal form (from South Africa to the Philippines) or its fundamentalist form (Iran). We should not forget that none of the Arab countries where popular uprisings have happened is formally democratic: they were all more or less authoritarian, so that the demand for social and economic justice is spontaneously integrated into the demand for democracy – as if poverty were the result of the greed and corruption of those in power, and thus it is enough to get rid of them. What then happens is that we get democracy, but poverty remains – what to do *then*?

To return to Rand, what is problematic is her underlying premise: that the only choice is between direct and indirect relations of domination and exploitation, with any alternative dismissed as utopian. But one should nonetheless bear in mind the moment of truth in Rand's otherwise ridiculously ideological claim: the great lesson of state-socialism really was that a direct abolition of private property and market-regulated exchange, lacking concrete forms of direct social regulation of the process of production, necessarily resuscitates direct relations of servitude and domination. Jameson himself falls short with regard to this point: focusing on how capitalist exploitation is compatible with democracy, how legal freedom can be the very form of exploitation, he neglects the sad lesson of twentieth-century leftist experience: if we merely abolish the market (including market exploitation) without replacing it with a proper form of communist organization of production and exchange, domination returns with a vengeance, and, in its wake, direct exploitation too.

What further complicates the situation is that the very rise of blank spaces in global capitalism is in itself also a proof that capitalism can no longer afford a universal civil order of freedom and democracy, that it more and more needs exclusion and domination. The case of the Tiananmen crackdown in China is exemplary here: what was squashed by the brutal military intervention in Tienanmen Square was not the prospect of a fast entry into the liberal-democratic capitalist order, but a genuinely utopian alternative possibility of a more democratic *and* more just society: the explosion of brutal capitalism after 1990 goes hand-in-hand with the reassertion of undemocratic one-party rule. Recall the classical Marxist thesis on early modern England: it was in the interest of the bourgeoisie to leave the *political* power to the aristocracy and keep for itself *economic* power. Maybe something homologous is going on in today's China: it is in the interest of the new capitalists to leave political power to the Communist Party.

How, then, are we to break out of this deadlock of post-political de-historicization? What to do after the Occupy movement, when the protests which started far away (Middle East, Greece, Spain, UK) reached the centre, and are now rolling back all around the world? One of the great dangers the protesters face is that they will fall in love with themselves, with the nice time they are having in the 'occupied' places – along these lines, at a San Francisco echo of the Wall Street occupation on Sunday, 16 October 2011, a man addressed the crowd with an invitation to participate in it as if it were a happening in the hippy style of the 1960s: 'They are asking us what our programme is. We have no programme. We are here to have a good time.' Carnivals come cheap – the true test of their worth is what remains the day after, how our normal daily life is changed. The protesters should fall in love with hard and patient work – they are only the beginning, not the end, so their basic message is: the taboo has been broken, we do not live in the best of all possible worlds, we are allowed, obliged even, to think about alternatives. In a kind of Hegelian triad, the Western left has come full circle: after abandoning so-called 'class struggle essentialism' for the plurality of anti-racist, feminist, etc., struggles, 'capitalism' is now clearly re-emerging as the name of *the* problem. So the first lesson to be drawn is: do not blame individuals and their attitudes. The problem is not corruption or greed, the problem is the system that pushes you to be corrupt. The solution is not 'Main Street, not Wall Street', but to change the system in which Main Street cannot function without Wall Street.

There is a long road ahead, and soon we will have to address the truly difficult questions – questions not about what we do not want, but about what we *do* want. What social organization can replace the existing capitalism? What types of new leaders do we need? What organs, including those of control and repression? The twentieth-century alternatives did not work, obviously. While it is thrilling to enjoy the pleasures of the 'horizontal organization' of protesting crowds with egalitarian solidarity and open-ended free debates, we should also bear in mind what Gilbert Keith Chesterton wrote: 'Merely having an open mind is nothing; the object of opening the mind, as of opening the mouth, is to shut it again on something solid.' This holds also for politics in times of uncertainty: the open-ended debates will have to coalesce not only in some new Master Signifiers, but also in concrete answers to the old Leninist question 'What is to be done?'

The conservative attacks are easy to answer. Are the protests un-American? When conservative fundamentalists claim that the US is a Christian nation, one should remember what Christianity really is: the Holy Spirit; a free, egalitarian community of believers united by love. It is the protesters who are the Holy Spirit, while on Wall Street they are pagans worshipping false idols. Are the protesters violent? True, their very language may appear violent (occupation, and so on), but they are violent only in the sense in which Mahatma Gandhi was violent. They are violent because they want to put a stop to the way things are continuing – but what is this violence compared to the violence needed to sustain the smooth functioning of the global capitalist system? They are called losers – but are not the true losers those on Wall Street, and were they not bailed out by hundreds of billions of dollars of our money? The protestors are called socialists – but the US already has socialism for the rich. They are accused of not respecting private property – but the Wall Street speculation that led to the crash of 2008 erased more hard-earned private property than if the protesters had destroyed property night and day: just think of the tens of thousands of homes foreclosed. They are not communists, if 'communism' means the system which deservedly collapsed in 1990 – and remember that the communists who are still in power today run the most ruthless capitalism (in China). The success of Chinese communist-run capitalism is an ominous sign that the marriage between capitalism and democracy is approaching a divorce. The only sense in which the protestors are 'communists' is that they care for the commons – the commons of nature, of knowledge – which are threatened by the system. They are dismissed as dreamers, but the true dreamers are those who think that things can go on indefinitely the way they are now, with just a few cosmetic changes. They are not dreamers; they are awakening from a dream which is turning into a nightmare. They are not destroying anything; they are reacting to how the system is gradually destroying itself.

The protesters should beware not only of enemies, but also of false friends who pretend to support them but are already working hard to dilute the protest. In the same way we have decaffeinated coffee, non-alcoholic beer and fat-free ice-cream, they will try to make the protests into a harmless moralistic gesture. In boxing, to 'clinch' means to hold the opponent's body with one or both arms in order to prevent or hinder punches. Bill Clinton's reaction to the Wall Street protests is a perfect case of political clinching; Clinton thinks that the protests are 'on balance . . . a positive thing', but he is worried about the nebulousness of the cause: 'They need to be for something specific, and not just against something because if you're just against something, someone else will fill the vacuum you create', he said. Clinton suggested the protesters get behind President Obama's jobs plan, which he claimed would create 'a couple million jobs in the next year and a half'. What one should resist at this stage is precisely such a quick translation of the energy of the protest into a set of 'concrete' pragmatic demands. Yes, the protests did create a vacuum – a vacuum in the field of hegemonic ideology, and time is needed to fill this vacuum in a proper way, since it is a pregnant vacuum, an open-ing for the truly New. The reason protesters went out onto the streets is that they had had enough of a world where to recycle your Coke cans, to give a couple of dollars for charity, or to buy Starbucks cappuccino where 1 per cent goes to the Third World is enough to make them feel good. After outsourcing work and torture, after the marriage agencies started to outsource even our dating, they saw that for a long time they were allow-ing their political engagements also to be outsourced – and they want them back.

The art of politics is also to insist on a particular demand which, while thoroughly 'realistic', disturbs the very core of the hegemonic ideology – which, while definitely feasible and legitimate, is de facto impossible (universal healthcare is such a case). In the aftermath of the Wall Street protests, we should definitely mobilize people around such demands – however, it is no less important to remain simultaneously *subtracted* from the pragmatic field of negotiations and 'realistic' proposals. What one should always bear in mind is that any debate here and now necessarily remains a debate on the enemy's turf: time is needed to deploy the new content. All we say now can be taken (recuperated) from us – everything except our silence. This silence, this rejection of dialogue, of all forms of clinching, is our 'terror', ominous and threatening as it should be.

This threat was clearly perceived by Anne Applebaum. The symbol of Wall Street is the metal statue of a bull in its center – and ordinary people have been receiving quite a lot of its shit in recent years. While the standard reactions of Wall Street itself are the expected vulgar forms of bullshit, Applebaum proposed in the *Washington Post* a more sophisticated, perfumed version, including references to Monty Python's *The Life of Brian*. Since her negative version of Clinton's call for concrete proposals stands for ideology at its purest, it deserves to be quoted in detail. The basis of her reasoning is the claim that the protests around the world are

> similar in their lack of focus, in their inchoate nature, and above all in their refusal to engage with existing democratic institutions. In New York, marchers chanted, 'This is what democracy looks like', but actually, this isn't what democracy looks like. This is what freedom of speech looks like. Democracy looks a lot more boring. Democracy requires institutions, elections, political parties, rules, laws, a judiciary and many unglamorous, time-consuming activities . . . Yet in one sense, the international Occupy movement's failure to produce sound legislative proposals is understandable: both the sources of the global economic crisis and the solutions to it lie, by definition, outside the competence of local and national politicians.

The emergence of an international protest movement without a coherent program is therefore not an accident: it reflects a deeper crisis, one without an obvious solution. Democracy is based on the rule of law. Democracy works only within distinct borders and among people who feel themselves to be part of the same nation. A 'global community' cannot be a national democracy. And a national democracy cannot command the allegiance of a billion-dollar global hedge fund, with its headquarters in a tax haven and its employees scattered around the world.

Unlike the Egyptians in Tahrir Square, to whom the London and New York protesters openly (and ridiculously) compare themselves, we have democratic institutions in the Western world. They are designed to reflect, at least crudely, the desire for political change within a given nation. But they cannot cope with the desire for global political change, nor can they control things that happen outside their borders. Although I still believe in globalization's economic and spiritual benefits – along with open borders, freedom of movement and free trade – globalization has clearly begun to undermine the legitimacy of Western democracies.

'Global' activists, if they are not careful, will accelerate that decline. Protesters in London shout, 'We need to have a process!' Well, they already have a process: It's called the British political system. And if they don't figure out how to use it, they'll simply weaken it further.[16]

The first thing to note is Applebaum's reduction of the Tahrir Square protests to calls for Western-style democracy – once we do this, it of course becomes ridiculous to compare the Wall Street protests with the Egyptian events: How can protesters here demand what we already have, namely democratic institutions? What is thereby lost from view is the general discontent with the global capitalist system which, obviously, acquires different forms here or there.

But the most shocking part of Applebaum's argumentation – a truly weird gap in argumentation – occurs at the end. After conceding that the undeserved economic consequences of global capitalist finances are due to their international character, beyond the grasp of democratic mechanisms which are by definition limited to nation-states, she draws the necessary conclusion that 'globalization has clearly begun to undermine the legitimacy of Western democracies'. So far so good, we might say: this is precisely what the protesters are drawing attention to – that global capitalism undermines democracy. But instead of drawing the only logical further conclusion, that we should start thinking about how to expand democracy beyond its state-multiparty political form, which excludes the destructive consequences of economic life, she performs a weird turn-around and shifts the blame onto the protesters themselves, who have started to raise these questions. Her last paragraph deserves to be repeated: '"Global" activists, if they are not careful, will accelerate that decline. Protesters in London shout, "We need to have a process!" Well, they already have a process: It's called the British political system. And if they don't figure out how to use it, they'll simply weaken it further.' So, since the global economy is beyond the scope of democratic politics, any attempt to expand democracy to its level will accelerate the decline of democracy. What, then, can we do? Engage in the existing political

---

16 Quoted from Anne Applebaum, 'What the Occupy protesters tell us about the limits of democracy', available at washingtonpost.com.

system which, according to Applebaum's account itself, precisely *cannot* do the job . . .

It is here that we should go all the way: there is no lack of anti-capitalism today; we are witnessing a vast expansion of critiques of the horrors of capitalism: books, in-depth newspaper investigations and TV reports abound on companies ruthlessly polluting our environment, on corrupt bankers who continue to get fat bonuses while their banks have to be saved by public money, on sweat shops where children work overtime, and so on. There is, however, a catch in all this overflow of critique: what is as a rule not questioned, ruthless as it may appear, is the very democratic-liberal framework of fighting against these excesses. The (explicit or implied) goal is to democratize capitalism, to extend democratic control into the economy, through the pressure of the media, parliamentary inquiries, harsher laws, honest police investigations, and so on – but never to question the democratic institutional framework of the (bourgeois) state of law. This remains the sacred cow that even the most radical forms of this 'ethical anti-capitalism' (the Porto Alegre World Social Forum, the Seattle movement) do not dare touch.

It is here that Marx's key insight remains valid, today perhaps more than ever: for Marx, the question of freedom should not be located primarily in the political sphere proper (Does a country have free elections? Are the judges independent? Is the press free from hidden pressures? Are human rights respected? and the similar list of questions various 'independent' – and not so independent – Western institutions apply when they want to pronounce a judgment on a country). The key to actual freedom rather resides in the 'apolitical' network of social relations, from the market to the family, where the change needed if we want an actual improvement is not a political reform, but a change in 'apolitical' social relations of production. We do not vote about who owns what, about relations in a factory, and so on, for all this is left to processes outside the sphere of the political, and it is illusory to expect that one can effectively change things by 'extending' democracy into this sphere – say, by organizing 'democratic' banks under people's control. Radical changes in this domain should be made outside the sphere of legal 'rights', and so on: in such 'democratic' procedures (which, of course, can have a positive role to play), no matter how radical our anti-capitalism, the solution is sought in applying the democratic mechanisms – which, one should never forget, are part of the state apparatuses of the 'bourgeois' state that guarantees the undisturbed functioning of capitalist reproduction. In this precise sense, Badiou was right in his claim that, today, the name of the ultimate enemy is not capitalism, empire, exploitation, or anything similar, but 'democracy': it is the 'democratic illusion', the acceptance of democratic mechanisms as the ultimate horizon of every change, which prevents the radical change of capitalist relations.

The Occupy protests are thus a beginning, and one must begin like that, with a formal gesture of rejection which is more important than positive content – only such a gesture opens up the space for the new content. So we should not be terrorized by the perennial question: 'But what do they want?' Remember that this is the archetypal question addressed by a male master to a hysterical woman: 'With all your whining and complaining – do you know at all what you really want?' In the psychoanalytic sense, the protests are effectively a hysterical act, provoking the master, undermining his authority, and the question 'But what do you want?' aims precisely to preclude the true answer – its point is: 'Say it on my terms or shut up!'

This, of course, does not mean that the protesters should be pampered and flattered – today, if ever, intellectuals should combine full support for the protesters with a non-patronizing, cold, analytical distance, beginning by questioning the protesters' self-designation as the 99 per cent against the greedy 1 per cent: how many of the 99 per cent are ready to accept these protesters as their voice, and to what extent? If we take a closer look at the well-known manifesto of the Spanish *indignados* ('angry ones'), we are in for some surprises. The first thing that strikes the eye is the pointedly apolitical tone: 'Some of us consider ourselves progressive, others conservative. Some of us are believers, some not. Some of us have clearly defined ideologies, others are apolitical, but we are all concerned and angry about the political, economic, and social outlook which we see around us: corruption among politicians, businessmen, bankers, leaving us helpless, without a voice.' They voice their protest on behalf of the 'inalienable truths that we should abide by in our society: the right to housing, employment, culture, health, education, political participation, free personal development, and consumer rights for a healthy and happy life.' Rejecting violence, they call for an 'ethical revolution. Instead of placing money above human beings, we shall put it back to our service. We are people, not products. I am not a product of what I buy, why I buy and who I buy from.' Who will be the agent of this revolution? While the entire political class, right and left, is dismissed as corrupt and controlled by the lust for power, the manifesto nonetheless consists of a series of demands – but addressed to whom? Not the people themselves: the *indig-nados* do not (yet) claim that no one will do it for them, that (to paraphrase Gandhi) they themselves have to be the change they want to see. It seems that Lacan's all too easy and dismissive remark on the 1968 protesters found its target in the *indignados*: 'As *revolutionaries,* you are *hysterics* who demand a *new master.* You will get one.'

Faced with the demands of the protesters, intellectuals are definitely not in the position of the subjects supposed to know: they cannot opera-tionalize these demands, translate them into proposals for precise and detailed realistic measures. With the fall of twentieth-century commu-nism, they forever forfeited their role as a vanguard which understands the laws of history and can guide the innocents along its path. The people, however, does not know either – the 'people' as a new figure of the subject-supposed-to-know is a myth of the party which claims to act on its behalf, from Mao's slogan to 'learn from the farmers' up to Heidegger's famous appeal to his old farmer friend in his short text 'Why Do I Stay in the Provinces?' from 1934 – a month after he resigned as the dean of the Freiburg University:

> Recently I got a second invitation to teach at the University of Berlin. On that occasion I left Freiburg and withdrew to the cabin. I listened to what the mountains and the forest and the farmlands were saying, and I went to see an old friend of mine, a 75-year-old farmer. He had read about the call to Berlin in the newspapers. What would he say? Slowly he fixed the sure gaze of his clear eyes on mine, and keeping his mouth tightly shut, he thoughtfully put his faithful hand on my shoul-der. Ever so slightly he shook his head. That meant: absolutely no![17]

One can only imagine what the old farmer was really thinking – in all probability, he knew what answer Heidegger wanted from him and politely provided it. So no wisdom of ordinary men will tell the protesters *warum bleiben wir* in Wall Street. There is no subject who knows, neither in the form of intellectuals nor ordinary people. So is this not a deadlock: the blind leading the blind, each of them presupposing that the others are not blind? No, because the respective ignorance is not symmetrical: it is the people who have the answers, they just do not know the questions to which they have (or, rather, are) the answer. John Berger wrote about

---

17   Quoted from 'Heidegger: The Man and the Thinker', available at stanford.edu.

the 'multitudes' of those who found themselves on the wrong side of the Wall (dividing those who are in from those who are out):

> The multitudes have answers to questions which have not yet been posed, and they have the capacity to outlive the walls. The questions are not yet asked because to do so requires words and concepts which ring true, and those currently being used to name events have been rendered meaningless: Democracy, Liberty, Productivity, etc. With new concepts the questions will soon be posed, for history involves precisely such a process of questioning. Soon? Within a generation.[18]

Claude Lévi-Strauss wrote that the prohibition of incest is not a question, an enigma, but an answer to a question that we do not know. We should treat the demands of the Occupy protests in a similar way: intellectuals should not primarily take them as demands, questions, for which they should produce clear answers, programmes about what to do. They are answers, and intellectuals should propose questions to which they are answers. The situation is like that of psychoanalysis, where the patient knows the answer (his symptoms are such answers) but does not know to what they are answers, and the analyst has to formulate a question. Only through such patient work will a programme emerge.

---

18 John Berger, 'Afterword', in Andrey Platonov, *Soul* (New York: New York Review Books, 2007), p. 317.

Notes on Contributors

Alain Badiou teaches philosophy at the École Normale Supérieure and the Collège International de Philosophie in Paris. In addition to several novels, plays and political essays, he has published a number of major philosophical works, including *Theory of the Subject*, *Being and Event*, *Manifesto for Philosophy*, and *Gilles Deleuze*. His recent books include *The Meaning of Sarkozy*, *Ethics*, *Metapolitics*, *Polemics*, *The Communist Hypothesis*, *Five Lessons on Wagner*, *The Adventure of French Philosophy*, *The Rebirth of History* and *Wittgenstein's Anti-Philosophy*.

Étienne Balibar is Professor Emeritus of moral and political philosophy at Université de Paris X–Nanterre and Distinguished Professor of Humanities at the University of California, Irvine. His many books include *Spinoza and Politics*, *The Philosophy of Marx* and *Politics and the 'Other' Scene*, and he is the co-author of *Race, Nation and Class* and *Reading Capital*.

Bruno Bosteels, Professor of Romance Studies at Cornell University, is the author of *Badiou and Politics*, *Marx and Freud in Latin America*, and *The Actuality of Communism*. He is also the translator of several books by Alain Badiou: *Theory of the Subject*, *Wittgenstein's Antiphilosophy* and *The Adventure of French Philosophy*. Between 2005 and 2011 he also served as the general editor of *Diacritics*.

Susan Buck-Morss is Professor of Political Philosophy and Social Theory at Cornell University. She is the author of *Dreamworld and Catastrophe: The Passing of Mass Utopia in East and West*, *The Dialectics of Seeing: Walter Benjamin and the Arcades Project* and *The Origin of Negative Dialectics: Theodor W. Adorno, Walter Benjamin and the Frankfurt Institute*.

Jodi Dean teaches political and media theory in Geneva, New York. She has written or edited eleven books, including *The Communist Horizon* and *Democracy and Other Neoliberal Fantasies*.

Adrian Johnston is a Professor in the Department of Philosophy at the University of New Mexico at Albuquerque and an Assistant Teaching Analyst at the Emory Psychoanalytic Institute in Atlanta. He is the author of *Time Driven: Metapsychology and the Splitting of the Drive*, *Žižek's Ontology: A Transcendental Materialist Theory of Subjectivity*, *Badiou, Žižek, and Political Transformations: The Cadence of Change*, *The Outcome of Contemporary French Philosophy: Prolegomena to Any Future Materialism – Volume One* and *Adventures in Transcendental Materialism: Dialogues with Contemporary Thinkers*.

Frank Ruda is a Research Associate at the Collaborative Research Centre on Aesthetic Experience and the Dissolution of Artistic Limits at the Free University of Berlin, Germany. He is the author of *Hegel's Rabble*.

Emmanuel Terray is a French anthropologist. A former Director of Research at the École des Hautes Études en Sciences Sociales (EHESS) in Paris, he is the author of *Marxism and 'Primitive' Societies: Two Studies*. His recent books include *Combats avec Méduse* and *Penser à droite*.

Slavoj Žižek is a Slovenian philosopher and cultural critic. He is a Professor at the European Graduate School, International Director of the Birkbeck Institute for the Humanities, Birkbeck College, University of London, and a senior researcher at the Institute of Sociology, University of Ljubljana, Slovenia. His books include *Living in the End Times*, *First as Tragedy, Then as Farce*, *In Defense of Lost Causes*, four volumes of the *Essential Žižek*, *The Year of Dreaming Dangerously*, *Less Than Nothing: Hegel and the Shadow of Dialectical Materialism* and many more.

Index